Economics and the Mind

Economics is often described as the science of choice or human action, but although both of these concepts are essentially mental, economists have paid little attention to the relevant developments made by philosophers of mind. *Economics and the Mind* brings together a range of leading scholars in the fields of economics, philosophy of mind, and psychology, and offers the first in-depth analysis of the intersections of economics and philosophy of mind.

The various questions that arise and are discussed in this book often involve thinking about problems or concepts in economics through the lens of philosophy of mind. What is the role of emotions in decision-making? How do we make choices, and stick to them, over time? What do behavioral economics and neuroeconomics imply about the nature of the individual? Must preferences always be transitive? Can we be free to choose not to be free? Does the typical economic agent have a will? How do we equalize utility or happiness if it's all "in our heads" – or is it? The chapters of this book attempt to answer these questions and many more.

Economics and the Mind paves the way to a new interdisciplinary approach to economics and philosophy of mind, and will be of interest to all scholars working in the intersections of these areas, as well as behavioral economics, decision theory, and neuroeconomics.

Barbara Montero is Assistant Professor of Philosophy and **Mark D. White** is Associate Professor of Economics. They are both at the College of Staten Island and CUNY Graduate Center, USA.

Routledge INEM Advances in Economic Methodology
Series edited by Esther-Mirjam Sent, the University of Nijmegen, the Netherlands.

The field of economic methodology has expanded rapidly during the last few decades. This expansion has occurred in part because of changes within the discipline of economics, in part because of changes in the prevailing philosophical conception of scientific knowledge, and also because of various transformations within the wider society. Research in economic methodology now not only reflects developments in contemporary economic theory, the history of economic thought, and the philosophy of science; but it also reflects developments in science studies, historical epistemology, and social theorizing more generally. The field of economic methodology still includes the search for rules for the proper conduct of economic science, but it also covers a vast array of other subjects and accommodates a variety of different approaches to those subjects.

The objective of this series is to provide a forum for the publication of significant works in the growing field economic methodology. Since the series defines methodology quite broadly, it will publish books on a wide range of different methodological subjects. The series is also open to a variety of different types of works: original research monographs, edited collections, as well as republication of significant earlier contributions to the methodological literature. The International Network for Economic Methodology (INEM) is proud to sponsor this important series of contributions to the methodological literature.

1 Foundations of Economic Method, 2nd Edition
A Popperian Perspective
Lawrence A. Boland

2 Applied Economics and the Critical Realist Critique
Edited by Paul Downward

3 Dewey, Pragmatism and Economic Methodology
Edited by Elias L. Khalil

4 How Economists Model the World into Numbers
Marcel Boumans

5 McCloskey's Rhetoric
Discourse Ethics in Economics
Benjamin Balak

6 The Foundations of Paul Samuelson's Revealed Preference Theory, Revised Edition
A Study by the Method of Rational Reconstruction
Stanley Wong

7 Economics and the Mind
Edited by Barbara Montero and Mark D. White

Economics and the Mind

Edited by Barbara Montero and Mark D.
White

Routledge
Taylor & Francis Group

LONDON AND NEW YORK

First published 2007
by Routledge
2 Park Square, Milton Park, Abingdon, Oxon OX14 4RN

Simultaneously published in the USA and Canada
by Routledge
270 Madison Ave, New York, NY 10016

Routledge is an imprint of the Taylor & Francis Group, an informa business

Transferred to Digital Printing 2009

Typeset in by Taylor & Francis Books

British Library Cataloguing in Publication Data
A catalogue record for this book is available from the British Library

Library of Congress Cataloging in Publication Data
Economics and the mind / edited by Barbara Montero and Mark D. White.

p. cm.

"Simultaneously published in the USA and Canada."

Includes bibliographical references and index.

1. Economics--Philosophy. 2. Economics--Psychological aspects. 3. Philosophy of mind. I. Montero, Barbara, 1962- II. White, Mark D., 1971-

HB72.E2725 2007

330.01'9--dc22

006018087

ISBN13: 978-0-415-77056-9 (hb)   ISBN10: 0-415-77056-4 (hb)
ISBN13: 978-0-415-49373-4 (pb)   ISBN10: 0-415-49373-0 (pb)
ISBN13: 978-0-203-96613-6 (ebk)   ISBN10: 0-203-96613-9 (ebk)

Contents

List of illustrations   *vii*
Notes on contributors   *viii*

Introduction   1
BARBARA MONTERO AND MARK D. WHITE

**PART 1: PHILOSOPHY OF MIND, NEUROECONOMICS, AND
PSYCHOLOGY**   **9**

1   Emotion: the gaping hole in economic theory   11
    GEORGE AINSLIE

2   Ainslie's bundling and resolute choice   29
    EDWARD F. MCCLENNEN

3   The economics of the sub-personal: two research programs   41
    DON ROSS

4   Behavioral economics, neuroeconomics, and identity   58
    JOHN B. DAVIS

5   Language, monetary exchange, and the structure of the
    economic universe: an Austrian–Searlean synthesis   75
    STEVEN HORWITZ

6   Putting the brakes on vehicle externalism: two economic
    examples   89
    DAN FITZPATRICK

PART 2: AGENCY, PREFERENCES, AND REASONS   **113**

7   There are preferences and then there are preferences   115
    CHRISOULA ANDREOU

8   Freedom from choice: reconsidering Sen's case for
    maximizing opportunities   127
    DAVID GEORGE

9   Does *Homo economicus* have a will?   143
    MARK D. WHITE

10 Rationalizing coordination: towards a strong
    conception of collective intentionality   159
    HANS BERNHARD SCHMID

11 Adding reasons up   180
    WILLIAM A. EDMUNDSON

12 Externalism, expensive tastes, and equality   201
    KEITH DOWDING

    Index   216

List of illustrations

1.1	Hyperbolic discount curves from two rewards of different sizes available at different times	13
1.2	Summed hyperbolic curves from a series of LL rewards and an alternative series of SS rewards	14
8.1	A conflicted agent's metapreference, preference, and choice	130
8.2	The prisoner's dilemma	132
8.3	From internal conflict to internal harmony	134
8.4	Restricting choice as a welfare-improving action	137
8.5	Preserving free choice as a means of expressing sacrifice	137
10.1	Pure coordination	162
10.2	Coordination, relabeled strategies	163
10.3	Coordination, relabeled, complete set of strategies	163
10.4	Coordination, unequal equilibria	164

Notes on contributors

George Ainslie is the author of *Picoeconomics: The Strategic Interaction of Successive Motivational States within the Person* (Cambridge, 1992), *Breakdown of Will* (Cambridge, 2001), and articles on motivational conflict that have appeared in the psychological, economic, philosophical, and legal literature. He is chief psychiatrist at the Veterans Affairs Medical Center, Coatesville, PA.

Chrisoula Andreou is Assistant Professor in the Department of Philosophy at the University of Utah. Her recent publications are in the areas of action theory, rational choice theory, and ethics. She is especially interested in dynamic choice problems, analyses of temptation, and Humean conceptions of practical reason.

John B. Davis is Professor of History and Philosophy of Economics at the University of Amsterdam and Professor of Economics at Marquette University. He is author of *Keynes's Philosophical Development* (Cambridge, 1994) and *The Theory of the Individual in Economics* (Routledge, 2003), and co-editor of the *Journal of Economic Methodology*.

Keith Dowding is Professor of Political Science at the London School of Economics. He has published seven books (four edited), as well as numerous articles in the fields of political philosophy, social choice, urban politics, public administration, and British politics. He is co-editor of the Journal of Theoretical Politics.

William A. Edmundson is Professor of Law and of Philosophy at Georgia State University. He is author of *Three Anarchical Fallacies* (Cambridge, 1998) and *An Introduction to Rights* (Cambridge, 2004), and editor of *The Duty to Obey the Law* (Rowman & Littlefield, 1999).

Dan Fitzpatrick is Research Fellow at the University of Hertfordshire, Hatfield, UK, and Research and Project Coordinator at the Program for Social Studies of Environment and Development, University of Social Science and Humanities, Vietnam National University, Hanoi, Vietnam.

David George is Professor of Economics at La Salle University and author of *Preference Pollution: How Markets Create the Desires We Dislike* (University of Michigan, 2001). His current research interests include the effect of market values on education and the connections between social class and identity.

Steven Horwitz is the Associate Dean of the First Year and Professor of Economics at St. Lawrence University in Canton, NY. He is the author of *Microfoundations and Macroeconomics: An Austrian Perspective* (Routledge, 2000) and numerous articles on Austrian economics.

Edward F. McClennen is Professor of Political Philosophy, Syracuse University. His publications include *Rationality and Dynamic Choice* (Cambridge, 1990) and "The Rationality of Being Guided by Rules," in *The Oxford Handbook of Rationality* (A.R. Mele and P. Rawling, eds, Oxford, 2004)

Barbara Montero is Assistant Professor of Philosophy at the College of Staten Island and the Graduate Center (City University of New York). She works primarily in the areas of philosophy of mind and metaphysics on issues related to physicalism and bodily awareness.

Don Ross is Professor in the Department of Philosophy and the Department of Finance, Economics and Quantitative Methods at the University of Alabama at Birmingham, and Professor in the School of Economics at the University of Cape Town, South Africa. His most recent book is *Economic Theory and Cognitive Science: Microexplanation* (MIT, 2005).

Hans Bernhard Schmid is Assistant Professor of Philosophy at the Universities of Basel and St. Gallen, Switzerland, and can be reached at Hans-Bernhard.Schmid@unibas.ch.

Mark D. White is Associate Professor of Economics at the College of Staten Island and the Graduate Center (City University of New York). He has written many articles and book chapters on economics and philosophy (in particular, Kantian ethics), and can be reached at profmdwhite@ hotmail.com.

Introduction

Barbara Montero and Mark D. White

> In explaining or assessing human action, economic theory presupposes a
> largely unarticulated account of rational, intentional action.
>
> (Coleman 1997, 183)

> The assumptions that are at the basis of economic theory must be consistent
> with the mechanisms that guide the workings of the human mind.
>
> (Rizzello 1999, xv)

Economics is often defined as the science of choice or human action. But
choice and action are essentially mental phenomena that cannot be understood fully without considering the nature of mind itself. Philosophers
typically take choice to involve beliefs, desires, intentions, and arguably even
free will. And they often distinguish actions from mere bodily movements by
holding that the former, but not the latter, are in some sense deliberate and
as such involve mental processing. Although philosophers have long
concerned themselves with the connections between choice, action, and the
mind, economists have tended to steer clear of what might appear to be an *a
priori* debate, either implicitly adopting a "black box" theory of mind or
taking an extreme behaviorist orientation and neglecting the role of the
mental entirely. At the same time, philosophers thinking about choice and
action have tended not to dirty their hands with the real-world applications
in which economists are specialized, whether theoretical or empirical. This
volume brings economists and philosophers of mind together to explore the
intersection of their disciplines in studying choice and action, as well as
identity, the social world, collective agency, and other philosophical concepts
as they are used in economic theory.

Economics and philosophy of mind are not complete strangers, of course.
A number of influential 17th- and 18th-century thinkers such as David
Hume, Adam Smith, and Anthony Shaftsbury all theorized about both the
mind and economics, but their views about one topic were not always relevant to their views on another. Hume, for example, is well known for his
argument that passions, not reason, motivate action, but his economic contributions were focused more on the economy at large than the behavior of
economic agents. And in the last half of the 20th century, axiomatic decision

theory (on the part of economists and mathematicians) and action theory (on the part of philosophers) have primarily developed in parallel with little interaction. In retrospect, it would seem that many connections were possible through the years, but they were rarely made.

In more recent years, some inroads have been made to bridge this gap, but help was sometimes needed from disciplines other than economics and philosophy. For example, George Ainslie, a contributor to the present volume, has brought insights from psychology (such as hyperbolic discounting) and neuroscience (such as results of functional magnetic resonance imaging, or fMRI) into the modeling of economic decision-making with his development of picoeconomics, in which opposing interests inside an agent's brain compete strategically for influence over eventual choices. Several of the other contributors to this book, such as Edward F. McClennen and Mark D. White, comment on aspects of Ainslie's analysis, a testament to his influence and the innovations he has made (and continues to make). Related to Ainslie's contributions are the even more recent developments in neuroeconomics, a field combining economics and neuroscience that works toward finding the neurological bases for economic activity, discussed by several of the authors herein, such as John B. Davis and Don Ross.[1] Of course, contributions from psychologists are not new to economics: the groundbreaking work of Daniel Kahneman and Amos Tversky (1979) documented many anomalies in the standard rational choice theory used by economics, and, together with the bounded rationality approach pioneered by Herbert Simon (1955), provides the foundation for modern behavioral economics (Jolls et al. 1998; Camerer et al. 2003), as well as ongoing work merging psychology with economics (Rabin 1998; Brocas and Carillo 2003, 2004).

Apart from the very important work incorporating psychology or neuroscience, there has been little cross-pollination between philosophy of mind and economics, but what work there is has led to extremely interesting conclusions. For example, contributor John Davis, in his 2003 book *The Theory of the Individual in Economics*, relies on certain philosophical views about personal identity to critically assess mainstream and heterodox economics for their conceptions of the individual. Also, Robert Sugden, with his theory of "team thinking" (1993), largely introduced into economics the philosophical concept of plural agency, an alternative explanation of social facts, action, and reality, favored by philosophers of mind such as Margaret Gilbert, Raimo Tuomela, Michael Bratman, and John Searle, and discussed by contributor Hans Bernhard Schmid in the present volume (see Chapter 10).[2] There is also fascinating work related to mind from the Austrian school of economics, largely based on an often-neglected book by Friedrich von Hayek titled *The Sensory Order* (1952), as well as his other writings that focus on human beings' imperfect ability to obtain and process information.[3] Peter Boettke and Robert Subrick (2002) and Steven Horwitz (2002) have written in this vein, as does Horwitz in the present volume (see

Chapter 5). Also, Salvatore Rizzello's book *The Economics of the Mind* (1999) (hopefully not be confused with the present volume!) incorporates the insights of both Hayek and Simon to explore the role of institutions in saving scarce cognitive resources among individual human agents.[4]

Several modern philosophers of mind have been getting attention from economists in recent years, as well. Daniel Dennett's work is extensively incorporated into the work of contributor Don Ross, particularly his 2005 book *Economic Theory and Cognitive Science: Microexplanation*, in which he uses Dennett's theory of intentional behavior to develop a unified science that integrates economic theory with cognitive and behavioral science, along the way discussing other topics in the philosophy of mind such as agency, selves, and consciousness. John Searle is perhaps the best-known philosopher of mind among economists, having been recently the subject of a conference session at the 2001 Allied Social Sciences Association meetings and a resulting mini-symposium in the March 2002 issue of the *Journal of Economic Methodology*, as well as an entire issue of the *American Journal of Economics and Sociology* (containing a contribution from Searle himself), later reprinted as a separate volume (Koepsell and Moss 2003). Several of the chapters in the present volume discuss aspects of Searle's writings, from his thoughts on collective agency (Schmid, Chapter 10), rationality (White, Chapter 9), and social reality (Horwitz, Chapter 5).

The book is split into two parts: the first part contains chapters discussing the intersection of philosophy of mind and economics primarily in relation to psychology and neuroscience, and the second part contains chapters about rationality, choice, and agency. Our modest hope is that these chapters (all commissioned specially for this volume) contribute to this very promising development in the intersection between the fields of economics and philosophy of mind.

Part 1: Philosophy of mind, neuroeconomics, and psychology

Our first chapter is by George Ainslie, whose "Emotion: the gaping hole in economic theory" argues that the effects of emotion on rational decision-making cannot be ignored, and can in fact explain many anomalies of choice that have been identified over the years by scholars such as Kahneman and Tversky. He argues that for most people in modern, developed countries, discomforts such as pain and hunger are often trivial problems, and instead most of their time and effort is spent on seeking out emotional experiences. After reviewing his theory of hyperbolic discounting, Ainslie shows how this characteristic of human beings' valuation implies that risk and novelty are treasured properties of emotional experiences, and demonstrates the importance of this for models of rational behavior. Throughout, Ainslie cites results from neurophysiology and behavioral science to support his argument, evidence of the vitality of this multidisciplinary endeavor.

In his chapter, "Ainslie's bundling and resolute choice" (Chapter 2), Edward F. McClennen responds to one aspect of Ainslie's conception of self-control put forward in his 2001 book *Breakdown of the Will*. In that book, Ainslie proposes that, to combat the inclination to choose (irrationally) present over future consumption due to hyperbolic discounting, agents can bundle choices together under the rubric of a rule or principle. For example, a dieter may say to himself, "If I have a donut today, I will probably have one everyday, so it is very important that I not have one today." But Ainslie cautions against a tendency of such exercises of willpower to result in a self-defeating rigidity, a position with which McClennen disagrees. Drawing upon his past work on rationality (McClennen 1990, 1997), McClennen describes his own favored approach to dynamic choice problems such as those Ainslie concerns himself with, one that emphasizes positive reinforcement of cooperative agreements between successive "selves," rather than the sanction-based approach favored by Ainslie.

Don Ross's chapter, "The economics of the sub-personal: two research programs" (Chapter 3), uses concepts from philosophy of mind, and especially some innovative ideas of Daniel Dennett's, to explain how we can and should view the relationship between two theories of sub-personal interaction: Ainslie's picoeconomics and the new field of neuroeconomics. Ross argues that these two fields should be seen as complementary, rather than rival, programs, and he explores the proper relationship between them. He compares this relationship to that between microeconomics and macroeconomics, which he argues (in Ross 2005) is not reductive in the sense that macroeconomic phenomena can be explained by microeconomic behavior (a widely held belief of many economists). Just as this relationship is more complicated than ordinarily believed, the relationship between picoeconomics and neuroeconomics is similarly complex, and Ross uses many examples from both fields to illustrate his thesis.

John B. Davis's chapter, "Behavioral economics, neuroeconomics, and identity" (Chapter 4), furthers the approach of his 2003 book by examining the concept of the individual held by the very popular field of behavioral economics. Behavioral economists criticize neoclassical economics for its limited notion of preferences, on which its conception of the individual is (problematically) based. But Davis argues that behavioral economics borrows its concept of personal identity from cognitive psychology, which in turn is based on John Locke's well-known, and much-criticized, account of memory, which leaves it no more secure than neoclassicism's version. Davis suggests that neuroeconomics may provide a way to supplement behavioral economics' conception of the individual. Ultimately, however, relying on several thought experiments devised by philosophers such as Derek Parfit, he questions this approach and offers a mixed evaluation of the role neuroeconomics should play in identifying the economic individual.

Turning to John Searle's theory of social reality, Steven Horwitz, in his chapter, "Language, monetary exchange, and the structure of the economic universe: an Austrian–Searlean synthesis" (Chapter 5), argues that the "symbolization" role that Searle attributes to language (and that serves as the foundation for social reality) has direct, if imperfect, parallels with the role of money in providing the foundation for economic reality. After summarizing Searle's concepts of social reality and the Background, Horwitz compares and contrasts these concepts with some central ideas in Austrian economics: Hayek's theory of spontaneous order, Mises's insights into the role of monetary exchange and calculation, and Menger's description of the origin of money. Horwitz's chapter emphasizes that money and markets play an essential role in the economic aspect of social reality and the development of other social and economic institutions.

In his contribution, "Putting the brakes on vehicle externalism: two economic examples" (Chapter 6), Dan Fitzpartick criticizes the idea, proposed by philosophers Andy Clark and David Chalmers (1998), that any process should count as mental if it saves us cognitive effort and would count as mental if it were to occur inside our heads. As Fitzpatrick points out, the central point of the notion of division of labor in economics is that it allows for greater output at lower inputs of labor, and this makes it more efficient to purchase most goods from others rather than self-produce them. But this should not make us think that the process involved is part of the mind. Based on recent work on cognitive integration, Fitzpatrick proposes his *integration principle*, which, he argues, saves the general concept of vehicle externalism without making it apply to cases such as tax preparation and Menger's theory of the origin of money (also discussed in Horwitz's chapter, Chapter 5).

Part 2: Agency, preferences, and reasons

Chrisoula Andreou's contribution, "There are preferences and then there are preferences" (Chapter 7), defends the following two claims concerning rationality against what appear to be serious counterarguments: the *transitive-preferences claim*, that a rational agent's preferences are transitive; and the *preferred-option claim*, that rationality requires choosing a more preferred option over one less preferred. Andreou argues that these two claims are referring to two different conceptions of "preferences," between which she distinguishes, explaining how the two senses are to be defined and utilized, and shows that the counterarguments are misguided. Against this background, she reassesses the implications of Kenneth Arrow's famous Impossibility Theorem regarding the feasibility of democratic social choice. She argues that this theorem, although often seriously misinterpreted, nonetheless may be inescapable unless reconsidered in light of her dual concepts of preference.

David George's chapter, "Freedom from choice: reconsidering Sen's case for maximizing opportunities" (Chapter 8), critically appraises the use of metapreferences in the writings of Nobel laureate Amartya Sen. Although perhaps the first economist to mention metapreferences into the economic literature in his famous 1977 article "Rational Fools," Sen has relied upon them minimally in the years since. Building upon his 2001 book, *Preference Pollution*, George here links metapreferences to Sen's notion of capabilities and explores the implications that follow. Drawing on the work of philosopher Harry Frankfurt (1971), George argues that recognizing the uniquely human ability to have preferences about one's preferences requires some significant revisions of Sen's conclusions about freedom and choice, in particular his exclusion of content- and context-dependent preferences from considerations of "true" freedom.

In his chapter, titled "Does *Homo economicus* have a will?" (Chapter 9), Mark D. White discusses the nature of free choice and rationality in economic theory, arguing that the standard economic decision-maker has limited agency or freedom of choice, because his choices are modeled as deriving directly from his preferences and constraints. After summarizing recent contributions from John Searle, R. Jay Wallace, and other philosophers critical of the standard desire/belief model of choice in action theory, White proposes integrating a sense of true, free choice into the model of economic decision-making. Generalizing a model developed previously in the context of Kantian morality (2004), White uses a probability distribution to incorporate a distinct faculty of the will into the economic model of choice, wherein a person's probability of making the "right" or preferred choice is representative of her character. He then speculates on how these probabilities may change over time, and compares his theory to those proposed by George Ainslie, Michael Bratman, and Robert Nozick.

Hans Bernard Schmidt's chapter, "Rationalizing coordination: towards a strong conception of collective intentionality" (Chapter 10), discusses the theory of collective intentionality or plural agency, popularized by Margaret Gilbert, Raimo Tuomela, Michael Bratman, and John Searle. By means of an especially conspicuous example, he argues that, because of its individualistic limitations, the standard economic model of human behavior fails to capture the basic traits of even the most elementary social phenomenon: coordination. Schmid then summarizes the existing theories of collective intentionality, including Robert Sugden's account of team thinking, and concludes that even though they point the way to an improved account of coordination, a more robust conception of collective intentionality is still needed. He identifies the core weakness in all of these theories as their strict avoidance of any sense of "group mind," and Schmid argues that the choice between individual mind and group mind is misguided, based on a narrow understanding of intentionality.

In his chapter, "Adding reasons up" (Chapter 11), William A. Edmundson defends the maximizing conception of rationality that economists are often criticized for using, and argues that maximization is essential for moral philosophers to use as well. Employing the dual concepts of reasons and requirements, Edmundson argues that maximization uniquely connects what we have reason to do with what we are required to do, but with important qualifications that he traces out throughout the chapter. In the process, he confronts specific alternatives to maximization, such as sanction theory, voluntarism, and universalizability, and John Broome's (2003) recent criticisms of maximization. He concludes by discussing the difficulties of translating the maximization framework, along with the reason/requirement dichotomy, into the area of positive behavioral psychology, using insights from the work of Kahneman and Tversky, such as their distinction between intuitive and supervisory cognitive systems.

The final chapter, Keith Dowding's "Externalism, expensive tastes, and equality" (Chapter 12), addresses a central debate within egalitarianism: exactly *what* should be equalized? If we want to equalize happiness (or something like it), we run into the problem of "expensive tastes": if one person requires expensive goods to be just as happy as someone else who only needs simpler things, are we required to satisfy the person with so-called expensive tastes? Dowding sets aside the political issue, as well as the issue of what to equalize, and instead turns his attention to the more essential problem of measuring happiness (by any name), or what it means to say that one person is *ever* as happy as another. He argues that, despite the common assumption that happiness is in the mind and therefore cannot be measured or compared between persons (internalism), all of our intuitions regarding happiness comparisons are actually based on external, observable behavior, and this type of evaluation allows local interpersonal comparisons of utility, and even rough global ones, despite the common belief that any such comparison is impossible (again, based on internalism).

Notes

1 See Camerer, Loewenstein, and Prelec (2005) for an excellent survey.
2 See Gilbert (1989), Tuomela (1995), Bratman (1999), and Searle (1990); Davis (2003) also discusses plural agents in his critique of current economic concepts of the self.
3 See, in particular, Hayek (1937, 1945).
4 See also Fitzpatrick's chapter in this book (Chapter 6) for a different approach to cognitive savings within philosophy of mind.

References

Ainslie, G. (1992) *Picoeconomics: The Strategic Interaction of Successive Motivational States within the Person*, Cambridge: Cambridge University Press.
—— (2001) *Breakdown of Will*, Cambridge: Cambridge University Press.
Boettke, P.J. and Subrick, J.R. (2002) "From the Philosophy of Mind to the Philosophy of the Market," *Journal of Economic Methodology*, 9: 53–64.
Bratman, M.E. (1999) *Faces of Intention: Selected Essays on Intention and Agency*, Cambridge: Cambridge University Press.
Brocas, I. and Carillo, J.D. (2003) *The Psychology of Human Decisions, Volume 1: Rationality and Well-Being*, Oxford: Oxford University Press.

—— (2004) *The Psychology of Human Decisions, Volume 2: Reasons and Choices*, Oxford: Oxford University Press.

Broome, J. (2003) "Reasons," in P. Pettit, S. Scheffler, M. Smith, and R.J. Wallace (eds.) *Reason and Value: Essays on the Moral Philosophy of Joseph Raz*, Oxford: Oxford University Press, 28–55.

Camerer, C., Loewenstein, G., and Prelec, D. (2005) "Neuroeconomics: How Neuroscience Can Inform Economics," *Journal of Economic Literature*, 43: 9–64.

Camerer, C., Loewenstein, G., and Rabin, M. (2003) *Advances in Behavioral Economics*, Princeton, NJ: Princeton University Press.

Clark, A. and Chalmers, D. (1998) "The Extended Mind," *Analysis*, 58: 7–19.

Coleman, J.L. (1997) "Rational Choice and Rational Cognition," *Legal Theory*, 3, 183–203.

Davis, J.B. (2003) *The Theory of the Individual in Economics: Identity and Value*, London: Routledge.

Frankfurt, H.G. (1971) "Freedom of the Will and the Concept of a Person," *Journal of Philosophy*, 68: 5–20.

George, D. (2001) *Preference Pollution: How Markets Create the Desires We Dislike*, Ann Arbor, MI: University of Michigan Press.

Gilbert, M. (1989) *On Social Facts*, Princeton, NJ: Princeton University Press (1992 reprint).

Hayek, F.A. (1937) "Economics and Knowledge," *Economica*, 4: 96–105.

—— (1945) "The Use of Knowledge in Society," *American Economic Review*, 35: 519–30.

—— (1952) *The Sensory Order*, Chicago: University of Chicago Press.

Horwitz, S. (2002) "Comment on Boettke and Subrick and Faulkner," *Journal of Economic Methodology*, 9: 81–86.

Jolls, C., Sunstein, C.R., and Thaler, R. (1998) "A Behavioral Approach to Law and Economics," *Stanford Law Review*, 50: 1471–1550.

Kahneman, D. and Tversky, A. (1979) "Prospect Theory: An Analysis of Decision under Risk," *Econometrica*, 47: 263–91.

Koepsell, D. and Moss, L.S. (2003) *John Searle's Ideas about Social Reality: Extensions, Criticisms and Reconstructions*, Malden, MA: Blackwell Publishing.

McClennen, E.F. (1990) *Rationality and Dynamic Choice: Foundational Explorations*, Cambridge: Cambridge University Press.

—— (1997) "Pragmatic Rationality and Rules," *Philosophy & Public Affairs*, 26: 210–58.

Rabin, M. (1998) "Psychology and Economics," *Journal of Economic Literature*, 36: 11–46.

Rizzello, S. (1999) *The Economics of the Mind*, Cheltenham: Edward Elgar.

Ross, D. (2005) *Economic Theory and Cognitive Science: Microexplanation*, Cambridge, MA: MIT Press.

Searle, J.R. (1990) "Collective Intentions and Actions," in P.R. Cohen, J. Morgan, and M.E. Pollack (eds.) *Intentions in Communication*, Cambridge, MA: MIT Press, 401–15.

Sen, A.K. (1977) "Rational Fools: A Critique of the Behavioural Foundations of Economic Theory," *Philosophy and Public Affairs*, 6: 317–44.

Simon, H.A. (1955) "A Behavioral Model of Rational Choice," *Quarterly Journal of Economics*, 69: 99–118.

Sugden, R. (1993) "Thinking as a Team: Towards an Explanation of Nonselfish Behavior," *Social Philosophy and Policy*, 10: 69–89.

Tuomela, R. (1995) *The Importance of Us: A Study of Basic Social Notions*, Stanford: Stanford University Press.

White, M.D. (2004) "Can *Homo Economicus* Follow Kant's Categorical Imperative?," *Journal of Socio-Economics*, 33: 89–106.

Part 1

Philosophy of mind, neuroeconomics, and psychology

1 Emotion

The gaping hole in economic theory

George Ainslie

1 Introduction

Economics is the study of choice among limited resources. This kind of choice is easy to conceive and, often, to study when the limiting factor is the physical availability of external goods. Choice among internal processes that are available at will is harder to conceive and almost impossible to study, which is undoubtedly why economists have thought very little about it. And yet the most prominent of these internal processes, the emotions, are also limited in regular ways, and could be said to be far bigger creators of value in modern societies than goods which are physically limited. I will suggest a conception of how emotions generate value that is based on what are now widely accepted research findings, and point out some likely implications for more conventional economics.

The best sources of economic data have been marketplaces, which have revealed a basic constraint on competitive choice-making: Successful marketplace behavior depends on assigning each good a value that declines exponentially with delay. People who do not buy and sell according to exponential discounting become what are called money pumps, since a more rational agent can buy from them when they undervalue a good and then simply wait until they overvalue the good to sell it back to them at a profit. Thus economic theories of choice have converged on the model that assigns this value according to exponential discount curves, rational choice theory (RCT). Formalized almost as an afterthought by Samuelson (1937), RCT has become the established theory of how people value goods in the absence of pathology. It has even been argued that some forms of pathology – that is, of self-destructive choice-making – can arise within the framework of RCT via an extremely steep discount function (Becker and Murphy 1988). Insofar as other fields assume that choice will stay constant over time in the absence of new information, they can be said to follow RCT as well, since concave discount curves from any other function predict change of preference between smaller, sooner (SS) and larger, later (LL) goods as a function of elapsing time.

However, an increasing number of cases have been brought to light where people regularly depart from RCT. I have argued that RCT describes a special case of human motivation that arises as people adapt to competitive marketplaces. Elementary motivation in humans and nonhumans alike is described by a non-exponential discount curve, one that creates conflict among successive evaluations. The resulting patterns of choice must be studied by analysis of this conflict, a micro-microeconomics or *picoeconomics* (Ainslie 1986, 1992).

A recent article by Jolls *et al.* (1998) catalogued cases anomalous for RCT under the rubrics of bounded (limited) rationality, bounded willpower, and bounded self-interest. I will use these three categories to describe the potential contributions of picoeconomics to macro/microeconomic theory. In particular, I will expand their bounded self-interest category to begin an examination of how occasions for emotion acquire value alongside other limited resources, a topic which by the extent of motivation involved represents a gaping hole in RCT and economic theory generally.

Of the three, bounded rationality has been the subject of the most research but represents the least problem for conventional theory. It describes what look mostly like simple perceptual or computational errors in estimating value – framing effects, endowment effects, and many of the inconsistencies of choice described by Kahneman, Tversky, and their collaborators (Kahneman *et al.* 1982). Some of these may actually represent evasions of self-control, such as the defense of sunk costs in order to postpone the realization of loss, or attempts to achieve self-control, such as choosing illiquid investments at the cost of poorer returns (Harris and Laibson 2001); but many seem to be innocent errors; that is, they do not seem to be motivated. Rational allowance for limited cognitive capacity has been well described in the literature on satisficing (starting with March and Simon, 1958).

2 Bounded willpower

According to RCT, bounded willpower should not even be observed, since there is no need for will in the first place. A rational agent simply maximizes her exponentially discounted prospects at all times, and would have no incentive to restrict her future range of choice. It was the failure of choice to retain its predicted consistency over time in the absence of new information that first made the need for a radical re-evaluation of RCT evident. I have ascribed this failing to the shape of the basic discount curve (Ainslie 1975, 2001). A large number of experiments have now confirmed that both humans and nonhuman animals tend to discount prospective events in hyperbolic rather than exponential curves (Green and Myerson 2004; Kirby 1997). Humans seem to achieve exponential discounting only in special situations, particularly where competition for quantifiable goods threatens to make them money pumps insofar as they fail. The highly bowed shape of hyperbolic curves predicts that SS goods will often be preferred temporarily over LL goods, in the period just before the SS goods become available (*impulsiveness*; see Figure 1.1). The relatively high tails of hyperbolic curves predict also that making sequential choices in *bundles* should increase the incentive to pick LL options (see Figure 1.2). That is, series of LL options will be more apt to be chosen over the series of their SS alternatives than is the single LL option of Figure 1.1 to be chosen over the single SS option. Furthermore, these high tails should motivate a person (or nonhuman, if given a simple method) to commit her future behavior so as to forestall temporary preferences for SS options. These effects have all been observed experimentally: Both human and nonhuman subjects switch preferences from LL to SS alternatives as the SS alternatives draw near, increase their tendency to pick LL alternatives when choosing whole series of rewards at once, and learn behaviors the only effect of which is to commit them to make LL choices (reviewed in Ainslie 2001 and 2005).

The greatest objections to hyperbolic discounting have been (1) that it lacks an adaptive purpose and therefore should have been selected against in evolution and (2) that as often as not people avoid the impulsiveness it predicts. Regarding the first objection, it is not possible to state positively why hyperbolic discounting should have evolved as the basic principle of evaluating future events. The idea that it motivates organisms to attend to immediate opportunities and threats is not adequate, since exponential curves would provide a more objective weighing of immediate versus

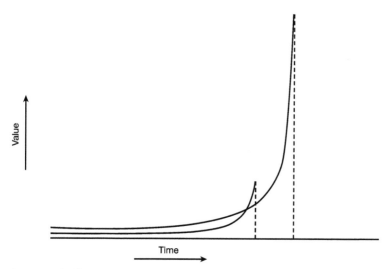

Figure 1.1 Hyperbolic discount curves from two rewards of different sizes available at different times.

The vertical bars represent the value of the reward when immediate, and each curve represents the discounted value of that alternative as a function of the time before it will be available. The smaller, sooner (SS) reward is temporarily preferred for a period just before it is available, as shown by the portion of its curve that projects above the curve from the larger, later (LL) reward.

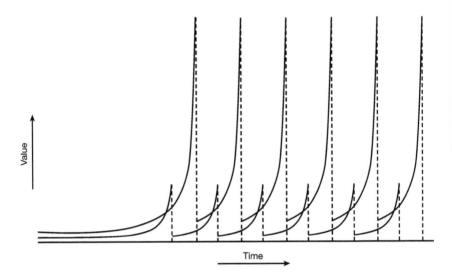

Figure 1.2 Summed hyperbolic curves from a series of LL rewards and an alternative series of SS rewards.

The curve from each reward represents the discounted value of that reward when summed with all the other rewards of the same size occurring later in time (to the right). The period of temporary preference for the series of all six SS rewards is about zero, but as time passes and there are fewer choices in the series, periods of temporary preference for the series of SS rewards get longer. The curves from the final pair of rewards show the same period of temporary preference that is depicted in Figure 1.1.

delayed events. Hyperbolic discounting might have been adaptive by making individuals follow instincts that lead them to sacrifice their own long-range interests for the sake of their offspring – to lure women into having babies and men into defending kin – but the hyperbolic shape was in place at least as early as rats and pigeons evolved, before there was much likelihood that an animal would recognize its long range interest in self-preservation. However, traits often survive not because they increase fitness but because they are not-too-costly side effects of traits that do. Hyperbolic discounting of prospective rewards is likely to have been a consequence of the more general hyperbolic principle of estimating sensory magnitudes, the Weber–Fechner law (Gibbon 1977), a consequence that was harmless until significant foresight evolved. And evolution requires time to fine-tune fitness. Organisms sufficiently foresighted to get in trouble from hyperbolic discounting have existed for no more than a hundred thousand years or so. Whatever the case may be, hyperbolic discounting is an empirical given, and any analysis of choice needs to include the motivational consequences of this discounting.

As for the second objection, when people avoid choosing SS over LL rewards, it is usually by self-control rather than spontaneous preference. The hyperbolic shape of spontaneous discount curves themselves suggests several means of self-control, such as finding external precommitments, diverting attention from likely sources of SS reward, and cultivating incompatible emotions that have some momentum; but the workhorse of self-control is willpower. The decrease in impulsiveness that results when choices are made in bundles suggests a mechanism for willpower, including a mechanism by which we can sometimes get our choices to approximate RCT. It also provides rationales for both the familiar experience of freedom of will and maladaptive overcontrol (compulsiveness). Again, these phenomena are described elsewhere (Ainslie 2001, 2005), and are only summarized here. Basically, an adequately self-observant organism – probably only a human – will come to see frequent temptation by SS rewards as creating an intertemporal variant of the repeated prisoner's dilemma. Of course, she will usually recognize this property under some other name, or have no name for it, just as interpersonal repeated prisoner's dilemmas that arise naturally have usually been recognized only tacitly even by effective players.[1] Once you have become aware of an intertemporal prisoner's dilemma relationship, even indirectly, giving in to a current temptation will make you expect to give in to similar temptations in the future, and thus reduce your expectation of getting a whole series of LL rewards rather than just the one currently at stake.

When you think your resistance to the current temptation is both necessary and sufficient to maintain the cooperation of your successive selves, you will have an incentive that constitutes willpower, without the involvement of any other faculty or organ. Since your estimate of necessity and sufficiency depends on your interpretation of past choices and on your prediction of future selves' interpretation of your current choice, your decision cannot be manipulated or even predicted with certainty from the incentives you face. Thus your will is imponderable, and, arguably, free.[2] However, the more your current choice matters as a precedent rather than as an experience in its own right, the more your evaluation of your choices will become lawyerly and, in the extreme case, compulsive. The observational benchmarks that predict whether you will go on cooperating with future selves come to define internal laws or personal rules, which are self-enforcing because your expectation of whole bundles of LL reward depend on your seeing yourself obey them.

Since this model of will depends on the recursive feeding back of choices and even of mooted choices, it will not be directly testable by controlled experiments until it is possible to observe the internal stages of choice. Neuroimaging has made some progress in locating the brain sites that are active when there is a prospect of reward and even when a subject is resisting an urge to consume a reward, but the results so far have not gone much beyond brain geography: When human subjects evaluate expected cash rewards, they not only discount them hyperbolically but generate correlated gradations of neural activity in identified brain centers such as the ventral striatum and posterior parietal cortex (Glimcher and Kable 2005). These regions are active also when smokers anticipate smoking (Monterosso *et al.* 2006). As both Berridge (1999) and I (Ainslie 1992: 101–14) have pointed out, a rewarding component is necessary for even aversive processes to be "attention grabbing" (Berridge 2004: 195), a component that he calls "incentive salience" and that I call very-short-range reward. There is evidence that the reward component that is common to both pleasurable and aversive processes involves GABAergic neurons in one part of the ventral striatum, the nucleus accumbens (Berridge 2004: 195). Similar is Bechara's (2006) concept of "primary induction," for which he finds the amygdala necessary. There are even some imaging studies of self-control. For instance, subjects choosing between SS and LL coupons with monetary exchange values have more lateral prefrontal activity when they choose the LL coupons (McClure *et al.* 2004). When smokers are instructed not to take available puffs on a smoke-delivery apparatus, the dorsal anterior cingulate cortex and supplementary motor area become differentially active (London *et al.* 2006). The medial prefrontal (orbitofrontal) cortex has been implicated in both temptation and its opposite, rational planning, depending on the method of observation (Davidson *et al.* 2000; McClure *et al.* 2004; Rolls 1999: 124–44; Volkow and Fowler 2000).

These neurophysiological data are encouraging. They confirm that some of the functional components of motivation that have been derived from behavioral research have specific locations. They increasingly support the notion that there is a marketplace in the brain of all processes available for choice, that is, that there is a common currency of reward, which makes all options comparable (Shizgal and Conover 1996). However, the direct observation of how the components of temptation and self-control interact still looks distant.

Meanwhile, I have argued that a favorite tool of the philosophy of mind, the thought experiment, can make common intuition usable to test models of willpower (Ainslie, forthcoming). Kavka's problem will serve as an example: You are offered a large sum of money just to intend to drink an overwhelmingly disgusting but harmless toxin. Once you have sincerely intended it, as verified by a hypothetical brain scan, you are free to collect the money and not actually drink the toxin (Kavka 1983). Philosophical discussion has revolved around whether you have any rational motive actually to drink the toxin once you have the money, and whether, foreseeing a lack of such motive, you can sincerely intend to drink it in the first place, even though you would drink it if that were still necessary to get the money. People usually say that it would not be rational to drink the toxin, but are then bothered by the counterintuitive possibility of defrauding themselves in this way.

The service of this thought experiment is to point out that there is a conceptual piece missing in the common theory of how people intend difficult behaviors. It is probably not possible to intend to drink if you expect to renege, but it is possible to commit yourself, more or less, not to renege. You do this by putting up a pledge of sufficient value; and the only pledge available to put up irrevocably in this situation is the credibility of your pledges in difficult choices in the future. This kind of pledge is recursive: The more you believe that you will keep it, the more you can keep it and the more you will subsequently believe you will keep it; the less you believe you will keep it, the less you can keep it, and so on. The pledge need not be deliberate, or even conscious. It is enough to notice that this choice resembles a kind of choice that comes up at other times. In that case your present choice will affect your prospect of making the similar future choices, whether you want it to or not. By the same token, your memory of similar past choices will tell you whether or not you have any such prospect to lose.

The current pledge need not put the set of all future pledges at risk, but if you don't relate it to a broader class of pledges – not just those involving toxins – you will probably expect it to be inadequate from the start. You won't feel as if anything else in your future is at stake. You will then have to throw in more collateral, as it were – to put a larger category of pledges at stake – if your intention is going to register on the scanner. This is a step that people facing stubborn urges speak of in many ways: You "get serious," you "solemnly vow," you "really mean it," you are "in earnest this time," and so on. But whichever way you speak (or think) about it, you have thereby related your current choice to the major category of choices where you are serious, earnest, and so on, and thus have put a big chunk of your credibility at risk. Once you have perceived your credibility with yourself to be at risk you have a rational incentive to drink the toxin. I submit that this unique ability to solve Kavka's problem supports the intertemporal bargaining model of willpower. Furthermore, the fact that people who think about the problem usually experience the incentive to drink the toxin only as a vague discomfort with the RCT solution (reneging) provides an illustration of the tacit nature of most intertemporal bargaining.

Higher processes

To recap my model thus far: hyperbolic discounting predicts a population of processes in partial conflict with each other, with outcomes determined by which of them is dominant when an irreversible choice can be made. These processes have grown to obtain rewards, and remain viable as long as they sometimes succeed. Processes that obtain quick rewards will be robust, and will dominate as long as they are not forestalled by earlier processes. These earlier, necessarily foresighted processes will be based on more attenuated reward values, but values that are more nearly proportionate to the "objective" rewards at stake. They have the advantage of acting before their shortsighted competitors, and, as I have described here, can often dominate even immediate alternatives when they seem to lead to whole bundles of rewards – the phenomenon of willpower.

There is nothing in this model to prevent the growth of foresighted processes that are generalists, brokers of reward that do not depend on specific sources of reward but forage for adequately long-lasting reward of any kind. Piaget (1937) described similar processes in his "tertiary circular reactions"; and, of course, if "ego functions" must compete in the internal marketplace they do so on this basis. These generalist processes are the financiers of the reward economy. The foresighted processes discern the greatest of rewards discounted over a relatively long time (the LL rewards) and plan how to forestall competing, faster rewards that are recognized as smaller from the perspective of distance (the SS rewards). The negatives in this model are always SS rewards, rather than nonrewards or inverses of reward, since in the absence of reward a process cannot compete for a person's participation. Addictive rewards such as drugs or self-destructive thrills turn negative over periods from hours to days; itch-like urges such as tics or irritating habits ("wanted" but not "liked" in Berridge's theory; see Berridge 1999) turn negative within seconds; urges for processes that never feel voluntary, like panic or the emotional component of physical pain, repeatedly lure and turn negative within a fraction of a second, as I have argued (Ainslie 2001: 51–61); but all compete for expression with the same positive currency. This should be called reward because its defining property is to make processes that it follows more likely to occur; but in modalities where it seduces only briefly it is radically different from pleasure.

Relevance to orthodox economics

Inter*temporal* bargaining connects the special case of rationality within competitive inter*personal* markets to the general case of hyperbolic valuation – in somewhat the way that relativistic physics defines a place for Newtonian physics while correcting its anomalies. The inter*temporal* bargaining model of decision-making that I have called picoeconomics suggests an infrastructure for the economics of inter*personal* transactions. The model of impulsiveness and will just described depicts the individual agents of micro-economics as populations in their own right, which, like collectives of individuals, must take their own diversities of interest into account. They will try to limit their choices to those that will stand up both to intermittent temptation and to compulsive application of personal rules. Someone trying to sell to such populations will discover markets both for rapidly paying goods that are harmful to them in the long run and for devices that restrict this market. These complex agents can sometimes follow personal rules to choose *as if* their discount curves were exponential, but often cannot do so. The lower the exponent (interest rate), the greater the strain on their resolve. Inter*personal* bargaining among members of a culture will result in a rough consensus about what degree of this strain a person can normally be expected to withstand (Ainslie 2001: 100–04).

3 Bounded self-interest, the entryway to emotional reward

Self-interest is said to be bounded – that is, limited – because of cases where individuals have behaved altruistically without any prospect of reward, or, as the argument about this case has progressed, without any increase in the prospective fitness of their genes. Even though altruistic choices can be required by personal ethics – in effect by personal rules (Rachlin 2002) – a strict utility theorist will still demand to know what source of reward such rules are protecting. The obvious answer is that the immediate basis of altruism is emotional; our motive is to enjoy the beneficiary's feelings vicariously, or at least not to suffer vicarious pain. Where someone's rules are lax it even happens that people give alluring but destructive presents so as to enjoy the immediate evidence of pleasure they seem to produce, despite credible information that later the beggar will indulge his drug habit or the fed animal will get sick. However, there is no generally accepted model of this emotional process. If altruism is mostly a way of getting occasions for vicarious pleasure, we need to ask what the nature of vicarious pleasure is.

But this question opens an even larger topic in turn. Vicarious pleasure is just one of many positive emotional experiences, ones that are not governed by bodily sensations.[3] And emotions are the preponderant goods of any modern society. As physical discomforts (hunger, cold, pain) have become trivial problems, most human effort has been directed toward obtaining some kinds of emotional experience and avoiding others. Even activities that aim at getting bodily sensations have a strong admixture of getting components that are not bound to these sensations. Food is enjoyed within the context of particular tastes that differ from one culture or one person to another. Pain is more or less aversive depending on its context and the person's attitude toward it (Beecher 1959 describes some extreme forms of this). It is true that people work for their money in order to buy facts – a good that is delivered or not, a service that is performed or not – but their valuation of what they buy often depends more on an emotion that it engenders than on any objective measure of well-being. Even money itself is apt to be valued for more than the goods and services that it will buy, a well-documented value that has been likened to a drug effect and that is not accounted for by standard economic theory (Lea and Webley forthcoming).

Thus the difficulty with RCT extends far beyond its excessive endorsement of selfishness. I submit that much of this difficulty comes from its anchoring basic value in the hard currency of external events – no longer a single font of value like gold or land, but nevertheless a set of external stimuli that are held even by psychologists to control the reward process. On the contrary, hyperbolic discounting raises the possibility that much reward is freely available to the internal marketplace, and is constrained mainly by the properties of intertemporal bargaining. Such a model makes no sense in a world of exponential discounting, of course, since that world lacks a rationale for intertemporal conflict. Given hyperbolic discounting, the elusive behavior of emotion can be particularly well explained.

Emotion as reward dependent

It is easy to study behavior toward durable rewards, events that reward reliably as long as the physiological potential (*drive*) exists, like food, sex, and relief of discomfort. When the internal process of reward is less tied to physical events, the valuation process becomes harder not only to observe but to conceive. What selective mechanism determines the value of processes that begin and end in the mind? Most value that does not arise from sensation arises from emotion, but emotions can be summoned deliberately. It is true that summoned emotion is usually paler than the kind that surprises us, but this property itself needs explanation. A process that is both a behavior subject to reward and a reward itself is in danger of falling into a positive feedback loop. What determines the competition of emotions in the internal marketplace, against each other and against more tangible sources of reward? This is a question that has begun to be answered at the neurophysiological level, but despite the birth of "neuroeconomics" the interaction of brain regions has so far told us little about how the currency of reward behaves.

In the meantime the hyperbolic form of future discounting offers at least a possible explanation (Ainslie 2001: 65–69, 161–97; 2005), which, again, is only summarized here. Reward that can be had just by opting for it will be limited by your hunger for it. This phenomenon, too, is easiest to see in the case of tangible rewards. A person with continuous, easy access to food will get significant enjoyment from eating only if she restrains herself from "grazing" and lets hunger build up. Hyperbolic discounting makes her value SS pleasures over LL ones when the SS ones are close, so her tendency will be to cash in small amounts of hunger as it develops rather than wait until the hunger is intense. In response people create strong restrictions by keeping food at a distance or making personal rules such as not to eat between meals. The motivation for such rules need have nothing to do with dieting; it may be enough that they permit sufficient build-up of hunger to make meals pleasurable.

The case of emotional reward is less obvious, but desirable emotions require infrequency to be strongly rewarding. However, unlike food, emotions are hard to restrict. You have continuous, easy access to them, and your attention moves too quickly to be controlled by personal rules, which themselves have to wait for the attention it takes to evaluate each proposed choice by the rules' criteria. A primitive kind of restriction develops naturally, in that a pattern of continuously opting for a given emotion – opting without occasion – will extinguish it. The real competition will be among emotions cued by intermittent occasions (as well as between these emotions and tangible rewards, of course). Strings of such occasions are supplied by *texts*, a necessary term despite its abuse by deconstructionists, which covers fictions, gambling games, news reports, memories – any sequential experience. All of these can pace the generation of emotions. However, some pacing patterns are the equivalent of grazing to satisfy hunger – "light fiction" or casual daydreams – while others have the power to build a high degree of suspense or longing. Having an emotion will be a more rewarding activity in the long run when the occasion is uncommon. News items, feats in sporting events, objects of collection, and victories in romance incite feelings in proportion to their perceived rarity.

Of course the rarity of an event may be subject to change precisely because it has served as an occasion for emotional reward; people learn to go looking for such instances. Occasions that you can voluntarily bring about sap the strength of emotions. People (and presumably nonhuman animals) wind up experiencing as emotion only those patterns that have escaped the habituation of voluntary access, by a selective process analogous to that described by Robert Frank (1988) for the social recognition of "authentic" emotions: expressions that are known to be intentionally controllable are disregarded, as with the false smile of the hypocrite. By this process of selection, emotion is left with its familiar guise as passion, something that has to come over you.

The role of facts

Belief has been increasingly recognized as a behavior in modern times, but the constraints that separate goal-directed beliefs such as self-delusions from what is experienced as make-believe have not been clear. Obviously the occurrence or non-occurrence of tangible rewards (those that satisfy hungers) will strictly shape beliefs about what will obtain them, as will the success or failure of instrumental beliefs (those that deal with getting testable goals). These shaping factors are experienced as facts – call them *instrumental* facts – and they leave little room for psychological construction. There are other facts that lack such practical tests of their validity but that are still useful in a way that make-believe is not (Ainslie 2001: 175–79). The property of factuality gets its non-instrumental importance from its selection of few occasions for emotional reward from many candidates. That is, non-instrumental facts get their importance by maintaining the rarity of occasions.

Other things being equal, texts that qualify as facts (by any stringent selective process, including communal folklore) are more potent than fictions, but facts can become cheap as well. News programs comb the world for facts which, if they happened close to you, would be overwhelmingly moving. There are all-sports channels, all-shopping channels, all-history channels, and so on. The impact of facts is reduced to that of fictions as they become infotainment, that is, when they stop being relatively rare. Ironically, one of the most potent factors that limit this cheapening of non-instrumental facts is instrumental value. The set of facts that are tools for tangible gain are often excellent disciplines for pacing emotional reward, partly because they inspire your neighbors to challenge you by competing for them, but more basically because they are limited in availability. Thus instrumentality, the value of facts for getting other goals, confusingly becomes a source of non-instrumental value. For instance, gambling for money has more kick than gambling for points, even when we gamble for money purely as recreation. And, in the United States at least, the variability of gasoline prices among stations makes the search for cheaper gas a challenging game; several acquaintances have admitted to a temptation to drive uneconomically far out of their way just for the sensation of winning at this game, even though they would not be playing it if it did not ostensibly save them money. Once we authenticate money as a prize, it becomes a tool for occasioning emotion as well, as does any text selected from the general ruck of texts by an adequately stringent process.

But rarity alone is not enough. Attention ranging freely as it does, it will inevitably move forward in a text in order to anticipate its occasions, and may thereby return the emotional reward sequence to a pattern of grazing. You can make a personal rule not to read ahead in a book, but memory or imagination will necessarily grow stale as repetition leads to anticipation and hence premature satiety; it must be refreshed by surprises – turnings that you cannot anticipate. With most emotional rewards, the only way to stop your mind from rushing ahead is to avoid approaches that can be too well learned. Thus the most valuable occasions will be those that are either not certain to occur or mysterious – too complex or subtle to be fully anticipated, arguably the goal of art. To get the most out of emotional reward, you have to either gamble on uncertainty or find routes that, although certain, will not become too efficient. In short, your occasions have to stay surprising, a property that has also been reported as necessary for activity in brain reward centers (for example Hollerman *et al.* 1998; Berns *et al.* 2001). Accordingly, surprise is sometimes said to be the basis of aesthetic value (Berlyne 1974; Scitovsky 1976). In modalities where you can mentally reward yourself, surprise is the only commodity that can be scarce.

Vicarious reward

Perhaps the source of the most robust occasions for emotion is not (mainly) a source of instrumental reward, but a source of patterns that are readily synchronized to our own emotional rhythms: the apparent experience of other people. I have argued elsewhere that the richest source of emotional occasions is to gamble on vicarious experience (Ainslie 1995; 2001: 179–86). Although a person is free to sample many sources of this experience, thus risking arbitrariness, the emotions suggested to her by a given perception are fixed – either the same emotions as her object is experiencing or, in the case of negative empathy, an obvious converse emotion like gloating at the object's chagrin. Recent neurophysiological data suggest that just watching another person generates highly specific signals about what she is experiencing via the stimulation of "mirror neurons" in your own cortex (Iacoboni *et al.* 1999). Empathy seems to be the hedonic exploitation of such a process, the modeling of another person's emotional choices by using your own (see a detailed hypothesis about this in Barnes and Thagard 1997). You adopt the criteria that you think the other is using to occasion emotion; for the time being, you entertain what you think would be her emotions. But, of course, they are hers only in the sense that you are having them according to a theory about her. They are happening in your brain. If you keep your model close to your observations, you can use it to occasion emotions just as you use your own situation.

Since emotions don't require a turnkey, just available appetite and adequately rare occasions to preserve this availability, you can sometimes experience the emotions you're modeling in the other person as substantially as the ones you have as yourself. To model the other people is to have their expected feelings; and nothing makes these vicarious feelings differ in kind from real ones. This, I argue, is the basis of the altruism that does not otherwise enhance your well-being. However, the impact of this phenomenon will be limited by the uniqueness of your relationship with the other person, just as the impact of texts in general is limited by their factuality; your vicarious experiences from strangers picked for the purpose will be little more than daydreams.

De gustibus disputare: *an addition to orthodox economics*

I began this chapter by repeating the truism that economics is the study of choice among limited resources. I then summarized some important implications of the hyperbolic discounting of expected value, leading to the point that intangible (emotional) reward is physically limited not by the availability of commodities but by internal states equivalent to hungers – call them the appetites or drives for these emotions – which permit self-reward at will as long as they are present. Because memory cannot be well controlled and positive emotions attenuate readily, good occasions for them must be adequately rare and surprising. Such occasions are the basic goods of the emotion-based sector of any economy.

Emotional occasions differ from other goods of commerce in several important properties:

1   They cannot be in assured supply without eventually losing their value. To maintain their freshness they must be at least partially unpredictable. To seek them deliberately you must accept gambles: works of fiction that have not become too familiar, chances for an exciting relationship, challenging tasks or sports, objects of collection that are competed for.
2   Instrumental tasks often make excellent pacers of emotional reward, but the best strategies for instrumental effectiveness are apt to differ from the best

strategies for emotional reward. The most efficient way of making a product may not be one that permits craftsmanship, and the most efficient way to solve a problem may not permit the savoring of the theoretical possibilities encountered. Efficiency experts delight in uncovering the flaws of methods that have been shaped by workers' tastes – and this criticism may sometimes be necessary not just for material efficiency but to maintain the specificity of the pacing criteria – but to be realistic economics needs to recognize the rationale of the emotional strategies, too. Actually this has somewhat happened, in analyses of what lottery structures are most popular or how game-like presentations enhance sales of tangible goods.

3   Because modern society values progress over mere cycles of appetite and satisfaction, people often feel obliged to control their impulses to seek risks. Adequately risky activities may then be selected only if they seem objectively productive. The result is a market for activities that have some rationale as productive but actually make their ostensible objects less certain: lotteries as ways to get rich, fights to impose peace, or complex methodologies that people are unaccountably loath to simplify. There often results an asymmetrical competition between making progress and putting that progress at risk, which cannot be resolved by weighing these purposes against each other because intermittent loss of the ostensible goal is necessary for maintaining the emotional payoff of this goal. The attempt to get satisfaction is called hedonically rational; the attempt to refresh appetite is stigmatized as irrational. The problem may be that society does not recognize that the value of such incentives as wealth or "objective" future prospects is subject to appetite. However, recognition that you are intentionally incurring losses is apt to undermine your perception of the task as instrumental and thus as unique. Our cultural ignorance may have itself been shaped by differential reward.

4   People develop tastes for emotional rewards just as they do for satisfying hungers. We are apt to find incitements to our favored emotions with the regularity of finding meals. Just as dictators are said to need an unbroken succession of enemy threats, there are people who seem always to have something to be angry about or, more rarely found, people who always find something at which to rejoice.[4] Emotional goods depend more on individual tastes than instrumental goods do, but for an individual they may have a steadier value.

5   Emotional goods depend on the probability structure of their occasions rather than on specific, turnkey powers as foods or drugs do. Desirable structure could be called texture, the availability of satisfactory patterns with which to occasion emotional reward. Hence on one hand emotional goods are much more substitutable for one another than are tangible goods, as one good becomes too predictable (loses its texture) or common or uncommon. Without a component that restrains premature satiation over time, they are highly susceptible to fashion.

With such a unique component, on the other hand, they may become unsubstitutable. Since a history of having been chosen is one feature that can make an emotional occasion unique, an occasion for emotional reward may acquire the status of a fact just by having been consistently chosen. Among many potential religious tenets with adequate textures, for instance, belief in one soon becomes self-confirming, since it both serves its purpose and has come to stand out from the others by being part of the person's history. Similarly, if someone gets emotional gratification from particular habits of hospitality to neighbors, frugal housekeeping, or just a daily routine, these habits may initially be shaped by an instrumental purpose but after some years no longer need this purpose, because the details of these specific habits have come to stand out as occasions.

Analysis of how emotional occasions are governed may certainly lead to the discovery of marketable goods, beyond what merchandizers have already discovered empirically. However, welfare economics may have a greater need for this analysis. Recognition of the self-generated nature of reward may lead to analysis of how the increasing systemization of modern institutions – trends toward uniform "best practices," thorough review, and zero risk – may be having a negative impact on the texture of people's lives. The monotony of factories has been notorious for a century, and many of the poor have always preferred life on the streets to the regimentation of institutions; but now automation has made it possible for centralized managements to impose data collection and customer relations routines on increasing numbers of employees, including doctoral-level professionals and ex-entrepreneurs, who, driven out of business by superior systemization, must seek jobs with their former competitors. Recognition of the role of texture may gradually transform welfare economics from a concern with inequalities of wealth to a concern that a person or system that can control the texture of others' lives often makes their days monotonous, without being held accountable for this cost.

4 Summary

The history of economics comprises increasingly sophisticated observations of people's choices in markets and theoretical models suggested by these observations. Because successful negotiation in markets depends on assigning each good a value that depends on its scarcity and declines exponentially with delay, economic theories of choice have converged on the model that assigns this value most effectively, rational choice theory (RCT). However, as physical discomforts (hunger, cold, pain) have become trivial problems in modern societies, most effort has been directed toward obtaining certain kinds of emotional experience and avoiding others. Events that are in limited supply still provide the occasions for these experiences, but since a person has some ability to assign meaning to these events and even to have the emotions without them, they have not been understood as goods (or bads) in a market. This understanding should be re-evaluated in light of mounting evidence that all of an individual's choices are determined in a single internal marketplace, and that this marketplace, in contrast to conventional markets, discounts delayed events hyperbolically rather than exponentially.

Hyperbolic discounting can explain the higher mental processes ("ego functions") that have heretofore not seemed derivable from elementary reward-seeking processes. It predicts a need for will, and offers a rationale for how willpower can arise simply from a person's interpretation of her own response to existing incentives. Hyperbolic discounting also leads to a theory in which emotions both generate reward and are selected by reward. Its implications make risk a positive factor in determining value, as well as giving scarcity a value beyond that created by its conventional role in the relationship of supply to demand. These constraints on emotional reward differ radically from the constraint of needing conditioned stimuli, the constraint that seems to be generally assumed. They make vicarious experience valuable in its own right, quite apart from the instrumental value of human relationships. Thus the inter*temporal* marketplace can be expected to create specific patterns of interaction with inter*personal* markets, patterns that may be responsible for many anomalies such as bounded willpower and bounded self-interest that contradict RCT.

Notes

1 Many situations ranging in importance from ordinary courtesy to whether wars will be escalated have been negotiated as repeated prisoner's dilemmas, but the formal game was described only in 1950 (Poundstone 1992).
2 As it becomes clearer that physical indeterminacy would make choices feel random rather than willed, authors trying to fit the experience of an originating will have searched for a process that would make choice among known incentives unpredictable, even by oneself. I have shown how recursive self-prediction can put the observing self in the middle of a chaotic process and thereby satisfy this test (background and argument in Ainslie 2001: 129–34, and forthcoming).
3 I will not deal with negative emotions here. I have argued elsewhere that the urge for grief or panic is like the urge for an addictive substance, only the cycle of reward and nonreward is extremely condensed (Ainslie 2001: 173–74).
4 Although anger is usually thought of as a negative emotion, it has many of the properties of a positive one (Lerner et al. forthcoming) and some people certainly cultivate it on a daily basis. There are people for whom even emotions that they consciously avoid seem to have a regular market value: the person who is constantly afraid of something despite the variability of actual threat (the customer of fear "mongers"), or always grieving at something.

References

Ainslie, G. (1975) "Specious Reward: A Behavioral Theory of Impulsiveness and Impulse Control," *Psychological Bulletin*, 82: 463–96.

—— (1986) "Beyond Microeconomics: Conflict among Interests in a Multiple Self as a Determinant of Value," in J. Elster (ed.) *The Multiple Self*, Cambridge: Cambridge University Press, 133–75.

—— (1992) *Picoeconomics: The Strategic Interaction of Successive Motivational States within the Person*, Cambridge: Cambridge University Press.

—— (1995) "A Utility-Maximizing Mechanism for Vicarious Reward: Comments on Julian Simons' 'Interpersonal Allocation Continuous with Intertemporal Allocation,'" *Rationality and Society*, 7: 393–403.

—— (2001) *Breakdown of Will*, Cambridge: Cambridge University Press.

—— (2005) "Précis of *Breakdown of Will*," *Behavioral and Brain Sciences*, 28: 635–73.

—— (forthcoming) "Thought Experiments that Explore where Controlled Experiments Can't: The Example of Will," in D. Spurrett, D. Ross, H. Kincaid, and L. Stephens (eds.) *Distributed Cognition and the Will: Individual Volition in Social Context*. Cambridge, MA: MIT Press.

Barnes, A. and Thagard, P. (1997) "Empathy and Analogy," *Dialogue: Canadian Philosophical Review*, 36: 705–20.

Bechara, A. (2006) "Broken Willpower: Impaired Mechanisms of Decision-Making and Impulse Control in Substance Abusers," in N. Sebanz and W. Prinz (eds.) *Disorders of Volition*, Cambridge, MA: MIT Press, 399–418.

Becker, G. and Murphy, K. (1988) "A Theory of Rational Addiction," *Journal of Political Economy*, 96: 675–700.

Beecher, H. (1959) *Measurement of Subjective Responses*, Oxford: Oxford University Press.

Berlyne, D.E. (1974) *Studies in the New Experimental Aesthetics: Steps Toward an Objective Psychology of Aesthetic Appreciation*, Washington: Hemisphere Publishing.

Berns, G.S., McClure, S.M., Pagnoni, G., and Montague, P.R. (2001) "Predictability Modulates Human Brain Response to Reward," *Journal of Neuroscience*, 21: 2793–98.

Berridge, K.C. (1999) "Pleasure, Pain, Desire, and Dread: Hidden Core Processes of Emotion," in D. Kahneman, E. Diener, and N. Schwartz (eds.) *Well-Being: The Foundations of Hedonic Psychology*, New York: Russell Sage Foundation.

—— (2004) "Motivation Concepts in Behavioral Neuroscience," *Physiology and Behavior*, 81: 179–209.

Davidson, R.J., Putnam, K.M., and Larson, C.L. (2000) "Dysfunction in the Neural Circuitry of Emotional Regulation: A Possible Prelude to Violence," *Science*, 289: 591–94.

Frank, R.H. (1988) *Passions within Reason: The Strategic Role of the Emotions*, New York: W.W. Norton and Company.

Gibbon, J. (1977) "Scalar Expectancy Theory and Weber's Law in Animal Timing," *Psychological Review*, 84: 279–325.

Glimcher, P.W. and Kable, J.W. (2005) "Neural Mechanisms of Temporal Discounting in Humans," paper presented at the Third Annual Meeting of the Society for Neuroeconomics, Kiowah Island, SC, September 16.

Green, L. and Myerson, J. (2004) "A Discounting Framework for Choice with Delayed and Probabilistic Rewards," *Psychological Bulletin*, 130: 769–92.

Harris, C. and Laibson, D. (2001) "Dynamic Choices of Hyperbolic Consumers," *Econometrica*, 69: 535–97.

Hollerman, J.R., Tremblay, L., and Schultz, W. (1998) "Influence of Reward Expectation on Behavior-Related Neuronal Activity in Primate Striatum," *Journal of Neurophysiology*, 80: 947–63.

Iacoboni, M., Woods, R.P., Brass, M., Bekkering, H., Mazziotta, J.C., and Rizzolatti, G. (1999) "Cortical Mechanisms of Imitation," *Science*, 286: 2526–28.

Jolls, C., Sunstein, C.R., and Thaler, R. (1998) "A Behavioral Approach to Law and Economics," *Stanford Law Review*, 50: 1471–1550.

Kahneman, D., Slovic, P., and Tversky, A. (eds.) (1982) *Judgment under Uncertainty: Heuristics and Biases*, Cambridge: Cambridge University Press.

Kavka, G. (1983) "The Toxin Puzzle," *Analysis*, 43: 33–36.

Kirby, K.N. (1997) "Bidding on the Future: Evidence against Normative Discounting of Delayed Rewards," *Journal of Experimental Psychology: General*, 126: 54–70.

Lea, S.E.G. and Webley, P. (forthcoming) "Money as Tool, Money as Drug: The Biological Psychology of a Strong Incentive," *Behavioral and Brain Sciences*.

Lerner, J.S., Tiedens, L.Z., and Gonzalez, R.M. (forthcoming) "Portrait of the Angry Decision Maker: How Appraisal Tendencies Shape Anger's Influence on Cognition," *Journal of Behavioral Decision Making*.

London, E.D., Monterosso, J., Mann, T., Ward, A., Ainslie, G., Xu, J., Brody, A., Engel, S., and Cohen, M. (2006) "Neural Activation during Smoking Self-Control," poster presented at the 68th annual meeting of the College on Problems of Drug Dependence, Scottsdale, AZ, June 20.

McClure, S.M., Laibson, D.I., Loewenstein, G., and Cohen, J.D. (2004) "The Grasshopper and the Ant: Separate Neural Systems Value Immediate and Delayed Monetary Rewards," *Science*, 306: 503–07.

March, J.G. and Simon, H.A. (1958) *Organizations*, London: John Wiley & Sons.

Monterosso, J., Ainslie, G., and London, E.D. (2006) "Delay Discounting Based on Activation in the Ventral Striatum," poster presented at the 68th annual meeting of the College on Problems of Drug Dependence, Scottsdale, AZ, June 20.

Piaget, J. (1937) *Construction of Reality in the Child*, trans. M. Cook, 1954, London: Routledge and Kegan Paul.

Poundstone, W. (1992) *Prisoner's Dilemma: John von Neumann, Game Theory, and the Puzzle of the Bomb*, New York: Doubleday.

Rachlin, H. (2002) "Altruism and Selfishness," *Behavioral and Brain Sciences*, 25: 239–96.

Rolls, E.T. (1999) *The Brain and Emotion*, Oxford: Oxford University Press.

Samuelson, P.A. (1937) "A Note on Measurement of Utility," *Review of Economic Studies*, 4: 155–61.

Scitovsky, T. (1976) *The Joyless Economy: An Inquiry into Human Satisfaction and Consumer Dissatisfaction*, Oxford: Oxford University Press.

Shizgal, P., and Conover, K. (1996) "On the Neural Computation of Utility," *Current Directions in Psychological Science*, 5: 37–43.

Volkow, N.D. and Fowler, J.S. (2000) "Addiction, a Disease of Compulsion and Drive: Involvement of the Orbitofrontal Cortex," *Cerebral Cortex*, 10: 318–25.

2   Ainslie's bundling and resolute choice

Edward F. McClennen[1]

1 Introduction

In an extensive series of books and articles, George Ainslie has presented a strikingly interesting theory about human deliberation and choice behavior. It is one that, he argues, sheds considerable light both on an important kind of human irrationality and also on how it can be at least partially overcome. I propose to compare what he has to say about this irrationality and its partial solution with an account I have offered about a parallel kind of irrationality and its solution. For the most part I will focus on the discussion he offers in his most recent book (Ainslie 2001) and my own views as developed in two works (McClennen 1990, 1997).

The irrationality with which Ainslie is concerned is predicated on an assumption that persons have a robust tendency to discount future goods hyperbolically rather than exponentially (Ainslie 2001: ch. 3). This leads them to exhibit dynamic inconsistency of their preferences over time. What they now prefer to do on a contemplated occasion some distance in the future turns out not to be what they prefer to do when that future draws nearer. The proposed solution to this problem, according to Ainslie, is for one to adopt a personal rule, prescribing choices that are in accordance with one's longer-term interests. Adherence to such a rule will be motivated by one's thinking of all the choices prescribed by the rule as bundled together, so that in adopting the personal rule one makes not just the single choice presented at that moment, but thinks of oneself as making a whole series of choices. Alternatively put, one conceives of the choice one now faces as setting a *precedent* – either for continual adherence to the personal rule or for continual abandonment of the rule.

One thing that is especially striking about this account, which relies on and adapts various economic concepts, especially those of decision and game theory, is that the proposed solution poses its own problem. The bundling technique, he argues, disposes the self to an undesirable kind of rigidity. It appears, then, that the self is poised between the Scylla of dynamic inconsistency and the Charybdis of a special form of self-imposed "enslavement," with little possibility of finding some equilibrium state in between that will enable the self to avoid both unfortunate outcomes.

Now, some time back I worked on a very special problem in decision theory, concerning the plausibility of what has been taken, from Von Neumann and Morgenstern on, as a key axiom of expected utility theory, the (strong) independence axiom, together with the principle in which it has typically been grounded in the context of dynamic choice theory – the separability principle. Separability requires that the choice made at any node in a decision tree must be the same as the choice that would be made were the agent to face a logically distinct tree, namely the truncated tree that begins *de novo* at that node (McClennen 1990: 106–07). My interest in the separability principle is that it provides the ground for the independence axiom, which in turn appears to preclude what otherwise appears to be a coherent and plausible way of discounting for risk and uncertainty (McClennen 1990: 67–73). As it turns out, however, some have thought there is a clear roadblock to working out an alternative account of non-separable preferences. This comes in the form of a pragmatic argument to the effect that a person whose choice behavior fails to satisfy the separability principle and the independence axiom will end up also violating a very secure and plausible principle that requires rejection of acts that are strictly dominated with respect to sure outcomes (Raiffa 1961). This is essentially a pragmatic argument. I have sought to show that it is fallacious (McClennen 1990: sects. 5.5, 10.4). More generally, I have argued that one can avoid pragmatic difficulties in general by choosing a plan covering the whole sequence of choices to be made and then *resolutely* executing that plan. Subsequently, I have explored the significance of such a possibility within the context of a general theory of resolute choice that would apply to a much wider set of choice problems, especially those in which one adopts a plan calling for two or more choices, and then finds oneself subsequently tempted to depart from that plan (McClennen 1997: 217–22).

Ainslie and I thus appear to have been exploring parallel problems and offering parallel solutions. The problems are parallel in that Ainslie is interested in a class of situations in which, due to the disposition to discount hyperbolically, one faces a problem of dynamically inconsistent preferences. My interest is in a class of situations in which, in virtue of a relaxation of the separability principle, one can be presented with a sequence of choices that, once again, poses a problem of dynamic inconsistency, which extends to cases in which one faces a temptation to depart from a rule adopted – where one now does not prefer to continue with the plan originally adopted. Such a preference reversal, in each case, can be characterized in the following manner: at time t_1, upon looking ahead, one prefers (at t_1) that x be chosen over y at time t_3, but at some time t_2, subsequent to t_1 but prior to t_3, one prefers (at t_2) that y be chosen over x at time t_3. Of course, such a preference reversal might plausibly and unobjectionably be the result of receiving new information, subsequent to t_1, about the remaining options. But the more interesting cases, upon which both Ainslie and I have focused, are those in which the reversal takes place without any new information being received. Alternatively put, we have both been concerned with a class of situations in which the disposition to settle upon what to do incrementally – deciding to cross each bridge only when we come to it – seems to be what poses a problem for the agent.

In each case, moreover, the suggestion is that the problem can be resolved by appeal to the notion of choosing in accordance with a personal rule or plan, where the rule or plan in question is the one that, antecedently, one prefers to follow. That is, Ainslie argues for bundling the sequences of choices to be made together, selecting the bundle that is most preferred, and then, at each choice point, choosing in the manner specified by reference to that preferred bundle. For myself, I do not appeal to the notion of bundling, but rather to the idea of adopting a plan that specifies a sequence of choices to be made, and then resolutely adhering to that plan; but this involves, in effect, settling antecedently upon what one regards as the most preferred sequence of choices one can make, and then, at each choice point, choosing in the manner that was called for by the preferred set of choices. In this respect, it could also be said that each of us has proposed that the agent adopt a more "holistic" or "global," as opposed to an incremental, way of choosing, when there are a number of repeated choices (for example, to abstain or to fail to abstain) over time.

In what is to follow, I want to look more closely at what Ainslie has to say about his bundling solution, and see in just what other respects our accounts do or do not coincide. To anticipate, I shall argue that, on closer inspection, our respective accounts diverge, and that they do so at a deeper level of conceptualization regarding the classes of dynamic choice problems upon which we have focused.

2 Multiple selves and bargaining

One can begin by noting that both Ainslie and I have sought to provide a grounding for our accounts of how to deal with preference reversals by appeal to a model in which the person is best analyzed in terms of multiple time-defined selves, between whom some sort of intertemporal tussle is taking place. Moreover, the model that Ainslie and I both utilize invokes a prisoner's dilemma game between the present self and some future self, in which failure to cooperate leaves the selves worse off than they need be if only they would cooperate, but where, nonetheless, the future self has motivation to defect from the agreement reached (Ainslie 2001: 90–94; McClennen 1997: 243–51). To be sure, the prisoner's dilemma game is a simplification of the problem that the time-defined selves face on each of our accounts, for it allows, simplistically, for only two options – cooperate or don't cooperate – without any consideration of the specific terms upon which the two or more selves end up agreeing.[2] Moreover, for the most part it conceptualizes the situation as involving only a present self and one future self. But even this simplified version suffices to show the nature of the problem.

This gives rise, predictably, to the idea that some sort of bargaining or negotiation needs to take place. That is, an agreement must be reached to the effect that the various time-defined selves will coordinate their choices. This would appear to provide both Ainslie and myself with an account of a kind of holistic choice, in which one settles upon a plan or rule or bundle of choices and then proceeds to execute it.

To be sure, the nature of the bargaining that takes place in each of our models is complicated by the fact that the selves in question exist sequentially, rather than simultaneously. That is, in Ainslie's model, as well as in my own, it is assumed that bargaining takes place between successive selves, so an account is needed as to how this is possible. Ainslie offers such an account by appeal to an ingenious experiment:

> Picture a lecture audience. I announce that I'll go along every row, starting at the front, and give each member a chance to say, "cooperate" or to say, "defect." Each time someone says, "cooperate," I'll award a dime to her and to everyone else in the audience. Each time someone says, "defect," I'll award a dollar only to her. And I ask that they play this game solely to maximize their individual total income, without worrying about friendship, politeness, the common good, and so on. I say that I will stop at an unpredictable point after at least 20 players have played, at which time each member can collect her earnings.
>
> (Ainslie 2001: 93)

Clearly, each successive person has a direct interest in the behavior of each subsequent player, and in trying to predict what future persons will do it will be relevant to see what each previous self has chosen, *as well as how one proposes to choose oneself*. Again, on this model any one person must recognize that their own choice sets a precedent for those who come later. Indeed, as Ainslie points out, one's own choice will be the most salient of previous choices for the next player in order. One certainly doesn't want one's choosing "defect" to trigger a whole series of subsequent defections – for one's final gains are directly proportional to how many of the players (including those still to come) are cooperative. Of course, if most of the previous players have chosen to defect, one cannot hope that one's being cooperative when one's turn comes up will have much influence on subsequent choices. Ainslie reports that on being questioned after the game ends, players generally indicate they used this kind of reasoning.

It can also be noted that a resolute agent is not committed to choosing between "all and nothing" plans. The plan adopted might allow for certain exceptions. Similarly, Ainslie supposes that one has more than just the extreme options of always doing something or never doing it. For example, in the case of drinking, one need not suppose that there are just two options: never drink alcohol or drink heavily. One might decide to adopt a more moderate personal rule. The problem of defining a compromise rule leads him into a very interesting discussion of "bright lines" – the possibility of there being some compromise between all or nothing that can be said to stand out in such a way that all those involved can coordinate upon it. Against this, however, he makes it clear that in some cases, specifically where the action is addictive, the introduction of a more flexible rule would presumably be ill advised: in such cases the only bright line is complete abstinence. Here, incidentally, is one clear difference between us, for I have not suggested that my model has any clear application to cases involving the potential for physical addiction. In particular, the problem of addiction does not arise in the context of the study of the dynamic inconsistency induced by dropping the separability axiom, or dealing with garden-variety temptations.

3 Strategic interaction and prediction

Another comparison that needs to be explored is that between the presuppositions of Ainslie's model and those associated with the strategic character of what is known as *sophisticated choice* (Strotz 1955). The most common form of a sophisticated choice involves the present self predicting what the future self would do if a certain future situation were to arise, and then acting now in a manner that precludes that situation from arising. This is the essence of what is known as a precommitment strategy, symbolized by the story of Ulysses and the Sirens. Because of its temporal priority, the present self is sometimes able, in effect, to block some later self from doing what the later self would most prefer to do. In this sense the present self is able to manipulate the situation to its own advantage and to the disadvantage of the later self. Thus Ulysses has himself tied to the mast, and the ears of his crew stopped up, so as to prevent the boat from being turned towards the Island of the Sirens. Notice that an essential feature of this approach is that the present self begins by first adopting a *predictive* stance toward its own future self. That is, the present self conceives of its future self as simply another being whose choice is to be (contingently) predicted, rather than another self with whom it must arrange to cooperate.

Of course, as Ainslie himself points out, such strategic maneuvering is not an exercise of willpower (Ainslie and Monterosso 2003: 837). Willpower involves a more complex process, in which the agent increases its self-control by bundling choices together. Suppose, for example, the agent prefers never smoking to repeatedly smoking, even though at any particular moment the preference is to smoke. By viewing the decision that is made at the moment as if it were a decision regarding what is to be done on an indefinitely large number of successive occasions, the preference for long-term abstinence can outweigh the preference for smoking at the present moment. But what would empower the "executive" self in this situation – that is, let the long-term preference take precedence over the preference of the moment? Ainslie suggests that the key here is to understand that the "marketplace" interaction between distinct time-defined selves gives rise, out of its own resources, to the requisite executive power (Ainslie 2001: 89). His appeal to executive power is somewhat puzzling, however. There is no executive power in the case of market interaction: only the operation of the invisible hand.

What, then, is the process? Ainslie argues that the best way for the present self to predict what it will do on future occasions is to observe what it does on this occasion. That is, it will take its present choice as *precedent-setting* for future choices, in a manner similar to that which occurs in Ainslie's audience game (2001: 93). The reasoning process, in the case of the single person, is something like the following: if I smoke now, I am all too likely to smoke on each occasion in the future when I am presented with the choice; I do not want to smoke repeatedly; so I will not smoke this time. Of course, it is not enough that the present self is able to bring to mind its preferences for repeated non-smoking; it must think that what it chooses on the present occasion *conditions*, in the sense of setting a real precedent for, its future choice behavior. If I smoke now, I am all too likely to continue to smoke; and if I refuse to smoke now I am likely to be able to continue with a policy of abstinence. This makes self-control – acting on principle – a matter of *self-prediction*: "personal rules represent self-enforcing contracts with your future motivational states," and keeping such a contract "depends on your seeing each current choice as a precedent that predicts how you're apt to choose among similar options in the future." And again: "personal rules are a recursive mechanism: they continually take their own pulse, and if they feel it falter, that very fact will cause further faltering" (Ainslie 2001: 87–89).

Ainslie correctly observes that this way of choosing is still strategic (2001: 62). The present self in effect supposes that the future selves will react this way or that, according to how the present self chooses. Since the predicted outcome of its choosing not to smoke now is preferred to the outcome of its choosing to smoke now, it chooses not to smoke now. On this model, the self does not simply react to how it expects the future selves to choose – as if that future choice behavior were an unconditional given; rather, it gauges the reaction of its future selves to each of the present possible choices (to smoke now or to not smoke now), and chooses that option whose outcome is most preferred given what it predicts will be the reaction of the future self to however it now chooses.[3] This suggests that the bundling approach is really only an "internal" version of the idea of precommitment. Still, this brings our accounts closer together, since my account of resolute choice explicitly rejects the idea of strategic maximization through external precommitment, and focuses instead on a genuinely cooperative approach involving internal commitments by the parties to the intertemporal choice problem.

4 What kind of model is involved?

Ainslie insists that bundling does not smoothly resolve the problem of hyperbolic discounting. Why? Short-range interests continually seek to evade personal rules by repeatedly proposing exceptions. As Ainslie puts it, the will, as expressed in the maneuver of bundling, is a recursive process that bets the expected value of one's future self-control against each of a series of successive temptations (Ainslie 2001: 89). This is, of course, fully predictable if the basic model is that of a process of sophisticated or strategic interaction in which the present self (the long-range interest) seeks to impose its will upon the future self (the short-range interest), which continually poses the problem of temptation.

However, his analysis is complicated by his making repeated appeals to a different model of interaction between long-range and short-term interests. What he does is to explicitly treat the "tussle" that arises between long-term concerns and the temptations of the moment as something that can also be analyzed in terms of an intrapersonal (that is, intertemporal) *bargaining* model, whose logical structure is that of the familiar indefinitely iterated prisoner's dilemma game – the very same logical structure that is found in his experiment with his audience, as already described. Each self has to choose whether to conform to a pattern of cooperative interaction – which if sustained will work to everyone's advantage in the end – or defect. Defecting promises additional benefits for the defector, but if it triggers defection on the part of subsequent selves, the defector would consequently lose thereby. Obviously the "best" solution for any self is to defect, while others continue to cooperate.

The first thing to note about the appeal to the iterated prisoner's dilemma game is that the model is not yet that which we encounter in classical bargaining theory. There is, in fact, in Ainslie's work no reference to the standard Nash model of bargaining (Nash 1953). Recognition that one is faced, as it were, with an all-or-nothing choice, either defecting all the time – that is, repeatedly giving in to the temptation of the moment – or never defecting, does not address the issue of the *distribution* of benefits from cooperation, which is the issue addressed in the standard theory of bargaining. Instead the resolution process is described in terms of establishing a "bright line." But the bright lines vary significantly from one situation to the next, and there is no general theory offered here as to how the compromise is reached. The discussion by Ainslie (2001: chs. 6, 7) offers some very original remarks about how to understand what is going on, but none of it fits very neatly with the usual accounts of bargaining.

Notice, in particular, that it is assumed in the idealized Nash bargaining model that thoroughly rational bargainers will not leave unrealized gains that they could cooperatively secure. This is usually expressed in terms of the idea that rational players will achieve a Pareto-optimal outcome. But on Ainslie's account the cooperation between long-term interests and the temptations of the moment is constantly being upset as the long-term and short-term interests tussle with one another. And where cooperation ends up being imperfect, one cannot hope that the outcome will be Pareto optimal.

In this regard, Ainslie's bundling concept can be more convincingly related to a model of indefinitely repeated interaction, in which cooperation is secured by a sense, on the part of each time-defined self, of the loss that comes from a failure to comply – a loss resulting from the subsequent defections of the other selves. That is, conformity to the rule (effective interaction) is secured by the present self realizing that defection will likely lead to "retaliatory" defections by the other selves on subsequent rounds. To be sure, Ainslie's model also presupposes that the self that is cooperative on the present occasion can likewise expect future cooperation – but still this expectation is qualified by the present self's own willingness to cooperate. That is, it must reckon with the consideration that subsequent selves are likely to switch to defection if it chooses defection. Here, it could be argued, then, it is the fear of a *loss* as a result of retaliation that motivates the self to not defect (that is, to cooperate).

I do not doubt that less than fully rational selves will likely have to rely upon the threat of retaliation. However, I have (controversially, to be sure) proposed an alternative model of interaction between fully rational agents, one that is predicated on the idea that it is the realization of the *gain* to be secured by cooperation that will motivate the successive selves to keep to the rule, and that for a thoroughly rational self this would suffice (McClennen 1997, 2001). That is, making threats and carrying them out (when defections occur) is a strategy that thoroughly rational interactors should not have to employ; it will only come into play when one has to deal with imperfectly rational selves.

5 The implications of thinking in terms of predicting

As I have already remarked, the most plausible way to interpret both the sophisticated choice model and the model of bundling are as models of *strategic* choice. In each case, the self bases his or her choice on an estimate of what he or she predicts the subsequent self will (contingently) do. What bothers me about this is exactly what bothers me about the standard model of *inter*personal interaction. The models in each case manage to make the business of rational interaction a matter of maximizing responses to (correct, contingent) predictions about the behavior of the other.

Such a view is, I suggest, predicated upon what I am tempted to characterize as a remarkably "autistic" conception of the reasoning process of a rational agent, according to which one conceives of one's own future self or another self as merely a conditioning variable whose value one needs to predict. That is, it is committed to a view in which one's own future choices or the choices of another self are just (hopefully) predictable *givens* that partially define the "natural" environment with which the self must contend. The problem is that agents who think this way cannot do as well as agents who can transcend this conceptualization, and see their problem as one calling for *coordinated* choices between rational selves, in order to realize the mutual gains that are possible. In this respect, it can be said that the standard theory is self-defeating. Persons who reason in the standard way have to expend valuable resources to provide each participant with the incentive to keep to whatever agreement they can reach. In contrast, those who can conceptualize their problem as one calling for cooperation between themselves and others can achieve an outcome that is clearly Pareto efficient relative to that which is achieved by the standard reasoners. The interpersonal and intrapersonal bargaining that Ainslie describes seems to clearly commit him to the less efficient form of interaction.

6 The downside of personal rules

Ainslie's rational agents are described as perpetually conflicted, as caught in a squeeze play between the self who seeks long-range gain and the self that wants to give in to the impulse of the moment. But the former of these selves is motivated by a long-term consideration that expresses itself in terms of the strategy of bundling and, as such, is supposed to *outweigh* the impulsive preference of the moment. Why, then, is there still a tussle? Why, given the reasonableness of the will, does it "break down"?

The argument here is powerfully presented. Considerable evidence is marshaled for the "breakdown" problem that the will can experience. However, the account offered is still puzzling. The device of personal rules was supposed to provide a way to undercut the dictatorial power of impulsive, short-range considerations. Whereas before there was nothing to counter short-term interests, now, at least, they have a serious contender. Granting that the long-term interests may not, or may only partially, succeed in overcoming short-term impulses, still it is surprising to discover that, on his account, the "solution" itself can itself become a problem. On his account the intertemporal tussle that takes place is between preferences that reflect long-term concerns based on rational reflection of what is really in one's interest, and impulsive preferences of the moment. Under that description it is odd to think of the bundling maneuver and the exercise of the "will" as having the negative features he ascribes to them. In particular, it is unclear why personal rules "can become prisons" (Ainslie 2001:145). Ainslie himself appears to be aware of the puzzle: he writes that personal rules

> are something we create for ourselves – if not deliberatively, at least under the influence of relatively long-range incentives. There's nothing we've discussed so far that suggests why a rational person, realizing at some level that she discounts the future hyperbolically, can't come close to maximizing her long-term rewards by bundling her choices into categories.
>
> (Ainslie 2001: 146)

However, he goes on to argue that a strong case can be made that there is a negative side to the use of personal rules – a negative side that is *inherent* in the utilization of personal rules – and that "the intertemporal bargaining model predicts that it will have serious side effects" (Ainslie 2001: 146). However, as real as the problems he mentions are, it is not at all clear why they flow from the model of personal rules that he has constructed. Perhaps the answer lies in the underlying assumptions about the interaction of selves, as I have discussed them here – in the conflictual dimensions of that interaction. But even so, I think, the story needs to be fleshed out more carefully. Ainslie has told us much about the nature of the breakdowns, but less about *why* breakdowns occur.

This marks the most important difference in our viewpoints. I have proposed resolute choice as a way of overcoming the problem of dynamic inconsistency, but I do not think of it as posing its own problem. Perhaps this difference is in part due to the fact that, as I have already mentioned, I make no claim to offer a theory that resolves the problems of addiction. In the various articles I have written on this subject, I have proposed resolute choice not as a solution to addictive choice, but as a device that enables a person to deal with preference change situations in a manner that does not carry with it the costs involved in an exercise of sophisticated choice (see, in particular, McClennen 1997). If the argument were that the earlier self could, by being resolute, impose its will on the later self, then I might also have to contend with the negative features of such a device. However, while I think sophisticated choice does carry with it the liability of a breakdown – precisely because it involves a strategic imposition by the earlier self on the choices of the later self – that is not true of resolute decision-making. My argument has been that what can motivate acting in a resolute fashion is precisely the recognition by the successive selves that in virtue of being resolute each time-defined self stands to gain, at the very least by a reduction in certain costs. On my account, cooperation need not be viewed as the result of a strategic move that is kept in place by costly precommitment and enforcement devices. Instead, I have supposed it is something that is predicated on, and enforced by, a mutual recognition of the gains to be secured thereby by each successive, and rational, self.

The model I have in mind for intrapersonal choice can be thought of as an *intra*personal adaptation of a model of *inter*personal cooperation. The latter model, of course, is not the one that economists employ. In a manner strikingly parallel to the one proposed by Ainslie, economists suppose that cooperation emerges out of a bargaining process, but poses a "free-rider" problem, in that any particular participant can do even better by defecting when others cooperate. Thus, in order to ensure cooperation, the arrangement must be backed up by some enforcement mechanism. Perhaps the introduction of such a mechanism can be thought of as an interpersonal analogue to what in Ainslie's intrapersonal model is the "overbearing" way in which willpower functions.

In the resolute choice model, what motivates the self is the realization that it has a choice between a variety of precommitment devices, each of which involves some sort of coercive device, or acting on a sense of the mutual gains, over and above those that enforcement devices can secure – gains to be realized by exercising willpower. In proceeding in this manner the rational agent could be said to make a rule-*guided* choice rather than a sanction-*goaded* choice.

7 Conclusion

I have, in effect, then, two main concerns about Ainslie's theory. The first is that his account of personal rules, and of "willpower," seems to me to rely too heavily upon something akin to the standard theory of rational deliberation. I find this theory too limiting, if not self-defeating. I think the problem with it is, at root, that the self is limited to having to employ only another version of what, following the economist Strotz (1955), can be described as a *sophisticated* choice approach. In contrast, the model of resolute choice that I have proposed is specifically intended to overcome the limitations of sophisticated deliberation, and to give an account of how the self does not have to settle for a second best – that is, a suboptimal – outcome. The second concern that I have is that it is not clear why, even on Ainslie's account of personal rules, their utilization *inherently* carries with it the negative features that he identifies. This is a part of the story that deserves to be developed more clearly. More needs to be said about why the will can break down. Despite my worries here, however, we are all indebted to Ainslie for an extremely interesting account of the problem of hyperbolic discounting of time, and how it can be at least partially resolved by the use of personal rules.

Notes

1 I would like to acknowledge here some very helpful comments from Professor Ainslie.
2 One could imagine, for example, that a bargain is struck in which one of the subsequent selves is allowed to deviate now and again, on specified rounds, from the cooperative scheme so as to secure, over the longer run, a greater share of the benefits that cooperation makes possible.
3 As it turns out, this connects with a model of interaction that was originally developed in Von Neumann and Morgenstern (1953: 148) but subsequently abandoned in favor of the Nash equilibrium model (Nash 1951). The Von Neumann and Morgenstern model, however, continues to have application to situations in which choices are made sequentially rather than simultaneously, which is the case in the situations in which Ainslie and I are interested.

References

Ainslie, G. (2001) *Breakdown of Will*, Cambridge: Cambridge University Press.
Ainslie, G. and Monterosso, J. (2003) "Will as Intertemporal Bargaining: Implications for Rationality," *University of Pennsylvania Law Review*, 151: 825–62.
McClennen, E.F. (1990) *Rationality and Dynamic Choice: Foundational Explorations*, Cambridge: Cambridge University Press.
—— (1997) "Pragmatic Rationality and Rules," *Philosophy & Public Affairs*, 26: 210–58.
—— (2001) "The Strategy of Cooperation," in C.W. Morris and A. Ripstein (eds.) *Practical Rationality and Preference: Essays for David Gauthier*, Cambridge: Cambridge University Press, 189–208.

Nash, J. (1951) "Non-Cooperative Games," *Annals of Mathematics*, 54: 286–95.
—— (1953) "Two-Person Cooperative Games," *Econometrica*, 21: 128–40.
Raiffa, H. (1961) "Risk, Ambiguity and the Savage Axioms: Comment," *Quarterly Journal of Economics*, 75: 690–94.
Strotz, R.H. (1955) "Myopia and Inconsistency in Dynamic Utility Maximization," *Review of Economic Studies*, 23: 165–80.
Von Neumann, J. and Morgenstern, O. (1953) *Theory of Games and Economic Behavior*, 3rd edn., New York: Wiley and Sons.

3   The economics of the sub-personal

Two research programs

Don Ross[1]

1 Introduction

The behavior of individual people has often been modeled by analogy with that of communities of people. Plato, Hume, and Freud, among many others, posited divided selves to explain a range of phenomena, especially moral compromise, weakness of will, self-defeating dispositions and actions, and feelings of equivocation. More recently, the philosopher Daniel Dennett (1978, 1987, 1991a) has explained both intentional behavior and consciousness by positing armies of stupid internal homunculi that compete with one another for control of the stories people tell about themselves to others, and thereby to themselves. Thomas Schelling (1978, 1980, 1984) has accounted for some common behavioral patterns that puzzle his fellow economists – notably apparent preference reversal over time – by reference to the dynamics of self-control. He models this by reference to sub-personal interests that form coalitions to capture a person's overall behavior, and which must make and regularly renegotiate trade-offs in order to preserve their bargains in the face of inducements to defect from other sub-personal interests.

If it makes sense to model behavioral dynamics by constructing sub-personal entities that are or have "interests," and behave so as to promote different ends in competition and cooperation with one another, then this entails some further assumptions. In particular, we must suppose that some things the sub-personal interests seek are scarce. This scarcity comes in first-order and second-order forms. Second-order scarcity is the scarcity of the goods and services from the environment that are needed to promote the interests, and in terms of which the interests are partly identified. First-order scarcity is scarcity of what might be called "personal resources." The person can only attend to a finite range of information and can only perform a finite range of actions. These are opportunity costs at the level of the whole person, but confront each sub-personal interest as supply constraints.

Dividing the person thus implies the possibility, at least in principle, of an economics of the sub-personal. The psychiatrist George Ainslie, who has built a model of internal bargaining among interests to explain addiction and compulsive behavior, has called this "picoeconomics" (Ainslie 1992).

Still more recently, the development of new technologies for (indirectly) observing internal brain regions while they compute decisions, including decisions about relative economic value, has produced a wave of research in so-called "neuroeconomics" (Montague and Berns 2002; Glimcher 2003). These new contributions directly raise a question for the economic theorist, one which embroils her in the foundations of the behavioral sciences in an unfamiliar way. The question is: how might neuroeconomics and picoeconomics be related to each other, and how are they together related to conventional microeconomics? In this chapter I will argue that the answer that is likely to seem most natural at first – that the three form a cascade of levels, with neuroeconomics at the bottom, in which generalizations from each domain ontologically validate and explain those from the domain one level above by relations of reductive decomposition – already shows signs of being too simple.

Ross (2005) argues that picoeconomics relates to microeconomics in the same way that post-war neoclassical microeconomics is related to macroeconomics – given the right construal of the latter relation, which is not the one found in standard histories of economic thought. Ever since macroeconomics was invented by Keynes and Hicks, economists have generally assumed that, at least in principle, it ought to reduce to microeconomics. It is not always obvious what they have in mind by this, or that they have in mind something clearly defined. Philosophers of science decompose the idea of reduction into several species, and no one kind of reduction applicable to a given domain necessarily implies that any of the others apply to it.[2] Sometimes reduction is mereological and explanatory: we seek to explain both the existence and the nature of composite (or "higher-level") kinds of things by showing how they are composed out of "lower-level" things whose existence and nature are taken for granted for the purposes of the explanation. Other reductions are intertheoretic. These kinds of reductions aim to show how one theory is a logical consequence of another. Typically, this amounts to showing that the reducing theory generalizes the reduced theory – or, as is also commonly said, that the reduced theory is a special case of the reducing one.

Almost all economists believe that macroeconomic objects and processes reduce to microeconomic ones in the first sense. Note that this is a metaphysical assumption, not something that economics shows. Nor is it something economists aim to show; if demonstrating the cogency of this sort of reductionism is anyone's job, it is one for philosophers.[3] Many economists do, however, hope to reduce macroeconomic theory to microeconomic theory, and some – rational expectations theorists – sometimes say they have pulled it off. This claim is misleading, however. Rational expectations macroeconomics borrows microeconomic modeling techniques, to be sure; but it does so by constructing theoretical fictions – infinitely lived agents and atomless measure spaces – that do not occur in any microeconomic generalizations (Ross 1999). This is not reduction as any philosopher of science would understand it. More to the point, it clearly has nothing to do with any sort of explanatory reduction. (In any case, few economists now expect rational expectations macroeconomics to be the whole or final account of macroeconomic phenomena, and many think it applies only to very special circumstances).

I argue (Ross 2005, forthcoming) on this basis that the relationship between microeconomics and macroeconomics is not reductive. Instead, I maintain, macroeconomics is explanatively basic relative to microeconomics, thus reversing the traditional picture of the relationship. Macroeconomic dynamics *create* microeconomic agents – roughly, whole people during the stretches of their biographies in which their behavior is consistent enough to satisfy the weak axioms of revealed preference, plus Houthakker's axiom. The interactions of these agents – their games – then feed back recursively into macroeconomic patterns. And so, similarly, microeconomic dynamics build picoeconomic agents – sub-personal interests – whose behavior feeds back into microeconomic patterns. The "raw material" for all of this is phys- ically constrained information flows in biological, social, and cultural systems, where the constraints in question vary systematically across these different kinds of systems.

This picture is apt to seem incredible to an economist trained in graduate school, like most, to think that any macroeconomic generalization is suspi- cious unless we can see at least in principle how it might have solid "microfoundations." However, this combines a legitimate concern for *unity* of science – for concern with avoiding commitment to types of objects and processes, and to theoretical generalizations, that are ontologically "stranded," and which thus must seem to be posited merely as ad hoc devices for writing down predictions – with a particular philosophical view about *how* unity must be achieved that does a poor, and increasingly poor, job of describing ontological and intertheoretic relationships found across the network of sciences. The non-reductionist account of unity as consisting in a network rather than a hierarchy with "top" and "bottom" levels is defended with reference to economics by Ross (2005) by appeal to *consilience*, that is, to the fact that it unifies observations and well-developed theories from the following domains:

- study of information-flow dynamics and control architectures in large neural networks and in brains (Kennedy and Eberhart 2001);
- study of the limitations on control through processing bottlenecks in complex distributed systems, most notably brains and markets (Siljak 1991);
- study of the social processes by which human infants are sculpted into people by pressures from adults for coherent stabilizing narratives (McGeer 2001; Ross 2006);
- study of coordination dynamics by evolutionary game theorists (Young 1998);

- study of economic behavior under experimental controls – especially the study of preference reversal phenomena (Ainslie 1992, 2001; Loewenstein *et al.* 2003);
- study of the dynamics by which market microstructures are differentiated, stabilized, and disrupted (O'Hara 1995).

Abstracted from the details of the argument, this view is bound to seem very radical to most economists. It indeed abandons methodological (and ontological) individualism, that is, the idea that explanatory progress consists in disassembling aggregates into atoms and their interactions. However, contrary to casual dogma asserted in some economic methodology and exploited to great effect in anti-economics tracts (for example Keen 2002), individualism has played no significant role in the detailed motivation of neoclassical theory. It is for this reason that my view can actually be conservative with respect to mathematical modeling technology: it encourages retention of the whole Samuelsonian economic formalism, but without requiring denial of any of the recently established empirical and experimental data on economic behavior. Specifically, in my framework an economic explanation, at any level of analysis (that is, pico, micro, or macro), continues to consist in identification of (static or dynamic) equilibria in the behavioral dispositions of sets of agents simultaneously maximizing the values of utility functions.

The purpose of this chapter is to indicate some implications of this view for the interpretation of the relationship between the two ongoing research programs that study sub-personal economic behavior: picoeconomics and neuroeconomics.

2 Neuroeconomics, picoeconomics, and reduction

A critic might worry that in promoting abandonment of microreductionist ambitions in economics I am looking for embarrassment. My suggestion, this critic might contend, is being pressed just at the moment when new technology will finally allow us to directly study the microfoundations of economic behavior (as opposed to having to infer these foundations, by means of models, from data that are mostly aggregate). The new technology this critic has in mind is the set of methods for monitoring brains while they guide on-line behavior: positron emission tomography (PET), transcranial magnetic stimulation (TMS), and, most importantly for now, functional magnetic resonance imaging (fMRI). These have made possible the thriving new sub-discipline of neuroeconomics, the study of the neural sub-strata of economic behavior.[4] What could be more reductionistic than looking for the basis of economic behavioral dispositions directly in the brain? If this seems promising, as the early successes of neuroeconomics certainly suggest it is, am I not calling for a halt to reductionistically motivated research just as it finally about to pay off?

We're indeed getting striking discoveries from neuroeconomics. Let me cite a small sample. Paul Glimcher and colleagues have shown that firing rates in monkey parietal motor neurons that control movements relevant to reward contingencies under uncertainty can be trained to encode the expected utility of each possible movement relative to the expected utilities of alternative possible movements (Platt and Glimcher 1999). Monkeys playing inspection games against computers robustly track Nash equilibrium, and Glimcher and his team have discovered how they do it: by adjusting behavior so as to keep the firing rate of the trained neurons constant. Fluctuations in rates closely predict those in computers programmed to track Nash equilibria in identical games (Glimcher 2003). Breiter and colleagues found correlates of utility tracked by elements of the human reward pathway (but with optimization defined by reference to prospect theory rather than classical expected utility theory) (Breiter *et al.* 2001). Montague and Berns (2002) report that the human orbitofrontal cortex responds to changes in the expected value of monetary rewards in accordance with a functional form that (given measured distributions of risk-aversion levels in groups of randomly drawn subjects) corresponds to the Black–Scholes model of portfolio option pricing. Also from Montague's lab comes the finding that neurons in dorsal striatum encode evolving expectations of reciprocity when sequences of games in which efficiency requires players to trust one another converge toward cooperative equilibria (King-Casas *et al.* 2005). This list of discoveries could be greatly extended.

What are the implications of this for the model theory of economics? First, note that the results support a Samuelsonian first-order theory as applied to the neurons themselves. That is, if we model individual neurons or groups of neurons as economic agents, they appear to compute optima under budget constraints; but the optima in question are relative to *their* utility functions rather than the utility function of the person they "serve." A given equilibrium in interactions among neurons may thus fail to correspond to equilibrium in the game being played by the person. So, as Berns suggests, "the interaction of different pools of neurons in the brain may result in phenotypic behavior that appears to be irrational, but it is possible that the rational agents are the neurons, not the person" (Berns 2003: 156).

As noted earlier, the idea that non-equilibrium behavior by people might emerge from equilibrium behavior by sub-personal agents pre-dates neuroeconomics; it is precisely the suggestion of Schelling, taken up and elaborated by Ainslie. Picoeconomics explains behavioral patterns by inferring internal agents (interests) playing games whose equilibria are the behavioral patterns to be explained. And so just as groups of rational people are subject to Arrowian cycles, so communities of rational internal interests can generate preference reversals and other microeconomic-level irrationalities in equilibrium (Kavka 1991).

This convergence suggests a straightforward proposal as to the relationship between picoeconomics and neuroeconomics: identify picoeconomic interests with neuronal agents to be discovered by neuroeconomics. On this idea, microeconomics will be given direct picoeconomic "foundations," and the model theory for Samuelsonian neoclassicism can simply be the standard 1950s one, but "shifted down a level." If this simple relationship turns out to predict the future course of research, it will amount to a vindication of reductionism from the microeconomic level down. This would not in itself refute my case against reductionism as between the macro and micro levels, but it would leave me in the awkward position of having to explain a basic asymmetry within the general class of economic phenomena, and to that extent would make non-reductionism as applied to macroeconomics look less plausible. In the next section I will argue, however, that the same considerations that undermine reductionism about macroeconomics also cast doubt on the simple relationship between neuroeconomics and picoeconomics (but without at all impugning the expected importance of the former).

3 Modules, rational fools, and people

I think that the simple account is in fact plausible for non-social animals with brains. (Animals without brains are simple agents, at least to the extent that cell regulation in them is broadly dictatorial.[5] Picoeconomics does not apply to such animals, and neuroeconomics obviously doesn't.) It might even be the right account for all non-*cultural* animals, which, on the strong notion of "culture" as going beyond imitation that I will endorse here, might be all or nearly all animals besides *Homo sapiens*. But I will argue that there are crucial aspects of human economics it must miss.

The neuronal groups modeled in neuroeconomics are, in the conceptual landscape of cognitive science, *modules* (Fodor 1983; Garfield 1987). This means that, although they receive input from elsewhere in the systems they're parts of, these inputs influence the values of parameters governing neuronal activity in a way that is fixed by neuronal architecture. This implies one sense of context insensitivity. Of course, which inputs are received by which neurons is sensitive to context, both that of the whole brain and that of the environmental contingencies to which the brain responds. What is context independent are the functions from axonal input parameters to neural activation responses themselves. This is what makes individual neurons, despite their impressive performance as equilibrium trackers, *stupid*. As Dennett has emphasized repeatedly over the years, the basic processing units in brains *have to* be stupid in this sense lest the kind of *non*-stupidity (plasticity and flexible context sensitivity) displayed by (some) whole organisms admits of no possible explanation (Dennett 1978: 109–26). Indeed, this alludes to the recurrent motivation for breaking agents up into dynamic systems of sub-agents in the first place: the kind of behavioral flexibility that often emerges as preference reversal and cognitive equivocation is explained as a product of the interactions of sub-systems that are themselves inflexible stimulus response machines.[6]

This kind of modularity admits directly of a description in the conceptual language of economics. What is insensitive to shifts in context in a module is its utility function. Modular output *is* sensitive to information about the global state of the system, but this information influences only whether and at what relative level of activity a module contributes its maximization efforts; context does not influence the *identity* of the modular utility function. Now, this is precisely the kind of agent that, according to Amartya Sen (1973, 1977, 1987), neoclassical economic theory has traditionally taken as the model of the person. According to Sen, neoclassical theory depicts people as "rational fools" who relentlessly maximize fixed and solipsistic preference functions while ignoring relevant shifts in social context. Though Sen greatly exaggerates the extent to which neoclassical theory – as opposed to some neoclassical theor*ists*, especially in the precincts of Chicago – incorporates any such model of people (Ross 2005: 126–40), he is right that it is an inaccurate model of them. However, a cognitive module, once conceptualized as an agent for purposes of representation in a neuroeconomic model, is exactly an instance of a rational fool.[7]

Not only are whole people not rational fools; there's a specific style of behavioral and constitutional configuration by which they implement sensitivity to social-contextual influences. Faced with overwhelming pressure to maintain coordination equilibria with ranges of conspecifics across many games that interact with one another in a general equilibrium network, they reduce their behavioral options by narrating *selves* that stabilize expectations (both their own and those of others) (Bruner 1992, 2002; Dennett 1991a). People police the stability of the selves of others by shunning those whose narratives they can't make sense of. It is for this reason that narrated selves represent real commitments rather than cheap talk. Shunned people forfeit the payoffs from coordination that are essential to the well-being of a social animal. Thus the self is a typical human being's most important investment, and many people will choose death over compromising their selves to the point of inducing what is popularly called "psychic trauma." The result, in each instance, is an agent with a utility function that is stable enough to give traction to economic analysis – and thus not so sensitive to contextual shifts as to be devoid of explanatory and predictive power – but is also not the utility function of a rational fool, in that an accommodation to the social pressures prevalent in its developmental environment is just what this agent *is* in the first place.

I spoke just now about "people" caring about their "selves." But once we understand the ontogenesis of the self in the way I suggested, this sort of talk multiplies entities beyond necessity. As the object with which others strategically interact, as the loci of the system-level utility function, as the entity that is praised, blamed, rewarded, punished, incentivized, owed money, and sent invoices, the self just is the person. This object should be distinguished from the organism that preceded it in existence, played a leading role in creating it, and may, in the case of people who suffer severe cognitive degeneration in old age, persist beyond it. Saying that people are not equivalent to their underlying biological phenomes is just a matter of semantic preference, of course, but it is a preference that seems to have good reasons behind it.[8] When we are applying economic theory the reason is especially clear: the selfless – more aptly, "non-enculturated" – organism has a different utility function from the person. (The person will in fact have many utility functions over the course of her biography; from the perspective of economics a person is a sequence of agents.) Infants are in no sense agents for the people they will become; their parents and other adults are such agents.

H. sapiens individuals and people, then, are products of different kinds of processes. The former are produced by biological processes alone: distally by natural selection and proximately by meiosis. People are sculpted into being by cultural processes operating within the constraints of biological (and chemical, and physical) possibility. Dualists were thus not entirely wrong in regarding them as differently constituted (though most historical dualists mistook this for the view that people are not subject to the laws of physics). Organisms are biochemical entities; people are virtual entities, assemblages of software running on biochemical hardware. The distinction between "virtual" and "physical" entities is much easier to make firm for ontological reductionists than for non-reductionists. But contemporary physics is not friendly to attempts to draw sharp lines here. The entangled particles of modern quantum theory have no greater definiteness of spacetime location or of Cartesian "extension" than computer programs (Ross *et al.* forthcoming; French and Krause forthcoming). Thus I use "virtual" here only to mark the less metaphysically portentous (indeed, obvious) point that some causally significant biological entities do not decompose into or cannot be simply identified with entities that people have traditionally regarded as unproblematically physical – and then to add the only slightly less obvious point that people are virtual in this sense, especially since they are *partly* constituted by behavioral dispositions stored in their cultural and technological environments rather than "in their heads" or "in their genes" (Clark 1997, 2003).

Here lies a deep source of trouble for the simple account of sub-personal agency that identifies neuroeconomic agents with picoeconomic agents. Neurons and neural groups are modular – rationally foolish – *because* they were designed directly by natural selection. Development and learning influence the relative power over behavior of a given neural structure (by influencing both brain wiring and the arrangement and number of neurochemical receptor sites) but not, as discussed earlier, the functional relationships between parameter values of inputs and neuroelectrical outputs; and *those* are what determine the utility function of a neuroen or neural group in neuroeconomics. By contrast, picoeconomic interests are theoretical constructs inferred from the equilibria represented by stabilized selves. That is, they're whatever agents turn up for identification with equilibrium strategies in the sub-personal games that generate a given self-as-equilibrium.

In that case they can't be identical to the neuroeconomic modules unless natural selection and ontogenetic development can, between them, anticipate macrocultural and microcultural evolution. But that is the hypothesis of Lamarck, and it is false.[9]

The reductionist might sniff victory here. If picoeconomic agents can't be identical with neuroeconomic ones because the former, but not the latter, are inferred theoretical constructs, she might say, then so much the worse for picoeconomics. Let us just study the behavior of the real entities and stop pretending to do science by telling just-so stories about sub-personal interests. This response undoubtedly speaks to and for the basic intuition behind reductionism, but for that very reason it begs the question. As Dennett (1991b) and many others have argued, attempts by "tough-minded" philosophers to ban all virtual objects – centers of gravity and population averages and mean molecular kinetic energies, and so on – from science have generally been ignored by scientists because they invariably involve throwing away good generalizations. Scientists do, of course, sometimes eliminate kinds of things that were previously endorsed. However, phlogiston and witches and vital spirits weren't eliminated because they were virtual – all of these things were thought to be fully substantive – but because they turned out not to do good explanatory work. Picoeconomic interests will likewise disappear from science if they don't pay their way by providing explanations and testable predictions of the phenomena, such as behavioral paths into and out of addiction, for which they're now invoked. But to assume this will be the outcome just because the interests can't, like neurons, be weighed, or looked at (because they don't reflect light) is to implicitly embrace a very simplistic picture of science.[10] Should the ethologists (such as Dingemanse et al. 2004) now studying animal personalities, and scoring outstanding behavioral predictions by doing so, cease their activities because personalities are not lodged in regions of the brain? Being virtual is a way of being real, not a way of being fictional.

4 Macroreduction

Even if all this is admitted, we nevertheless want a unified account of economic behavior, not a hodgepodge of accounts with mysteries at the interstices. If we think we are justified in constructing both neuroeconomic and picoeconomic agents, then we are required to try to discover the relationship between them. My claim to this point has just been that this relation isn't one of reductive identity. So how might we try to get a theoretical handle on the less simple actual relation?

I suggest we begin trying to understand the relationship between the economics of brains and the sub-personal economics of people by reference to the relationship between macroeconomic dynamics and the agents – among which are people – that are regulated by these dynamics. This will involve us in a digression from our immediate concern with the sub-personal.

I have already described, in very general terms, the way in which people are stabilized into being by the narratives that are told as responses to social pressures encouraging behavioral predictability against cultural backdrops.[11] The details of these kinds of processes are as variable as human cultures themselves. Some cultures tolerate substantial variation amongst selves, others relatively little. Some cultures demarcate private or "hobby" zones in which people can adopt new behavioral patterns whimsically; others suppress this. This variation notwithstanding, the possible processes are constrained by exogenous factors, especially biological ones – but also macroeconomic ones. Every culture encourages selves that care about whose children are whose and whose property is whose. Every culture encourages selves that keep some track of prices in relation to socially and individually available resources.

One very general kind of limitation on enculturation, as with any social or economic process, arises from informational dynamics. People cannot be reliably pressured into maintaining degrees of stability in areas of behavior or to degrees of detail that no one can monitor.[12] But what can and cannot be monitored, and by whom, varies with technology and economic organization. As modern societies became more economically complex, people could develop different selves for different sets of social circumstances (for example office and social club) to the extent that these circumstances could be relatively stably partitioned with respect to who was likely to be encountered where. It is a cliché that people experience greater autonomy in cities than in small villages, where all behavior that isn't private is known to all others.

However, while contemporary information-based economies provide greater autonomy to people (along several dimensions) than did their predecessors, there is at least one respect in which levels of monitoring are generally increasing in such economies. Information technology permits centralized databases about people to be compiled, comprehensively cross-indexed, and efficiently searched. The development of these databases is mainly driven at present by their value for determining credit offers and targeting marketing, but they are also used with increasing frequency to investigate job applicants and candidates for offices. At the same time, as Ainslie (2001) emphasizes, an increasing proportion of the information available both to and about people is quantitative, allowing comparative monitoring of people, both by others and by themselves, in ways and to degrees of detail that were not previously possible. These two trends increase pressure on people to tighten self-stabilization, in two senses: people are incentivized to define themselves along more dimensions and to notice finer departures from their established behavioral patterns. Where such departures can be noticed, they can and often will be resisted by "personal rules" that people legislate for themselves. As Ainslie explains, given the role played by sanctions, including self-sanctions, in maintaining the stability of selves, this predicts higher prevalence of compulsive behavior – that is, behavior people experience as aversively rigid self-management.

Behavioral economist Robert Frank (echoing both Marx and Hayek, but, unlike them, with carefully elicited evidence) argues that modern economic institutional life, and knowledge of economics, tends to sculpt people into approximations to neoclassical agency.[13] The neoclassical agent is not, pace Sen, a rational fool; but she is someone who tries to eliminate behavioral manifestations of cyclicity in her preference field – that is, to avoid being a potential money pump. Frank and his co-authors suggest that this should be explained by reference to ideological influence coming from institutionalized economic theory itself. However, the earlier reflections suggest a different account. The range over which a person's preference field is defined is a function of the dimensions over which enculturation is enforced (since, again, people are created by enculturation). Thus people can only worry about cycles among preferences over outcomes for which cultural books are kept. Then the more fine-grained, efficient and accessible the cultural books become, the smaller becomes the behavioral zone in which people are free to ignore the pressures to act like neoclassical agents.[14]

This is the sense in which I maintain that macroeconomic patterns drive microeconomic ones. The relationship is an instance of the more general class of causal structures that Friedman (1981) has called *macroreductive*. The idea of macroreduction is not to simply reverse the unidirectional (micro-to-macro) causal ordering of traditional reductionism. Rather, the idea is that we cannot explain macro – in this case macroeconomic – patterns by *fixing* the microeconomic agents *first* and then gluing them together. Satisfactory models must be recursive and dynamical (even if for many policy purposes static snapshots yield useful idealizations). In economics, the macro level has causal priority in just one sense: the entities that microeconomics studies, people, are brought into existence and prevented from dissipating by macro-level dynamics, into which their micro-level interactions feed back.

In many domains of inquiry that draw micro/macro distinctions, the boundary between the grains of analysis is vague. However economists (as usual) have operationalized it clearly. We do not think of the micro/macro boundary as being fixed independently of our models. Suppose one has constructed a model that generates reliable, quantitative, counterfactual-supporting predictions about the values of some variables. Call these the m variables. Then that model will hold fixed some other variables – call these the M variables – that will themselves change values over time (otherwise they wouldn't be variables), but on a longer timescale that is described by a distinct class of models.[15] Then the M variables are macro-variables relative to the m-variables and the m-variables are micro-variables relative to the M-variables. Thus the economist's micro/macro distinction is not metaphysical but structural; furthermore, it is indefinitely recursive.

Following Binmore (1998, 2005), let us now apply this to what has been said about cultures, people, and the biological organisms that implement people. The slowest dynamic scale relevant to economics is that at which natural selection re-engineers biological organisms and their cognitive modules. Call this the ecological scale. It determines the informational constraints that limn all economic processes. Its variables are statistical properties of whole populations of organisms. The micro-scale relative to it is that at which cultural institutions – patterns of self-generation – evolve; call this the institutional scale. Its variables are information-and-control transmission mechanisms that govern social possibilities. Against this backdrop, the next micro-scale is that at which social parameters, including the relationships amongst price levels, interest rates, growth rates, and so on, fluctuate; this is the domain of macroeconomic theory. Call it the social scale.[16] At the next micro-scale relative to it, traditional microeconomic variables fluctuate as consequences of games played amongst groups of networked particular people; microeconomics, now done mainly with the technology of game theory, studies this domain. Call it the personal scale.

Where do selves fit into this picture? Selves can't be re-narrated as fast as social contexts shift without destroying the point of having them. They are thus held fixed for particular applications of microeconomic analysis – just as neoclassical procedure has always had it. Selves are social products and statistical distributions of selves are social phenomena. I have argued that the rationale for the social production of selves is economic: it enables coordination on efficient equilibria to be achieved in what would otherwise be an intractable general equilibrium problem. Each culture's idea of the self is essentially one of that culture's economic institutions. This is the basis for my saying, peculiar as it might sound, that selves – people, then – are macroeconomic phenomena. (If Marxists want to smile here, I think they have a right to – but this a topic for another occasion.)

Picoeconomics is then the micro-scale relative to traditional microeconomics. The modeler studying games amongst sub-personal interests holds the properties of the self fixed during particular analyses; its stable traits constitute restrictions on picoeconomic equilibria. Of course, just as shifts at the microeconomic level can accumulate to cause phase-shifts at the macroeconomic level – this being the way in which micro-to-macro feedback happens – so picoeconomic dynamics can periodically disrupt the self and give rise to a new microeconomic agent with a new utility function. As long as the reforming addict must still struggle actively against temptation, she is the same agent as she was when she smoked, with her smoking interest being restrained by a coalition of others. When she no longer wants to smoke she has become a new agent; her smoking interest has been killed off and the preference profile correlated with the organism has altered.

In this framework, neuroeconomics does not study the ultimate foundational level, as the hypothetical reductionist who promoted the simple story supposed. Instead, it studies constraints on information flow at *all* scales. The modules it studies are products of ecological-scale dynamics. As has already been stressed, their parametric dispositions are held fixed for all economic analyses. But the network properties of the brain, which also interest the neuroeconomist (since they set the context in which the relative influence of modules will vary), are influenced by development, and hence by properties of the institutional scale and by the dynamics of the social scale. A person can't change her modules through behavior, although behavior influences the patterns of information flow in her whole cognitive network.

Connectionist models of mind, because of the affinity between neurons and nodes that they emphasize, encourage some people to think of the brain as non-modular. In connectionist systems, the most basic representations are in connection weights, and they are all plastic in response to learning. If our emerging theory of neural processing were like a connectionist model in this respect, then neuroeconomic descriptions would be implementation accounts of more abstract picoeconomic theories. However, connectionism is most accurately thought of as a technology for modeling learning dynamics at the *network* level. The early results from neuroeconomics are bearing out the expectation (among researchers who never got *carried away* by connectionism) that connection weights – roughly, synaptic properties, in the case of the brain – are not the most basic vehicles of content. Recall Glimcher's monkey neurons that track Nash equilibria. Prediction of reward value is surely contentful representation; and it seems that some groups of neurons in the nucleus accumbens are modules for predicting reward. I thus suggest that we for now think of the investigation of neural valuation as studying one (very rich, and absolutely binding) source of informational limits on picoeconomic adaptiveness.

Perhaps this is how we should think of neuroeconomic research in general. Picoeconomic hypotheses are inferences to the best explanation, and such hypotheses crucially require independent constraints. Let us sketch one example that is tentatively emerging from the conjunction of picoeconomic modeling and neuroeconomic research. Rachlin (2000) has produced a picoeconomic model of gambling addiction according to which the gambling interest in the addict recruits other interests to its coalition because it can capture the same rewards accruing to social interaction more cheaply in the short run than can the competing social interaction interest. Initially, the gambling interest strategically relies on discounting to sometimes get its way. It becomes consistently supreme in the addict because the more the system substitutes gambling for social interaction, the more costly the latter becomes by comparison with the former. This hypothesis predicts changes over time in the relative sizes of predicted rewards, as computed by some part of the system involved in behavioral governance. Thus if Rachlin's model is right, then some system in the brain had better be able to compute and track the required changes. Neuroeconomic research has already told us roughly where in the brain we should look for this sort of capacity. Several possibilities are open here. One is that we will find that rewards from social interaction are too diffuse to be stably integrated at a single neuronal site, but that gambling substitutes for some aspect, or, alternatively, some proxy, for social interaction in the response patterns of the reward prediction system. In this case Rachlin's picoeconomic hypothesis will be confirmed, and its informational basis refined, by neuroeconomic inquiry. Alternatively, if we look very hard for the neural patterns the hypothesis predicts and fail to find them, we will be motivated to seek a new picoeconomic model of the phenomena altogether.

These are early days, and neuroeconomics is bound to take directions no one can at present anticipate. My ambition in this chapter has been limited to explaining why I think we should not understand the new economics of the sub-personal in reductionist terms. Over the coming years, we can expect a flood of exciting neuroeconomic discoveries which admit of representation in exactly the mathematical structures with which economists are most familiar. We can thus predict that neuroeconomics will attract enormous attention, and that some enthusiasts will at some point pronounce it the only kind of economics worth doing. Induction on other recent episodes in the sociology of behavioral research should encourage tempering of such claims. Having its results spun in terms of simple-minded reductionism has certainly tarnished the image of evolutionary psychology, for example. No one should doubt that evolutionary psychology is important; but the idea that everything people do is an effort to maximize expected fitness in a vanished Pleistocene environment is a massive distortion of the sum of relevant findings. Similarly, people as economic agents are not the sums of their neurons, however much they are restricted in their strategic options by the sums their neurons compute.

Notes

1 I would like to thank Mark White, Barbara Montero, participants in 2005 symposia at the History of Economics Society/Allied Social Science Associations meetings, Eastern Economics Association annual meetings, and the Department of Economics seminar series at New York University for helpful comments.
2 See Ross et al. (forthcoming) for details.
3 The best existing attempt is Melnyk's (2003). Ross et al. (forthcoming) argue that the job cannot be done, because contemporary physics won't support it. But our disagreement here is more strictly technical, and has far fewer implications for the special sciences, than folk metaphysics would lead people to expect.
4 As of 2005 this sub-discipline is well enough established to be the business of a duly constituted academic society with annual meetings. See http://www.neuroeconomics.org.
5 This qualification is far from minor. See Lachmann et al. (2003).
6 Again, to be clear: this point does not suggest a return to the traditional mechanicism about nervous systems associated with the Sherringtonian tradition (Glimcher 2003: 55–144). Neurons are stimulus response machines only relative to parameterizations that are influenced by the global state of the whole brain, as Glimcher emphasizes. The same goes for ants, even on stories according to which ants are pure robots. The point is that individual neurons are as robotic as people have traditionally taken ants to be.
7 Dennett says that "people are not robots but they are made of robots" (Dennett 1996: 23). We can express the same point in a way that connects with themes from economics by replacing "robots" with "rational fools."

8 Consider, for example, debates in the United States over abortion and use of fetal stem cells. No one denies that an abortion terminates an organism of the species H. sapiens. The majority of people who do not regard abortion as murder deny that it kills a person. The point here is not to insist that the majority is ethically right and that therefore usage should accommodate its view. Rather, it is that a majority draws a distinction in practice, so it is convenient for thought and communication to lexically mark it.

9 This is not to contest the existence or importance of rich interactions among the environment, developmental pathways, and genetic constraints and potentials that are emphasized by developmental systems theorists (Oyama 2000). Rather, I am here pointing out that implementation of picoeconomic interests at the level of individual neurons or small neural groups would require not just complex causal pathways but backwards causation of the past by the future.

10 It is worth stressing here that the main technology for doing neuroeconomics, fMRI scanning, does not involve direct examination of neuronal behavior. Under fMRI, such behavior is statistically inferred from changes in brain hemoglobin.

11 For how to model this in game-theoretic terms, see Ross (2006).

12 This requires two kinds of qualification. First, as noted earlier, people rely on the stability of their selves for themselves. Thus most people stay broadly "in character" when they are alone. The point I am making here is that we should not expect to find cultures in which people are encouraged to make choices over alternative behavioral dispositions that are almost always private. There is, to my knowledge, no human culture that categorizes people (thereby setting up a choice dimension for self-narration) into those who masturbate lying down and those who do it sitting up. (According to Laqueur (2003), Europeans before the 17th century had no social concept of masturbation at all.) The other qualification is that not all monitors have the same status with respect to the private/public distinction. Many people behave very differently within their immediate families than with outsiders. But kin dynamics are different from, and complexly interrelated with, social dynamics (Fehr and Henrich 2003).

13 See Frank et al. (1993).

14 Unlike Frank and Marx, I don't think this should necessarily be deplored. No one knows whether the tendencies to compulsive behavior pointed out by Ainslie have higher costs in general than the inefficiencies and welfare losses that result from preference reversals.

15 Classes of models are theories (Ruttkamp 2002). Thus this framework finds that we're right to speak of macroeconomic theory, microeconomic theory, and picoeconomic theory.

16 This will seem strange to economists who think that macroeconomic theory should yield once-and-for-all quantitative relationships between its objects of inquiry. However, historical evidence suggests that although these relationships are stable enough to be held fixed throughout analytical exercises by microeconomists, on longer scales they jump in phase shifts between different equilibria. See Ormerod (1994) for a survey of literature and evidence

References

Ainslie, G. (1992) *Picoeconomics*, Cambridge: Cambridge University Press.
—— (2001) *Breakdown of Will*, Cambridge: Cambridge University Press.
Berns, G. (2003) "Neural Game Theory and the Search for Rational Agents in the Brain," *Behavioral and Brain Sciences*, 26: 155–56.
Binmore, K. (1998) *Game Theory and the Social Contract, Volume Two: Just Playing*, Cambridge, MA: MIT Press.

—— (2005) *Natural Justice*, Oxford: Oxford University Press.

Breiter, H., Aharon, I., Kahneman, D., Dale, A., and Shizgal, P. (2001) "Functional Imaging of Neuronal Responses to Expectancy and Experience of Monetary Gains and Losses," *Neuron*, 30: 619–39.

Bruner, J. (1992) *Acts of Meaning*, Cambridge, MA: Harvard University Press.

—— (2002) *Making Stories: Law, Literature, Life*, New York: Farrar, Strauss and Giroux.

Clark, A. (1997) *Being There*, Cambridge, MA: MIT Press.

—— (2003) *Natural Born Cyborgs*, Oxford: Oxford University Press.

Dennett, D. (1978) *Brainstorms*, Montgomery, VT: Bradford.

—— (1987) *The Intentional Stance*, Cambridge, MA: MIT Press.

—— (1991a) *Consciousness Explained*, Boston, MA: Little Brown & Co.

—— (1991b) "Real Patterns," *Journal of Philosophy*, 88: 27–51.

—— (1996) *Kinds of Minds*, New York: Basic Books.

Dingemanse, N., Both, C., Drent, P., and Tinbergen, J. (2004) "Fitness Consequences of Avian Personalities in a Fluctuating Environment," *Proceedings of the Royal Society of London B: Biological Sciences*, 271: 847–52.

Fehr, E. and Henrich, J. (2003) "Is Strong Reciprocity a Maladaptation?," in P. Hammerstein (ed.) *Genetic and Cultural Evolution of Cooperation*, Cambridge, MA: MIT Press, 55–82.

Fodor, J. (1983) *The Modularity of Mind*, Cambridge, MA: MIT Press.

Frank, R., Gilovich, T., and Regan, D. (1993) "Does Studying Economics Inhibit Cooperation?," *Journal of Economic Perspectives*, 7: 159–71.

French, S. and Krause, D. (forthcoming) *Identity in Physics: A Historical, Philosophical and Formal Analysis*, Oxford: Oxford University Press.

Friedman, M. (1981) "Theoretical Explanation," in R. Healy (ed.) *Reduction, Time and Reality*, Cambridge: Cambridge University Press, 2–31.

Garfield, J. (ed.) (1987) *Modularity in Knowledge Representation and Natural-Language Understanding*, Cambridge, MA: MIT Press.

Glimcher, P. (2003) *Decisions, Uncertainty and the Brain*, Cambridge, MA: MIT Press.

Kavka, G. (1991) "Is Individual Choice Less Problematic than Collective Choice?," *Economics and Philosophy*, 7: 143–65.

Keen, S. (2002) *De-bunking Economics*, New York: Zed Books.

Kennedy, J. and Eberhart, R. (2001) *Swarm Intelligence*, San Francisco: Morgan Kauffman.

King-Casas, B., Tomlin, D., Anen, C., Camerer, C., Quartz, S., and Montague, P.R. (2005) "Getting to Know You: Reputation and Trust in a Two-Person Economic Exchange," *Science*, 308: 78–83.

Lachmann, M., Blackstone, N., Haig, D., Kowald, A., Michod, R., Szathmáry, E., Werren, J., and Wolpert, L. (2003) "Group Report: Cooperation and Conflict in the Evolution of Genomes, Cells, and Multicellular Organisms," in P. Hammerstein (ed.) *Genetic and Cultural Evolution of Cooperation*, Cambridge, MA: MIT Press, 327–56.

Laqueur, T. (2003) *Solitary Sex*, Cambridge, MA: MIT Press.

Loewenstein, G., Read, D., and Baumeister, R. (eds.) (2003) *Time and Decision*, New York: Russell Sage Foundation.

McGeer, V. (2001) "Psycho-Practice, Psycho-Theory and the Contrastive Case of Autism," *Journal of Consciousness Studies*, 8: 109–32.

Melnyk, A. (2003) *A Physicalist Manifesto*, Cambridge: Cambridge University Press.

Montague, P.R. and Berns, G. (2002) "Neural Economics and the Biological Substrates of Valuation," *Neuron*, 36: 265–84.

O'Hara, M. (1995) *Market Microstructure Theory*, Oxford: Blackwell.

Ormerod, P. (1994) *The Death of Economics*, New York: Wiley.

Oyama, S. (2000) *Evolution's Eye*, Chapel Hill, NC: Duke University Press.

Platt, M. and Glimcher, P. (1999) "Neural Correlates of Decision Variables in Parietal Cortex," *Nature*, 400: 233–38.

Rachlin, H. (2000) *The Science of Self Control*, Cambridge, MA: Harvard University Press.

Ross, D. (1999) "Folk Theories, Models and Economic Reality: A Reply to Williams," *South African Journal of Philosophy*, 18: 247–57.

—— (2005) *Economic Theory and Cognitive Science: Microexplanation*, Cambridge, MA: MIT Press.

—— (2006) "The Economic and Evolutionary Basis of Selves," *Cognitive Systems Research*, 7: 246–58.

—— (forthcoming) *Economic Theory and Cognitive Science: Macroexplanation*, Cambridge, MA: MIT Press.

Ross, D., Ladyman, J., Spurrett, D., and Collier, J. (forthcoming) *Every Thing Must Go: Information-Theoretic Structural Realism*, Oxford: Oxford University Press.

Ruttkamp, E. (2002) *A Model-Theoretic Realist Interpretation of Science*, Dordrecht: Kluwer.

Schelling, T. (1978) "Ergonomics, or the Art of Self-Management," *American Economic Review: Papers and Proceedings*, 68(2): 290–94.

—— (1980) "The Intimate Contest for Self-Command," *Public Interest*, 60: 94–118.

—— (1984) "Self-Command in Practice, in Policy, and in a Theory of Rational Choice," *American Economic Review*, 74: 1–11.

Sen, A. (1973) "Behavior and the Concept of Preference," *Economica*, 40: 241–59.

—— (1977) "Rational Fools: A Critique of the Behavioural Foundations of Economic Theory," *Philosophy and Public Affairs*, 6: 317–44.

—— (1987) *On Ethics and Economics*, Oxford: Blackwell.

Siljak, D. (1991) *Decentralized Control of Complex Systems*, London: Academic Press.

Young, H.P. (1998) *Individual Strategy and Social Structure*, Princeton, NJ: Princeton University Press.

4 Behavioral economics, neuroeconomics, and identity

John B. Davis[1]

1 Introduction

Behavioral economics originated largely as a critique of neoclassical thinking about rationality and individual preferences. Largely overlooked by the proponents of this critique is the fact that preferences constitute the basis on which the personal identity of the individual may be understood in neoclassical theory, and thus that the behavioral critique has implications for how we might think about personal identity in economics. Moreover, since the implicit account of personal identity in neoclassical theory in terms of preferences is circular and empty (Davis 2003), and since some account of personal identity is ultimately necessary to be able to talk about individuals in economics, also overlooked is the question: Does behavioral economics, in addition to what it offers for thinking about rationality and choice, offer a secure foundation for thinking about personal identity to fill the gap left by neoclassical theory? Alternatively, might it rather be the case that behavioral economics makes no improvement on the neoclassical account of individual identity, and thus follows neoclassical theory in begging the question of what makes individuals individual in economics? In light of these questions, it is interesting not only that cognitive psychology, from which behavioral economics is drawn, possesses a widely shared view of what constitutes personal identity, but that this view involves a reinterpretation of the very same philosophical foundations that underlie the unsuccessful neoclassical view of identity, namely John Locke's understanding of identity in terms of memory. Can Locke's memory view of identity, then, be taken up and reinterpreted in behavioral economics in such a way as to escape the problems that arise in connection with neoclassical theory?

Here I first argue that cognitive psychology's adaptation of Locke's view offers behavioral economics an escape from one difficulty inherent in the neoclassical account, but that as a purely cognitive theory it still leaves unresolved another difficulty as an account of identity. However, just as cognitive psychology has employed neuropsychology as one route of development, so an increasingly influential route of development for behavioral economics is neuroeconomics, understood as the combination of neuroscience and behavioral theory (cf. Camerer *et al.* 2005). Thus, second, I argue that the relatively recent interest on the part of behavioralists and experimentalists in neuroeconomics represents a possible further step toward developing an alternative account of personal identity. This further step, moreover, goes to the heart of the neuroeconomics program, and thus evaluating it as a possible step in developing an account of personal identity provides insights both into the status of individuals in a revised preference approach to choice and rationality and also into the prospects for developing neuropsychological foundations for economics.

Section 2 briefly summarizes the emergence of behavioral economics as a set of critiques of neoclassical thinking about preferences and rationality, emphasizing what has been termed alternative or nonconventional approaches within non-expected utility theory, and then comments on how this development bears on thinking about individual identity in terms of preferences. Section 3 explains how personal identity is understood in cognitive psychology on the self-as-memory view, and distinguishes this approach from Locke's account of identity in terms of memory. Section 4 looks at how behavioral and experimental economics have inadvertently come upon the self-as-memory conception of the individual, reviews Vernon Smith's ideas on the subject as a particularly clear expression of this thinking, and argues that this conception still leaves one key problem unaddressed. Section 5 turns to neuroeconomics' conception of the individual as a potential further step in the self-as-memory view, considers what it might assume about the relationship between mind and brain, and then compares this view to a similar view advanced by Derek Parfit in his analysis of personal identity. Section 6 briefly introduces social psychology as a framework for additionally enlarging the neuroeconomics conception of the identity of the individual as applied to economics and law.

2 The behavioral economics critique of preferences

Though behavioral economics involves a wide and diverse set of critiques of the descriptive and normative adequacy of standard expected utility theory, over time these critiques have reflected less and less optimism as to whether standard expected utility theory can be retained as a general framework for understanding rationality and choice. In early contributions – for example Maurice Allais's (1953) discovery of common consequence and common ratio effects at odds with expected utility theory's independence axiom, or the evidence of preference reversals showing how orderings can depend on preference elicitation procedures (Lichtenstein and Slovic 1971) – the emphasis generally rested on seeing violations of the standard framework as anomalies, and then on revising the standard framework so as to be able to accommodate them in a more general theory. Thus, according to Chris Starmer, as a result of the accumulation of considerable evidence contradicting the independence axiom in particular:

a wave of theories designed to explain the evidence began to emerge at the end of the 1970s. Most of these theories have the following features in common: (i) preferences are represented by some function $V(.)$ defined over individual prospects; (ii) the function satisfies ordering and continuity; and (iii) while $V(.)$ is designed to permit observed violations of the independence axiom, the principle of monotonicity is retained.

(Starmer 2000: 337)

Starmer calls "theories with these properties *conventional theories*," and states that the "general spirit of the approach is to seek 'well behaved' theories of preference preserving monotonicity that are nonetheless consistent with observed violations of independence" (Starmer 2000: 337–38). In order to deal with the disconfirming empirical evidence, then, in time-honored instrumentalist fashion the conventional approach "models choice as preference maximization and assumes that agents behave *as if* optimizing some underlying preference function . . . [though] there is no presupposition that the model corresponds with any of the mental activities actually involved in making choices" (Starmer 2000: 349).

Others, however, saw abandoning descriptive adequacy as inconsistent with the general goal of providing more realistic explanations of choice under risk, and by the end of the decade what Starmer calls a nonconventional approach had emerged that proposed alternatives to standard theory rather than attempting to revise it. The most influential of these alternative theories was prospect theory, developed by Daniel Kahneman and Amos Tversky in what became one of the most highly cited articles in *Econometrica* (Kahneman and Tversky 1979). In general, nonconventional theories depart from the traditional framework by adding a procedural element to choice behavior in supposing that individuals rely on decision heuristics or rules sensitive to context to frame their choices.[2] Thus in prospect theory choice is a two-phase process, with prospects "edited" in the first phase using different decision heuristics, and choices then made in the second phase from a restricted or reformulated class of prospects.

This two-phase process reflects the distinction made in the psychology subfield of behavioral decision research between investigation of judgment processes, which people use to estimate probabilities, and choice processes, which people use to select among actions given their judgments (Camerer and Loewenstein 2003). The two-phase analysis makes it possible to look at gains and losses relative to reference points and ultimately introduce well-observed phenomena at odds with standard framework predictions such as diminishing sensitivity and loss aversion (Tversky and Kahneman 1991). More generally, prospect theory opens the door to the investigation of a variety of descriptive and procedure invariance failures that cast doubt on the traditional idea that individuals possess stable and coherent preferences. Taken as a whole, then, the "one feature common" to all nonconventional theories that distinguishes them from those approaches meant to preserve a revised standard expected utility framework is that "none of them can be reduced to, or expressed purely in terms of, a single preference function $V(.)$" (Starmer 2000: 339).

Thus, what appears to have occurred over the course of several decades in behavioral research is that the search for an alternative theory of choice under risk has gradually become an increasingly important if not the main objective of researchers in place of the original goal of repairing standard expected utility theory. One reflection of this is that researchers refer less to experimental results as violations and anomalies, and now consider the possibility that standard expected utility theory is more likely a special case within a more general alternative theory rather than a general theory itself. However, more may be involved than simply a change in focus if, as Starmer puts it, an increasing number of behavioral researchers are willing to assume that individual choice under risk cannot be explained in terms of a single preference function, since it is not clear that approaches which abandon this assumption fall into the same class as those that maintain it. Indeed, since having a single preference function is the way in which individuals are defined in neoclassical theory, supposing that choice cannot be explained in such terms raises the issue of whether behavioral economics (at least the nonconventional approaches) fundamentally departs from the neoclassical theory of the individual, and thus constitutes a significantly different approach to understanding individuals.

This deeper issue has been closer to the surface than it may initially seem in the form of a debate between behavioralists and experimentalists over the character of preferences consequent upon assuming the two-phase analysis of choice. Thus, on the one hand, those on the nonconventionalist side suppose that preferences are not the indifference curves of textbooks, but are highly malleable and dependent on the context in which they are elicited (Camerer and Loewenstein 2003), so that choice involves processes whereby individuals effectively "construct" their preferences (Payne *et al.* 1992; Slovic 1995). On the other hand, those likely to be conventionalists hold the "discovered preference hypothesis," a term coined by Charles Plott (1996), which assumes that individuals have coherent and stable preferences, though they are not necessarily always revealed in their decisions, but can be "discovered" to underlie their apparent preferences after individuals engage in information gathering, deliberation, and trial-and-error learning. Proponents of the "discovered preference hypothesis," we might thus say, depart from the instrumentalist "as if" view in saying that individuals have a single preference function $V(.)$ but that it is descriptively available only under the correct experimental procedures. While this shifts the debate away from the merits of instrumentalist reasoning regarding individuals to a consideration of the experimental controls needed to avoid confounding effects associated with laboratory subjects failing to act consistently with their underlying preferences, there are good reasons to suppose that it does not succeed in rescuing the conventionalist view (cf. Cubitt *et al.* 2001).

Where, then, does this leave thinking about the individual? If we are to assess behavioral economics as a whole, what we find is a general retreat from the neoclassical conception in the case of nonconventionalist approaches, together with a set of defenses of the traditional single preference function $V(.)$ basis for the individual in the case of conventionalist approaches that has gained an at best limited success. In neoclassical theory the traditional axiomatic treatment of preferences permits assigning the individual a single utility function, which allows for an account of the personal identity of the individual (albeit faulty) in terms of the notion of "own" preferences. However, this prospective foundation for identity ceases to be even an issue if it is not even possible to say that individuals possess a single preference function $V(.)$ in the first place. The important question, it thus seems, is what account of the individual and personal identity might be put forward by the nonconventionalists, who have not been reluctant to entirely cut the umbilical cord to the traditional neoclassical basis for understanding individuals in terms of preferences. As no such alternative account appears yet to have been fully worked out, the following section turns to the resources naturally available for one in the treatment of the individual and personal identity developed by cognitive psychologists.

3 Cognitive psychology and personal identity in terms of memory

Cognitive psychologists investigate individuals apart from their interactions with other individuals, focus on their mental representations, and regard individuals' mental representations as being either perception-based or meaning-based. The self is understood in terms of two kinds of mental representations which individuals can have of themselves: perception-based self-images and meaning-based self-concepts (Kihlstrom and Klein 1994). Since individuals have memories of their self-images and self-concepts, over time the self may be identified with the individual's collection of remembered self-images and self-concepts, and accordingly cognitive psychologists have explained the self in terms of memory, and characterized the self as one's memory for oneself (Klein 2001).

The well-known antecedent for the view that identity is based on memory is Locke's definition of personal identity as continuity in one's own memories (Locke 1975 [1694]). Philosophers generally regard Locke's definition as an inadequate explanation of personal identity on the grounds of its being circular (cf. Perry 1975). The self cannot be explained in terms of its remembering its *own* memories since this presupposes that which is to be explained. Cognitive psychologists, however, are not interested in how individuals might be seen to construct their own personal identities through what they remember about what they believe to be their own past experiences, but are, rather, interested in how third-party social scientists might attribute identity to individuals in terms of observed memory reports expressed by those individuals, irrespective of whether those reports accurately recall individuals' past experiences. In effect, cognitive psychologists make use of an alternative concept of memory essentially like the one developed by philosophers to overcome Locke's circularity problem, namely quasi-memory or q-memory (Parfit 1984), that only requires that an individual's memory seem to that individual to have been his or her memory, whether or not it in fact was.[3] Individuals are then identified in terms of their real memories and perhaps "false" memories, as observed by cognitive psychologists. This strategy escapes Locke's circularity problem, and provides a working framework in which to develop a more detailed analysis of the different forms of memory as they pertain to the individual's identity.

The broad distinction between two kinds of mental representations – perception-based and meaning-based – is first associated with two forms of memory that the individual exhibits: (1) episodic memory and (2) semantic memory (Tulving 1983). Within these two forms of memory there are memories that then relate to the self and memories that do not. Episodic memory is experiential memory, and may be either autobiographical, involving an individual's memories of experienced self-images, or non-autobiographical, involving an individual's memories of experiences that included no awareness of oneself. For example, an autobiographical episodic memory is remembering oneself seeing a friend, while a non-autobiographical episodic memory is just remembering seeing a friend. Semantic memory is context-free memory that in itself makes no reference to an experience.[4] As with episodic memories, there are semantic memories that relate to the self, and thus involve an individual's self-concepts, and semantic memories that do not relate to self. For example, a semantic memory that relates to the self is remembering that one was born in a certain year, while a semantic memory that does not relate to oneself is remembering that Africa is a continent. Generally, then, cognitive psychology's self-as-memory view encompasses both autobiographical episodic memories that involve mental representations in the form of self-images, and semantic memories that relate to the self involving mental representations in the form of self-concepts.[5]

An important assumption in cognitive psychology's general theory of memory is that both episodic and semantic memory take the form of declarative knowledge ("knowledge that"), and can always be represented by individuals in propositional form. Though this is not immediately obvious with respect to episodic memory, the standard argument is that any episodic memory must be representable in propositional form on the grounds that one cannot remember an experience unless one can remember *that* one has had that experience. At the same time, in contrast to memories that take the form of declarative knowledge, individuals also have memories that take the form of procedural knowledge ("knowledge how") that in itself is not represented propositionally (Anderson 1976). Further, whereas episodic and semantic memory can exhibit the self, procedural knowledge *per se* is thought not to include references to the self, as, for example, when one remembers that the way to operate a particular device is to follow certain instructions.

Nonetheless, for essentially the same reasons that episodic memory is representable in propositional form, so procedural knowledge is thought to be also. That is, one cannot remember how to do something unless, at least in principle, one could say *that* such and such was how to do something. And when individuals exercise memories regarding procedural knowledge they also remember *that* they have certain skills and capabilities. Cognitive psychologists have characterized these cases as involving a kind of "meta-knowledge," which itself is declarative or propositional in form, but whose object is procedural rather than declarative knowledge, as, for example, when one remembers one knows how to drive a car (Bandura 1977).

These latter points gain greater meaning when their general purpose is made clear. Thus, by including meta-knowledge memories about one's own skills and capabilities along with episodic autobiographical memories and semantic memories involving the self as kinds of propositional declarative knowledge, *all* forms of memory somehow involving the self can be treated as propositional declarative knowledge. Or, as it has been influentially put, when we think of the self as memory, we think of the self as a knowledge structure (Kihlstrom and Klein 1994). This conclusion is important by virtue of what it excludes. Specifically, whatever cannot assume the form of propositional declarative knowledge cannot be an object of memory. For example, should primitive single-cell animals be conditioned to respond to certain stimuli, this conditioning cannot properly be termed remembering, because it could never take the form of propositional declarative knowledge (Bennett and Hacker 2003: 156). Or, should human individuals exhibit patterns of conditioned functioning about which they can never become conscious, these also cannot be properly termed remembering. This basic conclusion underlies the main general theory of memory in cognitive psychology, the generic associative network model known as the Adaptive Control of Thought (ACT) model (Anderson 1983), which organizes memory as a system of declarative knowledge, and which makes it possible to explain the self as a set of such memories within this framework.

Within the general ACT framework, not surprisingly, there are competing models of the structure and organization of the overall memory system, and also, therefore, competing ACT models of the self as memory. The differences between these competing models are not important here.[6] Suffice it to say that empirical studies in cognitive psychology that employ the self-as-memory view attempt to support one or another model in experiments on well-identified phenomena such as self-reference effects (in which individuals engage in some sort of self-referent encoding task) or priming actions (in which memory paths are activated in connection with certain cues). Reference to these sorts of phenomena, of course, recalls research in behavioral economics in terms of framing heuristics, editing, and so on, that has played a role in nonconventionalist approaches to individual decision-making, and one might accordingly expect behavioral economists also to start from a self-as-memory view of the individual. But it appears that behavioral (and experimental) economists have only begun to make use of the cognitive psychology approach to memory and individual identity inadvertently by way of other concerns. The following section thus turns to how elements of an account of personal identity in terms of memory show signs of emerging in behavioral and experimental economics in connection with efforts to understand recent experimental results inconsistent with standard economic assumptions.

4 Personal identity in behavioral economics

A surprising though now widely accepted result of recent work in the economics laboratory is that, contrary to what economists have believed for over a century, individuals do not behave in an exclusively self-interested manner in their economic interaction with others, but in certain specific circumstances consistently deviate from self-interested behavior by emphasizing reciprocity in their interaction with others – for example in competitive markets with incomplete contracts, and also in situations involving public goods where there are strong material incentives to free ride but also opportunities to punish free riders (Fehr and Gächter 2000). One implication of this is that social context matters (or, more concretely, institutions), since it appears to determine the circumstances under which one observes self-interested behavior or reciprocity. A second, less frequently noticed implication, however, is that memory also matters, because behaving in a reciprocal way towards others requires that individuals remember their past interactions with them. Thus, economists' recent empirical discovery that reciprocity is fundamental to certain types of economic behavior has opened the door to making cognitive psychologists' research on memory a new concern of economics.

One good reflection of this new thinking can be found in the work of Vernon Smith. Though Smith is more an experimentalist than a behavioralist, he shares the latters' general view (one at odds with rational choice theory and conventionalist theories of individual decision-making) that individual behavior cannot be properly explained without reference to its human psychological foundations. Here I draw attention to his position in his "Experimental Methods in Economics," a contribution to the *Cognitive Science Encyclopedia* (2003), which as an encyclopedia contribution presumably represents views that Smith believes should be taken as authoritative in economics. Much of Smith's discussion focuses on two experimental games whose reciprocity results have been highly replicated in the literature, the ultimatum game and the trust game. In interpreting what these games show, Smith succinctly combines the two implications of reciprocity behavior noted earlier as follows: "context matters because all memory involves relationships and is associative" (V. Smith 2003: 1070). Here the term "associative" refers to the ACT model, a reference which is further supported by comments Smith makes, on priming effects and on the logic of how cues trigger memories, that draw on Gazzaniga *et al.* (1998), a standard cognitive psychology source which adds elements of neuroscience to the investigation of memory via neuropsychological studies of brain-injured patients and brain-imaging studies of normal individuals. Or, more explicitly, Smith states – echoing his oft-stated principle that institutions matter – "context is important," specifically because of "what is known about the autobiographical character of memory and the interaction between current and past experience in creating memory" (V. Smith 2003: 1072). Thus he argues that individuals' behavior in ultimatum and trust games exhibits reciprocity because individuals operate in contexts that not only require they remember their past interactions with other players but also require that they autobiographically remember these past interactions as their own experiences. Individuals, that is, employ what is described in cognitive psychology as episodic autobiographical memory in their interactions with others, and accordingly operate with perception-based mental representations of themselves, or self-images.[7] Smith also asserts that the design of experiments provides players with "different instructional-procedural contexts" (V. Smith 2003: 1072). On the argument of Kihlstrom and Klein (1994), this would generate procedural knowledge for individuals, which, when it pertains to the self, could take the form of meta-knowledge which individuals could additionally use to state propositions to be remembered about themselves and games.

Thus Smith sees a cognitive psychology understanding of memory as central to understanding interactive individual behavior. But he also has a particular view of the origins and development of this behavior which goes beyond a purely behavioral framework, and which draws on neuropsychology and evolutionary psychology. Neuropsychologists treat the mind as a system of circuitry organized in interacting modules that are specialized for various functions, and evolutionary psychologists regard this mental circuitry as the product of millions of years of human evolution.[8] One such module, Smith believes, is the "cheater-defector module" for social exchange, which evolutionary psychologists see as adaptive to a skill in making judgments about who can and cannot be trusted among individuals with whom one interacts. In a laboratory ultimatum and trust games context, then, individuals employ this module when they exhibit reciprocity, so that the reliance on memory in social interaction has its basis in the evolution of human biology and psychology. Further, in a passage in an earlier draft version of his Cognitive Science Encyclopedia contribution – then titled "Experimental Methods in (Neuro) Economics" – which was omitted from the final published version, Smith speculatively suggested how one might connect this larger framework and its emphasis on memory to a concept of the self: "personal identity is defined by some combination of inherited mental characteristics and our developmental experience" (V. Smith n.d.: 10). We might interpret this as saying that having a personal identity is the result of an evolutionary process that has reinforced the operation of our mental cheater-defector module by the development of enhanced memory processing. Thus while reconceptualizing the self was not Smith's original entry point – rather it was to explain experimental evidence regarding reciprocity at odds with the self-interest postulate – his effort to explain these results nonetheless leads to an understanding of the self which departs from the traditional neoclassical conception that treats individuals as uninflu-enced by context, and which integrates core cognitive psychology concerns in this regard with respect to the role of memory.

Whether Smith's views will be widely adopted by other experimentalists and behavioralists remains to be seen, but his picture, together with the more fully developed account to be found in cognitive psychology, points us toward an alternative behavioral conception of the individual. But applying this understanding of identity to the individual in economics still leaves one essential aspect of individuals unexplained: namely their independence from one another. Cognitive psychology puts this issue aside, because it by assumption investigates the individual apart from other individuals to focus on individuals' mental representations *per se*. But mainstream economics concerns individuals who interact with one another in markets, and thus its conception of the individual needs to include not only an account of what individuals are, but also an explanation of how they are distinct from one another. In this regard, cognitive psychology may be of little help if its self-as-memory view relies on quasi-memories which may be both the individual's memories and those of others the individual nonetheless believes to be his or her own. Indeed, cognitive psychologists have also developed "connectionist" models of social memory in which non-experien-tial semantic memories are formed and shared across individuals, thus blurring the lines between one individual and the next, at least with respect to this form of memory (E. Smith *et al.* 1999). Thus cognitive psychology's view of the self does not seem to provide a sufficient basis for explaining individual identity in economics, and something additional is needed if behavioral economics is to offer an account of the individual to fill the gap left by neoclassicism. In the following section I argue that those who see neuroeconomics as a logical extension of behavioral economics may see this additional needed element in the existence of the human body.

5 Neuroeconomics and identity

Neuroeconomics, understood as the combination of neuroscience and behavioral economics (cf. Camerer *et al.* 2005), represents a strategy for grounding the behavioral regularities that cognitive science has established in brain structures. That is, the regularities in behavior we observe are caused by the ways in which the brain works. While this general idea has long been entertained, the recent development of brain-imaging technolo-gies has now made it possible to investigate the idea more systematically. Thus neuroscientific research examines how different areas of the brain are activated when an individual is active in different ways. Since we may observe individuals' memory reports just as we can observe other types of behavior, neuroscientists argue that in principle we should be able to link memory behavior to particular areas of the brain. This, then, would locate all an individual's memories in the individual whatever their origin, whether or not they are autobiographical, and irrespective of whether social memory models are correct. Then individuals would not be identified strictly in terms of their memories but rather in terms of their "embodied" memories.[9] What, then, does this further conception of the individual involve?

First, the relation of psychological states to brain states is fundamental to both the neuroeconomics conception of the individual and indeed to neuroeconomics itself. There are different possible views here, and I begin with the most radical in order to dismiss it as not reflective of behavioral and neuroeconomics thinking as it is currently constituted. This radical view is a form of reductionism termed eliminative materialism or eliminativism, particularly as developed by Steven Stich (1983) and Patricia Churchland (1986). Actually, eliminative materialism is not reductionist in the sense of reducing or translating all psychological predicates into brain predicates, which proponents accept cannot be done, but rather reductionist in the sense that it aims to remove all psychological predicates and explanations from science on the grounds that such "folk psychology" notions as belief, desire, feeling, pain, memory, and so on are fictitious entities that have no place in science, much as was previously learned about such now-abandoned notions as phlogiston, ether, and so on.

But whatever the merits – or demerits (cf. Hacker 2001) – of eliminative materialism, it does not appear to reflect the goals of behavioral economists, who see neuroeconomics as an opportunity to reform the vocabulary of psychology used in economics rather than an occasion for abandoning such vocabulary altogether. Thus, even on the professedly "radical" interpretation of the neuroeconomics research program (Camerer *et al.* 2005), what is recommended is a replacement of the traditional neoclassical constructs of preferences and beliefs by such neuroeconomics constructs as affective versus cognitive processing and automatic versus controlled processing. These latter constructs may not be traditional folk psychology concepts, but neither are they concepts that may be explained purely in terms of neural functioning. Rather they constitute a sort of hybrid kind of concept whose purpose is to reconfigure the descriptions of psychological activity economists employ in such a way as to more closely reflect neural processing, and in this respect simply reflect recurrent efforts in the history of the field of psychology to re-specify and refine the field's categories and concepts. Indeed, neuroeconomic explanations of behaviors of particular interest in economics, such as loss aversion or hyperbolic discounting, remain well within the orbit of these new behavioral explanations. Thus neuroeconomics is clearly not a reductionist program in the strong eliminativist sense.

Nor indeed, moreover, does neuroeconomics appear reductionist in any significant sense. While some proponents may be carelessly tempted to suggest that psychological states can be translated into brain states, the program as a whole seems more committed to showing that brain states underlie psychological states, so as to be able to provide a more secure grounding to evidence regarding psychological regularities. Thus I suggest that the standard view among proponents of neuroeconomics is that psychological states are supervenient on brain states, meaning that psychological states depend on brain states but are not reducible to them, just as is widely argued in the case of other science–science relations such as biology and chemistry. Alternatively, psychological states are emergent upon brain states in the sense that they exhibit characteristics that cannot be ascribed to their associated brain states. That is, as in many other fields that have developed at the point of intersection between existing sciences, neuroeconomics as the combination of economics and neuroscience seems destined to adopt the widely held view of the relative autonomy of related sciences.[10]

Second, then, at issue is whether the body as the location of memories secures independence and personal identity for individuals. Here the challenge is more significant, though I will argue that what is at stake in this case is how one chooses to proceed in further expanding this conception rather than whether that conception fails altogether. Indeed, the question of whether the body secures personal identity has been extensively debated by philosophers in connection with a series of provocative thought experiments concerning brain transplants (one person's brain in another person's body), fission or split-brain transplant cases (one brain divided and transplanted into two bodies), brain fusion cases (distinct brains combined in one body), and teletransporter cases (bodies destroyed and identically rematerialized elsewhere).[11] All of these cases challenge the basic idea that one individual is indeed one individual by imagining improbable but conceivable circumstances in which the person becomes two persons or the reverse. The effect of their discussion on philosophers, it seems fair to say, has been to lead many to conclude that no definitive view of personal identity is likely possible. Perhaps most representative of this consensus is Derek Parfit (1984), whose own view of the individual – a brain-based psychological continuity theory – fairly closely matches the behavioral economics–neuroeconomics conception of the individual. Thus here I briefly describe his view in order to comment on the status of that conception.

Parfit's teletransporter cases are designed to violate identity while leaving in its place a weaker form of connectedness for individuals across change.[12] Were it possible for an individual to be destroyed and a perfect replica of that individual created elsewhere, our usual intuition is that the replica is not us – identity does not hold – but that we nonetheless have more interest in that replica of ourselves than in an entirely different individual. Parfit terms our replicas our descendent selves, and argues that in the absence of personal survival or personal identity proper we still care about the survival of our descendent selves. In effect, Parfit's approach is a second-best-type strategy in that he gives up personal identity to place a lesser substitute in its place. On the one hand, this reflects philosophers' general skepticism about whether an adequate account of personal identity is possible, while, on the other hand, it reflects increasingly realistic dilemmas modern medical science may soon encounter regarding human identity. These same issues, however, also arise for the neuroeconomics conception of the individual, since its addition of the brain (from neuroscience) to the self-as-memory account (from cognitive science) leaves it in the same situation Parfit and others describe, where changes in the bodily basis for being an independent individual inevitably raise questions regarding the continuing independence and identity of that individual. Thus the neuroeconomics conception, at least as currently developed, also arguably fails to account for personal identity.

This all may strike some as a rather unsatisfactory resolution of the identity issue on the grounds that the effect of Parfit's arguments is to essentially drop the issue of individuals having a personal identity. Yet from another perspective Parfit's arguments carry a more positive message, since they could also be interpreted to mean that the brain-based psychological continuity conception of the self is only incomplete – not necessarily mistaken – as an account of personal identity. That is, if we suppose, as seems reasonable, that some account of identity needs to be supplied for particular domains of social investigation such as economics or the law, but that we cannot guarantee personal identity in the abstract, we might go on to adopt assumptions specific to those domains that effectively "close" our account of identity, recognizing that any such account is relative to the purposes for which it is developed, and thus is more on the order of a contingent account of identity, not a solution to the "pure" problem of personal identity. In the brief final section, then, I sketch such a strategy for conceptions of the individual in economics, in order to indicate how the neuroeconomics conception of the individual might yet provide a partial basis for thinking about the individual in economics.

6 Social psychology's social interactionist perspective

What Parfit's arguments challenge is the numerical identity assumption underlying personal identity, namely that an individual is one and the same person across change. Another way of capturing this idea of numerical identity is to say that individuals remain distinct and independent of one another across change – what may be understood as a matter of being able to individuate persons (Davis 2003). Consider, then, the different sorts of strategies that might be used to individuate persons. One could first reason in terms of properties of individuals *per se*, and attempt to show that certain properties successfully distinguish particular individuals from one another. This route is taken by neoclassicism that emphasizes individuals' subjectivity, and takes individuals to be distinct in virtue of each having their own individual subjective states. The behavioral econonomics–neuroeconomics conception also takes this route when it makes individuals' memories necessarily their own in virtue of their location in independent brains. However, both accounts fail as means of individuating persons – the neoclassical conception in virtue of its circularity problems and the neuroeconomics conception in virtue of Parfit-type problems. Thus we need to consider an alternative strategy for establishing individuation.

In this case, rather than reason from the properties of individuals *per se*, we might ask whether the independence and distinctness of individuals is a function of individuals' interaction with one another. Arguably this is the general view in social psychology, which in contrast to cognitive psychology begins from the assumption that individuals' psychological states must be understood socially. On this view, roughly speaking, individuals occupy different positions, the occupation of which distinguishes them *vis-à-vis* one another. This is not the place to examine the adequacy of this strategy, and accordingly I restrict myself to linking this idea to the notion that identity conceptions may be "completed" relative to fields of investigation in which they operate. Taking economics and law, then, as social interactionist types of investigation, both may be said to invest agents with certain capacities – the capacity to choose and trade in economics and the capacity to act as a legal and moral agent in law. Such capacities can be said to distinguish individuals from one another as independent beings, because both economics and the law presuppose that these capacities are independently exercised in the ideal case. Supposing individuals have such capacities, then, does not solve the "pure" problem of personal identity. But were societies in fact to be organized according to economic and legal systems meant to ensure that individuals generally had such capacities, then individuals would effectively have personal identities understood in part in terms of those capacities and in part in terms of whatever substantive conceptions of individuals were employed (such as, for example, a brain-based psychological continuity theory). In this case, having a personal identity is a contingent matter reflecting how societies are organized, and not something that can be said to hold apart from any and all social-historical circumstances.

From this perspective, the emerging behavioral economics–neuroeconomics conception of the individual receives a mixed evaluation. On the one hand, since it draws on the first individuation strategy described earlier, it can ultimately no more provide a fully satisfactory account of personal identity than can Parfit. But, on the other hand, since the cognitive psychology foundations of this conception are not necessarily incompatible with the social interactionist perspective of social psychology, the door is still open to enlarging this conception in such a way as to provide an understanding of how individuals conceived in the first instance in terms of memories and brains might have personal identities in social settings. Further discussion of these strategies for a "social embedding" of the identity of the individual, however, must be postponed to another occasion.

Notes

1 The author is grateful to Barbara Montero, Mark White, and the participants of the 2004 Amsterdam–Cachan History and Methodology of Economics Workshop for comments on a previous version of this chapter.
2 In this respect they recalled Herbert Simon's earlier, neglected approach. See Sent (2004) for a comparison of the origins and nature of the "old" and "new" behavioral economics.
3 Thus one might have been told about an experience one does not remember, and subsequently come to believe one remembers it.
4 Though one may remember the experience of learning a semantic memory, as a semantic memory it can be remembered independently of the experience of learning it.
5 For a substantially similar but nonetheless slightly different classification of forms of memory from the perspective of philosophy, see the pioneering discussion of Norman Malcolm (1963).
6 A key difference is whether a memory item is stored independently of other memory items, as in the independent storage model, or whether there are groupings and clusterings of memory items, as in hierarchical organization models (Kihlstrom and Klein 1994). Note that it is important to take the term "storage" metaphorically.
7 This is not to say that Smith thinks non-autobiographical episodic and semantic memory are not involved in games. Surely they are. He simply does not employ these additional categories in emphasizing players' reliance on experiential memory.
8 Smith refers to the often-cited Cosmides and Tooby (1992) for this argument.
9 A precursor view is that of philosopher Sydney Shoemaker, who thought Locke's memory argument for identity presupposed the body, so that the memory criterion for identity depends on bodily continuity (Shoemaker 1984).
10 See Dupré (2001) for a defense of this view.
11 Locke actually considered the mind transplant case in his prince–cobbler example. His memory-as-identity definition led him to conclude that the prince was still the prince with his mind in the body of the cobbler, and vice versa. The fission and fusion cases are due to Wiggins (1967); Parfit (1984) develops the teletransporter case.
12 Similar conclusions arguably follow from the fission and other cases.

References

Allais, M. (1953) "Le Comportement de l'homme rationnel devant le risque: Critique des postulats et axiomes de l'école americaine," *Econometrica*, 21: 503–46.
Anderson, J. (1976) *Language, Memory, and Thought*, Hillsdale, NJ: Erlbaum.
—— (1983) *The Architecture of Cognition*, Hillsdale, NJ: Erlbaum.
Bandura, A. (1977) "Self-Efficacy: Toward a Unifying Theory of Behavioral Change," *Psychological Review*, 84(2): 191–215.
Bennett, M. and Hacker, P. (2003) *Philosophical Foundations of Neuroscience*, Oxford: Blackwell.
Camerer, C. and Loewenstein, G. (2003) "Behavioral Economics: Past, Present, Future," in C. Camerer, G. Loewenstein, and M. Rabin (eds.) *Advances in Behavioral Economics*, Princeton, NJ: Princeton University Press, 3–51.
Camerer, C., Loewenstein, G., and Prelec, D. (2005) "Neuroeconomics: How Neuroscience Can Inform Economics," *Journal of Economic Literature*, 43: 9–64.
Churchland, P.S. (1986) *Neurophilosophy: Toward a Unified Science of the Mind/Brain*, Cambridge, MA: MIT Press.

Cosmides, L. and Tooby, J. (1992) "Cognitive Adaptations for Social Exchange," in L. Cosmides and J. Tooby (eds.) *The Adapted Mind*, New York: Oxford University Press, 163–228.

Cubitt, R., Starmer, C., and Sugden, R. (2001) "Discovered Preferences and the Experimental Evidence of Violations of Expected Utility Theory," *Journal of Economic Methodology*, 8: 385–414.

Davis, J.B. (2003) *The Theory of the Individual in Economics*, London: Routledge.

Dupré, J. (2001) *Human Nature and the Limits of Science*, Oxford: Oxford University Press.

Fehr, E. and Gächter, S. (2000). "Fairness and Retaliation: The Economics of Reciprocity," *Journal of Economic Perspectives*, 14(3): 159–81.

Gazzaniga, M., Ivry, R., and Mangun, G. (1998) *Cognitive Neuroscience: The Biology of the Mind*, New York: Norton.

Hacker, P. (2001) "Eliminative Materialism," in S. Schroeder (ed.) *Wittgenstein and Contemporary Philosophy of Mind*, London: Routledge, 60–84.

Kahneman, D. and Tversky, A. (1979) "Prospect Theory: An Analysis of Decision under Risk," *Econometrica*, 47: 263–91.

Kihlstrom, J. and Klein, S. (1994) "The Self as a Knowledge Structure," in R. Wyer and T. Srull (eds.) *Handbook of Social Cognition, Vol. 1: Basic Processes*, 2nd edn., Hillsdale, NJ: Erlbaum, 153–208.

Klein, S. (2001) "A Self to Remember: A Cognitive Neuropsychological Perspective on How Self Creates Memory and Memory Creates Self," in C. Sedikides and M. Brewer (eds.) *Individual Self, Relational Self, and Collective Self*, Philadelphia: Psychology Press/Taylor and Francis, 25–46.

Lichtenstein, S. and Slovic, P. (1971) "Reversals of Preference between Bids and Choices in Gambling Decisions," *Journal of Experimental Psychology*, 89: 46–55.

Locke, J. (1975 [1694]) *An Essay Concerning Human Understanding*, ed. P.H. Nidditch, Oxford: Clarendon Press.

Malcolm, N. (1963) "Three Forms of Memory," in *Knowledge and Certainty*, Englewood Cliffs, NJ: Prentice-Hall, 203–21.

Parfit, D. (1984) *Reasons and Persons*, Oxford: Clarendon Press.

Payne, J., Bettman, J. and Johnson, E. (1992) "Behavioral Decision Research: A Constructive Processing Perspective," *Annual Review of Psychology*, 43: 87–131.

Perry, J. (ed.) (1975) *Personal Identity*, Berkeley: University of California Press.

Plott, C. (1996) "Rational Individual Behaviour in Markets and Social Choice Processes: The Discovered Preference Hypothesis," in K. Arrow, E. Colombatto, M. Perlman, and C. Schmidt (eds.) *The Rational Foundations of Economic Behaviour*, Basingstoke: Macmillan, 225–50.

Sent, E.-M. (2004) "Behavioral Economics: How Psychology Made Its (Limited) Way Back into Economics," *History of Political Economy*, 36: 737–62.

Shoemaker, S. (1984) "Personal Identity: A Materialist Account," in S. Shoemaker and R. Swinburne (eds.) *Personal Identity*, Oxford: Blackwell, 67–132.

Slovic, P. (1995) "The Construction of Preferences," *American Psychologist*, 50: 364–71.

Smith, E., Coats, S., and Walling, D. (1999) "Overlapping Mental Representations of Self, In-Group, and Partner: Further Response Time Evidence in a Connectionist Model," *Personality and Social Psychology Bulletin*, 25: 873–82.

Smith, V. (2003) "Experimental Methods in Economics," in L. Nadel (ed.) *Cognitive Science Encyclopedia*, London: Nature Publishing.

—— (n.d.) "Experimental Methods in (Neuro) Economics," unpublished.

Starmer, C. (2000) "Developments in Non-Expected Utility Theory: The Hunt for a Descriptive Theory of Choice under Risk," *Journal of Economic Literature*, 38: 332–82.

Stich, S. (1983) *From Folk Psychology to Cognitive Science*, Cambridge, MA: MIT Press.

Tulving, E. (1983) *Elements of Episodic Memory*, Oxford: Oxford University Press.

Tversky, A. and Kahneman, D. (1991) "Loss Aversion in Riskless Choice: A Reference-Dependent Model," *Quarterly Journal of Economics*, 106: 1039–61.

Wiggins, D. (1967) *Identity and Spatio-Temporal Continuity*, Oxford: Blackwell.

5 Language, monetary exchange, and the structure of the economic universe

An Austrian–Searlean synthesis

Steven Horwitz[1]

1 Introduction

With recent developments in psychology, behavioral economics, and even neuroeconomics, the relationship between the human mind and the economy has become a more frequent topic of research within economics. Such research can, as the fields just suggested indicate, take a number of forms. However, one fundamental philosophical issue remains how we move from the minds of distinct choosing individuals to the agreed-upon reality of the social world. How can it be that we all recognize certain social institutions and practices in the absence of explicit collective agreement on their functioning?[2] Phrased somewhat differently, how do those separate minds communicate to create social reality? One obvious answer is the use of language. However, language can only go so far in the creation of economic reality.

In previous work I have explored the parallels between the mind and the market through the lens of the analogies between language and monetary exchange (Horwitz 1992a, 1992b, 2004). In this chapter, I build on these previous contributions by bringing together the work on the nature of mind and society by the philosopher John Searle with Hayekian insights about spontaneous order and Misesian insights about the fundamental role of monetary exchange and calculation in the market.[3] More specifically, I will argue that Searle's description of the "symbolization" role of language as providing the foundation for the reality of the social universe is quite analogous to the symbolization role played by money prices in providing the foundation for the reality of the economic universe. Searle's description of the institutional order of the social world as emerging from collective intentionality, the assignment of function, and constitutive rules can be applied quite easily to the institutional order of the market, with money prices performing the symbolization function of language. It is monetary exchange that allows for the emergence of the institutional reality of the social world of the market.

2 Searle on mind, language, and society

My title for this chapter very consciously adapts a chapter title from Searle's 1998 book *Mind, Language, and Society*. That chapter is titled "The Structure of the Social Universe," and explores Searle's vision of the link between his philosophy of mind and the external world of society. Or, as he puts it there, "our main problem in this chapter is to explain how there can be an epistemically objective social reality that is partly constituted by an ontologically subjective set of attitudes" (Searle 1998: 113). That is, how can social institutions, which are often real because we think they are real, actually *be* real given that the "thinking" emerges from distinct human beings with distinct perceptions of the world? The key to the answer lies in the symbolization function of language. It is language that enables us both to "bridge minds" and to create a social reality that is distinct from the physical properties of objects. Searle begins his exploration of social and institutional reality interestingly enough with the puzzle of money, and how the physical facts about paper currency are not what endow it with the property of money; rather, it is a set of *social facts* that do so. Searle is interested in understanding how we get such "social facts." The key part of the answer is that social facts are facts because people believe they are facts. Those green pieces of paper are money largely, though not totally, because we believe they are money. How does that come about?

The first conceptual tool needed is Searle's distinction between "observer-independent" and "observer-dependent" or "observer-relative" features of the world (Searle 1998: 116). The former refers to those things that cannot be reduced to further intentionality. For example, the physical properties of a chair (for example its mass) are observer independent. It is true that objects have certain physical properties regardless of what we think and believe about them. What makes the physical object a "chair" is that we have come to a set of beliefs about what a chair does and that we recognize that the object at hand fulfills those functions sufficiently to qualify as a chair. As Searle notes, those beliefs themselves are observer independent, but they together create observer-dependent phenomena. The facts of the social world are observer dependent, but they are no less facts.

The other three tools necessary to understand social reality are collective intentionality, the assignment of function, and the idea of "constitutive rules" (Searle 1998: 118–24). Collective intentionality refers to the ability to say "we intend that X." Searle argues that it is possible to take "we intend" as a "primitive," in the sense that one can still uphold the idea that intentions must be located in the mind of individuals, but that doing so "does not require that all intentionality be expressed in the first-person singular" (Searle 1998: 120). The way Searle gets around these issues is to note that almost all forms of human cooperation are also acts of collective intentionality, for example the performance of a symphony orchestra.[4] He also notes, importantly, that even forms of human conflict require cooperation at a higher level. Sporting events, a legal trial, or even a good argument all involve agreement on what counts as doing those things. Searle does not use this language at this point in the argument, but what he is pointing out here is that collective intentionality in all of its forms rests upon agreement over the "rules of the game." To collectively intend to do X, especially where X may involve conflict, requires prior agreement and ongoing cooperation as to the rules that make what is being done qualify as X. Along these lines, Searle then distinguishes between "social facts," which refer to physical cooperation that manifests collective intentionality (for example an Amish barn-raising), and "institutional facts," which move us beyond "sheer physical cooperation" to things such as "own[ing] property, get[ting] married, and form[ing] governments" (Searle 1998: 121).

The *assignment of function* refers to our ability to use objects as tools. Searle argues that "all functions are observer-relative . . . . They only exist relative to observers or agents who assign the function." The assignment of function presupposes that there is a purpose at work, rather than just mere causation: "functional attribution situates the causal facts within a teleology" (Searle 1998: 122). Those purposes, or that teleology, are the creation of human actors; there are no observer-independent functions. Functions must be "attributed," and thus must be done by humans because they presuppose a purpose. They are observer dependent; they do not exist in nature. Even, using an example of Searle's, attributions of function to physical phenomena involve purpose: when we say the "function" of the heart is to pump blood, as opposed to just saying that it "does" pump blood, we are invoking a view that continued life is good and that death and disease are bad.

Finally, the concept of *constitutive rules* refers to the way in which some facts of the social world are only facts by virtue of a set of rules that make them possible. Some rules refer to pre-existing actions (driving on the right side of the road), but other kinds of rules *create* actions. To take Searle's example, there can be no such thing as "playing chess" without the rules of chess; that is, what makes what people's actions "playing chess" is that they are following the rules of chess. Alternately, just having a basketball and two hoops and running around on the court does not constitute "playing basketball." If two teams began kicking the ball around, trying to hit the backboard support to earn points, we would not call that basketball. It is the rules that create the institutional reality. Searle formalizes this as "X counts as Y in context C" (Searle 1998: 124).

These three elements together create the institutional reality of the social world. They explain, for example, why pieces of green paper function as money and why certain verbal utterances have the effect of creating legal relationships. The power of institutional reality comes in, according to Searle, because this formalization of the constitutive rules can be iterated. The X in formulation "X counts as Y in C" may well be a Y in an earlier formulation; for example, "handing over a $20 bill counts as making payment" and "that green piece of paper counts as a $20 bill." Searle uses the example of the levels of nested constitutive rules that go into the making and enforcing of a contract. One could do the same with almost any social institution.

What is of note here is the way in which we can take the fairly simple mechanism of a constitutive rule and "create a fantastically rich social structure by interlocking operations of the mechanism and complex iterations of the mechanism, piling one on top of another" (Searle 1998: 130). Social and institutional reality is the interconnecting of constitutive rules that enable the assignment of function with the end result being many forms of collective intentionality. In this conception of the social world, each element of the structure is dependent on a whole set of other constitutive rules that define the terrain for that element.

The social world that is built up this way creates what Searle calls "the Background," which is comprised of non-intentional capacities, such as, in his example of going out to eat, "what constitutes eating, what constitutes a meal, what constitutes a restaurant" (Searle 1992: 176). I can have a desire to eat a meal at a local restaurant, and I can have sets of beliefs about what restaurants and meals are, but what *counts as* eating, a meal, or a restaurant in a given circumstance is open to interpretation, and the meaning of my desire to have that meal in any specific circumstance will depend greatly on the nature of those Background capacities.

In order to do what one was asked to do in any given situation, one must bring to it a "Background of human capacities [that] will fix different interpretations, even though the literal meaning of the expression remains constant" (Searle 1992: 179). Searle argues that the Background is not removable by progressive interrogation. That is, the list of things that are part of the Background is not finite, mostly because many of them are in the form of negative restrictions. To use another example from Searle, when one orders a steak at a restaurant one takes it for granted that it "will not be encased in concrete, or petrified" (Searle 1992: 180). One could go on indefinitely about the "nots" that are taken for granted as Background to all purposive action (what Searle calls "Intentionality"), and the particular "nots" will vary, to some degree, from person to person and, certainly, from culture to culture. The unenumerable nature of the Background is further illustrated by the point that each Background capacity can itself only be understood against a further set of Background capacities. This is not a vicious infinite regress; rather it reflects the fact that all attempts to engage in and understand purposive action rely on this sort of unarticulatable Background.

This interlocking structure of rules that constitutes society is analogous to Intentionality and the Background. The meaning of any individual element of the social structure depends upon a whole Background of other elements. This is the result of the iterative process of those constitutive rules. The complexity of the social world that results is what enables us to, in turn, gain more control over the physical world. Following the rules of payment and contract allows us to manipulate the physical world in ways that enhance our lives. More generally, the innovations that have made human life longer and better are the result of the interconnected constitutive rules of the market and science.[5]

The very final piece of Searle's understanding of social reality is the fundamental role played by language. This role is twofold. First, all but the simplest of human thought is linguistically structured (Searle 1998: 152). We cannot have thoughts unless they are structured in language. Language is the set of "constitutive rules" of thought. Therefore, all acts of intentionality, whether collective or not, must start with language. To complicate matters further, language itself is a form of institutional reality in that what counts as "English" is an institutional fact. It is, in Searle's terms, the imposition of a function on the physical phenomena of the noises that humans make. However, Searle argues that language is the "fundamental human institution in the sense that other institutions . . . require language, or at least language-like forms of symbolism, in a way that language does not require the other institutions for its existence" (Searle 1998: 153). More specifically, it is the capacity of language to facilitate "symbolization" that makes it so fundamental. As noted earlier, the function of institutions is not something that can be derived solely from the physical facts of the situation (such as money). The "status function" of objects and institutions must emerge from the collective intention that they have that function, and having that collective intention requires some way "to represent to themselves the fact that the object has the status function" (Searle 1998: 154). To the extent we do this by using processes of symbolization, Searle argues we are using those symbols as a linguistic device. At the bottom of the social world, then, is our linguistic-symbolization capacity. It is that capacity that separates us from the other social animals (Searle 1998: 134). Monetary exchange is the extension of that capacity to the market where there are limits to the ability of language to perform the necessary symbolization.

3 History, institutional reality, and unintended consequences

For F. A. Hayek (1989), social and economic institutions, such as markets and prices, are orderly phenomena that emerge as the unintended consequences of human action. Social institutions are the product of human action, but not human design, and we need to rely on social institutions to coordinate our behavior by serving as intersubjective nodes of communication and coordination because there are limits to human knowledge that are a consequence of the nature of the brain and the mind. And given the limits to our knowledge, we are unable to design intentionally such institutions and we must allow maximum scope possible for them to evolve from the actions of individuals, unhampered by human hubris.[6] One way of understanding the limits to our ability to design institutions is that human social institutions, what Searle calls "institutional reality," must emerge out of the actual historical practices of human actors and cannot be imposed *ex nihilo* by the state or any other organization. One needs to be careful with Searle's concept of collective intentionality and continually recognize that it is at best metaphorical and, of necessity, backward looking. It cannot be understood, as Searle sometimes seems to suggest, as meaning that a specific legal or social act is what creates the general acceptance of a practice. This is how Searle sometimes appears to understand collective intentionality. At best, it must be used metaphorically to reflect the fact that a historical process has evolved to the point where the formulation "X counts as Y" has come to common acceptance.

The problem with Searle's formulation, to a Hayekian, is that institutional reality is *not* the direct result of anyone's intentions. Rather, institutions emerge as unintended consequences of choices made by actors all along the evolutionary path of the institution in question. The circumstances that make X count as Y today are likely not the result of anyone's current, or even past, intentions. Searle's argument that the individual mind can assert the first person plural form of intentionality is certainly correct, but in a literal sense it is not necessarily the case that "we intend" for X to count as Y in context C. Again, his use of the phrase "collective intentionality" in the context of the actual evolution of institutions is, at best, metaphorical. Searle's own example of the evolution of money is a case in point.

To say that "we intend that these specific green pieces of paper count as money" under particular circumstances is a bit misleading, as the way in which those *particular* things came to count as money was not necessarily the result of anyone's explicit intention during the process. Carl Menger (1892) argued over a century ago that the emergence of the precious metals as money was an unintended consequence of self-interested exchange. No one ever need say, "I intend" or "we intend" that gold becomes money. The desire to hold more saleable goods in order to more easily engage in sequences of barter exchanges will lead actors to acquire stocks of goods that they believe others find desirable. To the extent they are correct, their attempts to stock up on those goods are imitated by others as they see the easier time the innovators have making exchanges. As they demand the good for its exchangeability rather than its direct utility, they make the good even more marketable, enhancing its exchangeability even further. This process slowly converges on a small number of goods (such as the precious metals) as being the most useful for this process of indirect exchange.

The key to seeing what a Hayekian perspective can bring to Searle is to distinguish Searlean "Intention" from Hayekian "intentions." Searle might argue that the use of some object in indirect exchange is "taking it as money," and thus Intentional in his sense. To be precise, however, that person is only taking it as a *medium of exchange*. To be *money*, the good should be a *generally accepted* medium of exchange. Part of Menger's theory is how goods go from just being "taken as a medium of exchange" to the general acceptability that characterizes genuine moneys. It is important, then, to observe that no one in this process need ever *intend* that the specific good(s) they are using as a medium of exchange become money. That gold became *generally accepted* as a medium of exchange was an unintended consequence of other human action. The move from Intention at the level of individual action to the emergence of a social institution that may be the result of no one's intentions suggests that there is something about the interactions of Intentions that is greater than the sum of its parts. This is the Hayekian spontaneous order approach.

Searle might reply that, although this may have been true historically, what makes those green pieces of paper count as money today is the declaration by the state that they are legal tender. Hence, there is an explicit act of collective intentionality that underlies this institutional fact: "the creation of legal tender by the Treasury when it states that the currency it issues is legal tender is like a performative in that it creates the fact it describes" (Searle 1998: 115). The problem with this view is twofold. First, there are numerous historical examples, including in the evolutionary story Searle (1998) tells, of money being perfectly serviceable without the state declaring it legal tender or undertaking any sort of intentional act of defining what is or is not money. It can be an aspect of institutional reality that X is money without an explicit performative statement. The "general acceptance" part of money need not be, and has not been, the product of anyone's Intentionality. Second, where legal tender laws or other explicit statements of collective intentionality attempt to create the institutional reality of money, they cannot do so unless actors have already accepted the reality of that good serving as money.[7] Imagine a state attempting to declare lettuce to be money, or imagine even a sizeable minority of the population doing so. In neither case will this be successful unless traders as a whole already are using lettuce as money. It is not the performative that creates the reality; rather it is the process by which that practice has been accepted that creates the institutional reality. The sorts of explicit performatives that Searle uses in his money example are neither necessary nor sufficient to create the institutional fact of money, and this claim holds true for institutional facts in general.

In some sense Searle recognizes this point implicitly in his example of the wall (Searle 1998: 124–26). Searle imagines a group of people who create a wall around the area in which they live in order both to keep themselves in and to keep intruders out. He notes that it has two of the features of institutional reality: the assignment of function and collective intentionality. But, he argues, that function is related to the physical properties of the wall; for example, it is sufficiently high that it cannot be scaled. Then Searle adds a wrinkle: suppose the wall decays, leaving only a circle of stones. Further suppose that the inhabitants continue to "treat the line of stones as if it could perform the function of a wall" (Searle 1998: 125). One simply does not cross this line of stones. Searle argues that this wrinkle is the uniquely human aspect of institutional reality, namely our ability to agree upon the status of a particular object, which in turn assigns it a function. The physical properties of the stones do not keep the inhabitants in; rather, it is their collective agreement on what the stones *mean* or *symbolize* that does so. As noted earlier, our capacity to use language, or language-like processes, to engage in symbolization enables us to assign "status functions" this way.

At the center of these issues are the questions of size and longevity. We can imagine situations where a small number of people need to agree upon a social fact for a short period of time. Consider two siblings agreeing that a line on the floor of their shared bedroom will function as a wall. Explicit agreement can work here where communication is face to face and where the agreement is understood to bind only the parties making the agreement. When we think about genuine social institutions neither of these conditions holds. In large and complex human societies, there is no way to ensure that the communication emanating from the center will get to those who need to know this social fact. In addition, how will this necessarily bind those who do not get the communication? The Menger–Hayek approach offers a way around both problems through the assertion that effective social facts and institutions must emerge from actual practice, rather than being promulgated from the top or the center, in heterogeneous and complex societies.

The relevance for the current discussion is that it is not any old line of stones that can acquire the status function of a wall, but only one that actually *did* have certain physical properties at one point in time. If members of the group decided to lay another line of stones elsewhere, I submit that it would be very difficult, if not impossible, to assign those stones the status function of a wall. Our ability to engage in the symbolization process that assigns a status function is crucially dependent on history. We cannot declare any old object to be money anymore than we can, by inventing a new word, automatically make it part of a language. The symbolization that characterizes institutional reality must be part of a historical evolutionary process where those who are to make use of the symbolic representation have already *de facto* made use of the underlying non-symbolic process or object.

The implication of this perspective on Searle's argument is that institutional reality must grow from the ground up and cannot be imposed from the top down. Searle is correct that the process by which institutional reality is created allows for increased complexity through increased abstraction and symbolization. However, the process that produces this result must grow out of the day-to-day practices of the participants. Whatever anyone might want institutional reality to be, the de facto practices of the individuals will matter a great deal more than any de jure definitions.[8] A further implication is that we are simply not smart enough to create an institutional reality of our own invention. What constitutes collective intentionality, what brings about the constitutive rules, and what assigns the function, which are all three jointly necessary to produce institutional reality, are undesigned processes of social evolution.

4 Monetary calculation and the order of the market

Many of the same processes Searle identifies in the production of institutional reality are at work in an analogous way in what we might call the production of "economic-institutional reality." To see this, we need to understand that there is a powerful analogy between the use of language and the process of monetary exchange that produces the money prices of the market. Those prices serve as tools for economic calculation by market actors. Our ability to engage in any real intentionality in the realm of the market is a function of our ability to calculate using the money prices produced by decentralized processes of exchange. Money prices are symbolic representations that acquire economic reality through a process completely analogous to Searle's description of institutional reality. They have collective intentionality, the assignment of function, and constitutive rules, and thus serve as markers of what is real within the realm of the market. As I have argued elsewhere (Horwitz 1992b), monetary exchange is both an analog to, and an extension of, our language-using capacities. Monetary exchange and the prices that it produces enable us to communicate that which cannot be put into words but is nonetheless central to economic coordination. The constellation of money prices is the Background to entrepreneurial action.

The prices that are produced by monetary exchange are central to the institutional reality studied by economics. In the Austrian tradition, the epistemic role of prices has been most clearly articulated in Hayek's work, especially in the 1930s and 1940s as part of his participation in the debate over economic calculation under socialism, itself launched by Mises's (1920) article denying that calculation was possible under planning. Mises argued there that in the absence of prices for the means of production, socialist planners would be unable to make any sort of rational decision about how to use resources. In a world where the means of production are neither perfectly substitutable nor usable for the production of only one output, choices must be made as to how inputs will be applied to outputs. Money prices are necessary to engage in such calculations, and those money prices can only emerge from monetary exchange, which itself is conditioned on the existence of markets and private property in the means of production. Hayek (1945) added that the reason market prices are able to facilitate calculation in this way is that they enable us to more effectively use each other's knowledge than would planning. The various, and decentralized, acts of exchange that comprise the marketplace are a form of communication whereby the prices that emerge through that pushing and pulling are signals about our preferences and knowledge. We do not need to know why oranges in Florida are in short supply; we need only watch the price to be led to take the "right" action given that they are indeed in short supply.

As important as this point is, in that same article Hayek makes an argument even more relevant to the issue at hand. He notes that a great deal of the knowledge that matters for economic action is knowledge of the "circumstance of time and place" (Hayek 1945: 80). The contextuality of knowledge matters here because context cannot be known by an external observer trying to collect that knowledge and manipulate it in the form of "data." The meaning that a particular price has, or that a certain flow of inventory has, depends on the context in which that piece of knowledge sits. That context is lost when prices are treated as objectifiable and interchange-able pieces of data. This argument is strengthened when we recognize that a good deal of market-relevant knowledge is also tacit – things we know but cannot articulate (Polanyi 1958). We might know when is the right time to pull off the clutch when driving a standard shift car, but when we try to explain what it is that we know to someone else, we cannot articulate it. The same might be said of how we keep our balance on a bicycle. In both cases, there is no doubt that we possess knowledge, but it is not knowledge of the sort that we can convey directly to others.

Implicit in Hayek's emphasis on "time and space," and more explicit in the work of Lavoie (1985, 1986), is the claim that much economic knowledge is of this sort. An entrepreneur who has worked in a particular industry for many years will have acquired a great deal of experience and wisdom that she may not be able to articulate but which nonetheless accurately guides her decision-making. If asked to offer a complete and explicit explanation for her decision to buy some input today, she might not be able to do so, but might well say, like the driver or bicyclist, "I know it but I cannot describe precisely what it is that I know." However, what it is that she does know is made available to others in the form of the prices that her decisions affect. In buying that input, she contributes to movements in the price that signal to others that the resource has become more valuable and that they need to take that into account in their own decision-making processes. By exchanging money for the input, and thus causing the money price to change, the entrepreneur has engaged in a form of communication that goes beyond language by enabling tacit knowledge to be taken into account by others. Monetary exchange is an extra-linguistic social communication process.

Searle's three elements of institutional reality are at work in the monetary exchange process that is the foundation of the market. There is collective intentionality, with the recognition that it is in the sense that is appropriate to spontaneously ordered institutions as noted earlier. We have come to a collective understanding that markets order our economic lives and we generally agree that the institutional context of the market means that certain acts have certain meanings. There is the assignment of function in the way in which we understand prices to have a function beyond their phys-ical properties in written or spoken form. Finally, money prices are very effectively understood as resulting from constitutive rules. There cannot be money prices absent the set of rules that define markets and monetary exchange. As we noted earlier, what makes basketball "basketball" is not the physical equipment involved but the following of the rules of the game. The same is true of money prices. One can assign numbers to goods and try to make them into prices, but without the process of monetary exchange, and the rules that constitute it, underlying them those prices are meaningless. This is just another instance of the broader claim about the historicity of social institutions made in the previous section.

An illustration of the parallel to language can be found in the Hayek–Lange exchanges in the debate over the feasibility of economic calculation under socialism in the 1930s and 1940s.[9] Lange's (1936) argument for the feasibility of planning was that in order to allocate resources rationally one need not have genuine money prices. Prices were necessary, but Lange argued that price, in this context,

> may mean either price in the ordinary sense, i.e., the exchange ratio of two commodities on a market, or it may have the generalized meaning of "terms on which alternatives are offered" . . . . It is only prices in the generalized sense which are indispensable to solving the problem of the allocation of resources.

> (Lange 1936: 59–60)

This notion of price emerges from perfectly competitive/general equilibrium models where prices are parametric to the choices of individuals. Utility or profit maximization requires the "givenness" of prices, suggesting that Lange's "terms" would be sufficient to solve such models. Lange misconceived the problem facing real market and planned economies by importing notions of price from the static models of economists.

In order for prices to play a role in coordinating economic action, they must emerge from actual practice, that is, from "games" played according to the constitutive rules of the market. Just because one attaches a number to an object, that does not make it a price. What a price means, in Searle's terms, is that this number "counts as" a price in the context of monetary exchange. Lange's "terms" or the parametric prices of economic models are not prices in the sense relevant to institutional reality because they did not emerge from those constitutive rules. Because they are not prices in the sense that we collectively understand prices, they are unable to fulfill the functions that prices are supposed to. Like the game played with basketball equipment that is not basketball, the prices in Lange's argument might look like prices, but cannot have the meaning attached to them that prices emerging from acts of exchange do. Exchange using money enables actors to share their knowledge through the prices that emerge. Prices created outside the contextual and tacit knowledge of actors are, literally, meaningless and thus irrelevant for understanding how human economic action unfolds.

Searle's understanding of the centrality of language can be linked to our understanding of the linguistic-like functions of money exchange. In a quote discussed earlier, Searle argues that language is the: "fundamental human institution in the sense that other institutions . . . require language, or at least language-like forms of symbolism, in a way that language does not require the other institutions for its existence" (Searle 1998: 153). Monetary exchange can be seen as a "language-like" institution in the way that Searle notes. Recall that the centrality of language was due to its ability to help us create symbols, which are necessary to attribute status functions to things where those functions are not part of their physical composition. The example of money is, again, illustrative. Language enables us to make clear that money symbolizes value in ways that can be utterly disconnected from the physical properties of the money object, or, in the case of electronic forms of money, where they have no physical properties at all. Specific words, or groups of words together, become symbols of our collective intentionality. This is what prices and groups of prices do in the market.

These prices form the foundation for the economic calculations of producers and consumers that drive the market process. It is not just that we create meaning when we buy and sell and thus affect prices; we also interpret meaning when we look at prices on the market and act based on them. Producers decide on what and how to produce based on their interpretations of the prices in the marketplace, both as they look backward via profit and loss accounting and as they look forward through budgeting. Producers, often via their accountants, are interpreters of the language of money prices and use those interpretations to allocate resources. Calculations of profit and loss can fruitfully be understood as attempts to search for meaning within the data of the marketplace. The producer wants to understand how the rest of the market has assessed her acts of production, and profit and loss accounting enables her to grasp that meaning. This is the backward-looking function of the network of prices. The forward-looking budgeting activities of producers are an attempt to navigate the uncertain future through the use of prices as social guideposts. In the same way that social facts and institutional reality serve as anchor points for our actions in the world more generally, so prices provide that guidance for producers in the market. The meaning of words such as "marriage," "property," or "contract" enables us to predict the actions of others and imagine the results of our own actions. In the process of entrepreneurial planning, prices serve this same function. They are foundational for any meaningful economic reality.

The complex structure of capital and vast array of consumer goods that characterize modern market economies result from extensive symbolization processes that ultimately rest on the language-like features of monetary exchange. Just as we have built up a broader institutional reality by the repeated application of Searle's "X counts as Y in context C" formula, so has economic reality been built by repeated application of the process of monetary calculation using money prices. When entrepreneurs engage in monetary calculation they are using these prices in ways analogous to how all purposive action requires the Searlean Background.

The market is a special case of the institutional reality creation process described by Searle, and it is one that relies as much on the process of monetary exchange as "natural language" to be the foundational symbolization process. Economic processes including exchange certainly involve the use of natural language, but natural language is not sufficient to generate the institutional reality of the market economy. It must also include the language-like features of monetary exchange and the money prices it produces. These prices become surrogates for a great deal of historical and contemporaneous knowledge possessed by market actors. Like other entities with status functions, money prices are the sediment or crystallization of knowledge from the past and present, the details of which are both inaccessible and unnecessary to serve their purpose. Just as the wall from Searle's example evolves into a line of rocks serving the same purpose, so prices change and evolve in response to the exchange activity of individuals, leaving the current price to reflect that unknown past.

5 Conclusion

John Searle's approach to the interrelationships among mind, language, and society offers strong parallels to the way in which Austrian economists have understood the nature of the economic universe. From an Austrian perspective, the role of monetary exchange as the necessary basis for the evolution of a rich and complex economic order is as a Searlean "language-like" way to facilitate the symbolization process necessary to produce institutional reality more generally. Searle's conception of this process adds a richness to the Austrian view and helps to place it in the context of institutional reality more broadly. The market order is seen as a particular piece of institutional reality that is constituted by a particular set of rules, where the symbolization process takes place through monetary exchange precisely because a good deal of the knowledge "in play" cannot be captured in natural language. Monetary exchange extends the institutional reality making function of language into a new realm, which enables us to create even more complex social orders than we could do with natural language alone. Bringing together Searle's work with that of the Austrians makes clear both the role of the market in creating a large piece of social reality, and why markets cannot be dispensed with as a result, and in doing so enhances our understanding of the evolution and function of social and economic institutions.

Notes

1 The author thanks the editors for helpful suggestions and comments along the way.
2 This is a slight reworking of Menger's (1985 [1883]) foundational question for the methodology of the social sciences.
3 Boettke and Subrick (2002) also pursue an Austrian–Searlean connection, though one much more focused on the philosophy of mind.
4 I will return to this point later, in the context of unintended forms of social cooperation.
5 That science is a social process with its own internal constitutive rules should not be lost in this discussion. Our ability to directly manipulate the physical world is the result of the institutional reality of the social process of science.

6 For more on the relationships among Hayek's theory of mind and his economic
   theory and political philosophy, see Horwitz (2000).
7 This argument is normally credited to Mises (1980 [1912]) as "the regression
   theorem." Boettke (1996) extends this idea to cultural phenomena more generally.
8 DeSoto's (2000) work on the differences between de facto and de jure property
   rights in Latin America is illustrative of this point.
9 See Horwitz (1996) for a more complete elaboration of issues raised here.

References

Boettke, P.J. (1996) "Why Culture Matters: Economics, Politics and the Imprint of
   History," reprinted in *Calculation and Coordination: Essays on Socialism and
   Transitional Political Economy* (2001), London: Routledge, 248–65.
Boettke, P.J. and Subrick, J.R. (2002) "From Philosophy of Mind to the Philosophy
   of the Market," *Journal of Economic Methodology*, 9: 53–64.
DeSoto, H. (2000) *The Mystery of Capital*, New York: Basic Books.
Hayek, F.A. (1945) "The Use of Knowledge in Society," reprinted in *Individualism
   and Economic Order* (1948), Chicago: University of Chicago Press, 77–91.
—— (1989) *The Fatal Conceit: The Errors of Socialism*, W. W. Bartley III (ed.),
   Chicago: University of Chicago Press.
Horwitz, S. (1992a) *Monetary Evolution, Free Banking, and Economic Order*, Boulder,
   CO: Westview Press.
—— (1992b) "Monetary Exchange as an Extra-Linguistic Social Communication
   Process," *Review of Social Economy*, 50: 193–214.
—— (1996) "Money, Money Prices, and the Socialist Calculation Debate," *Advances
   in Austrian Economics*, 3: 59–77.
—— (2000) "From *The Sensory Order* to the Liberal Order: Hayek's Non-Rationalist
   Liberalism," *Review of Austrian Economics*, 13: 23–40.
—— (2004) "Money and the Interpretive Turn: Some Considerations," *Symposium*,
   8: 249–66.
Lange, O. (1936) "On the Economic Theory of Socialism," abridged in B. Lippincott
   (ed.) (1964) *On the Economic Theory of Socialism*, New York: McGraw-Hill, 57–
   143.
Lavoie, D. (1985) *National Economic Planning: What is Left?*, Cambridge, MA:
   Ballinger Publishing Company.
—— (1986) "The Market as a Procedure for the Discovery and Conveyance of Inar-
   ticulate Knowledge," *Comparative Economic Studies*, 28: 1–29.
Menger, C. (1892) "On the Origin of Money," *Economic Journal*, 2: 239–55.
—— (1985 [1883]) *Investigations into the Method of the Social Sciences with Special
   Reference to Economics*, New York: New York University Press.
Mises, L. (1920) "Economic Calculation in the Socialist Commonwealth," in F.A.
   Hayek (ed.) (1935) *Collectivist Economic Planning*, London: Routledge, reprinted
   (1975) Clifton, N.J.: Kelley Publishing, 87–130.
—— (1980 [1912]) *The Theory of Money and Credit*, Indianapolis: Liberty Press.
Polanyi, M. (1958) *Personal Knowledge: Towards a Post-Critical Philosophy*, Chicago:
   University of Chicago Press.
Searle, J.R. (1992) *The Rediscovery of the Mind*, Cambridge, MA: MIT Press.
—— (1998) *Mind, Language, and Society: Philosophy in the Real World*, New York:
   Basic Books.

6 Putting the brakes on vehicle externalism
Two economic examples

Dan Fitzpatrick

1 Introduction

In contemporary philosophy of mind, vehicle externalism (also known as active externalism, architecturalism, or environmentalism) is, in simple terms, the claim that the structures and mechanisms that allow an individual to possess or undergo various mental states and processes are sometimes structures and mechanisms that exist beyond the head or the skin of that individual. Along with other forms of externalism, vehicle externalism stands in opposition to a long tradition of internalism, the claim that the mind (or all mental states) is contained within the skull. Clark and Chalmers (1998) and others see the roots of internalism in the philosophy of Descartes and claim that this Cartesian prejudice prevails in contemporary philosophy of mind.

Although critical of Clark and Chalmers's account of vehicle externalism, the aim of this chapter is not to oppose vehicle externalism in favor of some internalist alternative; instead, using two economic examples, I will show, among other things, that a cornerstone of Clark and Chalmers's account, namely their *parity principle*, in untenable. In line with some recent work on cognitive integration (Menary 2006a, 2006b), I will be proposing its replacement with what I call the *integration principle*, which I claim is necessary if vehicle externalism is to avoid cognitive bloat. But first I will briefly introduce Clark and Chalmers's position and outline my strategy for resolving the problems that arise from their position.

Clark and Chalmers's challenge to the internalist opposition to vehicle externalism is the *parity principle,* according to which, if the external structures that underwrite the process were inside the head, we would have no problem claiming the process to be a cognitive one (Clark and Chalmers 1998: 8; Clark 2005). Of course it would be impossible for the external structures to actually be present in the same form inside the head; the pencil and paper I use to perform a calculation, for example, is not literally implanted inside my head. Instead, what Clark and Chalmers are referring to in their use of the parity principle is a parity of function between a cognitive process that uses a part of the world outside the head and a cognitive process that occurs solely inside the head. To use the calculation example again, calculation using pencil and paper, that is, using an external process in the cognitive task of calculation, is functionally on a par with calculation inside the head, a wholly internal process; as we have no problem describing the latter process as a cognitive one, we should therefore have no problem describing the former process involving pencil and paper also as a cognitive process.

Another important feature of Clark and Chalmers's account concerns why external structures are recruited to underwrite processes inside the head. To illustrate this point, let us look at the example of a person trying to complete a jigsaw. It is a common occurrence for individuals, when attempting to complete a jigsaw puzzle, to physically manipulate jigsaw pieces; this physical manipulation or rotation of pieces facilitates the completion of the jigsaw puzzle. Were these individuals to try to complete the jigsaw puzzle solely by mentally rotating the pieces inside their heads, jigsaw puzzles would be much more difficult (or impossible) to complete.

Clearly, such examples are intended to illustrate that the use of structures outside the body can greatly enhance our cognitive abilities, thereby allowing cognitive tasks to be completed that would otherwise be impossible, or, at least, would not be possible without much greater internal cognitive input. For the sake of clarity, throughout this chapter I will refer to this general point concerning either the enhancement of cognitive abilities or the saving of cognitive resources as *cognitive enhancement*. It is clear that in the absence of cognitive enhancement there would be no rationale for the use of external vehicles by an individual; from the standpoint of vehicle externalism, there would be no point in the individual physically rotating the jigsaw piece if there was not some payoff in terms of cognitive enhancement.

We now have two of the central features of Clark and Chalmers's version of vehicle externalism, cognitive enhancement and the parity principle. These provide us with the basis for claiming whether or not an instance of their version of vehicle externalism has occurred. I will also be examining other pertinent features of Clark and Chalmers's account later. While I accept that cognitive enhancement is a necessary feature of vehicle externalism,[1] later I will argue that the parity principle leads to cognitive bloat and ought to be dropped in favor of an alternative.

If one accepts the parity principle, cognitive enhancement and the possibility of vehicle externalism,[2] there would appear to be an abundance of examples of vehicle externalism to be found in economic activity. For instance, among the reasons why individuals may be said to engage in certain economic transactions is because they do not want to go to the effort of producing the required good or service themselves. In certain circumstances the savings involved can be almost exclusively cognitive. For instance, although I may have the ability and knowledge required to produce a computer program that I need, I do not want to go to the effort of doing so when either I can contract someone else to do it for me or I can purchase one off the shelf. This is an instance of what I called cognitive enhancement, in this case recruiting external structures in order to save the internal cognitive resources required to write the program myself.

Another reason for engaging in an economic transaction is that it would not be possible or feasible for an individual to produce the required good or service on her own. For example, if I cannot write computer programs (it may be cognitively beyond me because I lack the training or I do not have the aptitude), I can contract someone else to do it for me or I can purchase one off the shelf. Again, this is an instance of what I call cognitive enhancement – in this case recruiting external structures in order to complete cognitive tasks that I, on my own, would otherwise not be able to achieve using internal resources alone.

I will be arguing that such economic transactions also cohere with the parity principle in that they are a part of the world that functions in a process that results in the completion of a cognitive task. To reuse the example, there is a parity of function between coming up with a computer program using one's own internal resources and coming up with a computer program using external structures. Although I find this sort of claim to be counterintuitive, I will show that the point about economic transactions being cognitive processes involving external vehicles is perfectly in keeping with the parity principle and with Clark's other writings on extended mind.

I will also examine a second type of economic example that fits Clark and Chalmers's account. This concerns the way certain economic phenomena emerge and, in turn, facilitate our abilities to deal with other economic agents. Here I have in mind a development of the standard Mengerian story concerning the emergence of money (Menger 1892). According to Menger, money emerges as a response to the inefficiency of pure barter. In addition to other problems associated with pure barter, as soon as the number of goods rises above a relatively small number, the number of exchange rates required between goods becomes impossibly high. When money emerges along Mengerian lines, these difficulties disappear. This scenario is a perfect candidate for Clark and Chalmers's account of vehicle externalism; money is just one of those mechanisms in the (economic) environment that under-writes a process whereby, when comparing prices, we are able to deal with the multitude of exchange rates between as many goods as we like without cognitive overload. This example clearly exhibits cognitive enhancement in that money either saves us extraordinary cognitive effort or possibly allows us to engage in activity that otherwise would, using our internal resources alone, be cognitively impossible.

This example of the emergence of money is also consistent with Clark and Chalmers's parity principle in that there is a functional parity between the use of money and the calculation of multiple exchange rates inside the head. The cognitive task here involves calculating the best value for what one has to offer as part of a putative transaction. One of the cognitive processes involved in the completion of that task is comparing prices. In the absence of money, we would have to calculate prices using a multitude of exchange rates between different goods. As I will explain in more detail later, money, in effect, resolves this problem by reducing all exchange rates to one exchange rate, namely a monetary one.

Despite the coherence of these examples with Clark and Chalmers's extended mind thesis, I find their inclusion in any account of vehicle externalism to be implausible and counterintuitive. Although I am generally sympathetic to vehicle externalism, I think that advocating a form of vehicle externalism on the basis of the parity principle, as Clark and Chalmers have done, extends vehicle externalism in a way that leads to cognitive bloat, as I will show. Later I will be suggesting a substitute for the parity principle, the *integration principle*, that will avoid this cognitive bloat and will also allow us to clearly discriminate between true cases of vehicle externalism and those that are not. I will argue that this will not be the mere substitution of one principle for another; instead, I will be advocating a fundamental change of orientation away from the extended mind hypothesis towards a position known as *cognitive integration*.

Although Clark at times has indicated a concern with cognitive bloat, his own version of vehicle externalism provides fertile ground for it, as the economic examples I am putting forward illustrate. I will be arguing that a reorientation of vehicle externalism away from the extended mind hypothesis and in favor of cognitive integration will solve these issues of cognitive bloat. In addition, I will argue that the integration principle I put forward is more appropriate than the parity principle in that it rules out examples involving cognitive bloat but does not require relinquishing vehicle externalism.

2 Vehicle externalism

As I outlined in the introduction, externalism in philosophy of mind is the view that, broadly speaking, not all aspects of the mind are completely contained within the head of the person whose mind it is. Externalism is further broken down into two forms. Content externalism is the view that the content of a mental state can be dependent on aspects of the world outside the head of the person whose mental state it is. There has been much discussion about this form of externalism in the literature (Putnam 1975; Burge 1979), but I will not be discussing it here. Instead I will be concentrating solely on vehicle externalism.

Vehicle externalism is the view that cognitive processes are not always contained within the head but can involve external structures or mechanisms that are outside the head of the individual. Vehicle externalism belongs to a family of positions, such as active externalism, environmentalism, and extended mind; to avoid confusing the reader and for the purposes of clarity, I propose restricting the discussion here to vehicle externalism and the extended mind hypothesis. Because Clark equates the extended mind hypothesis with vehicle externalism (2005: 1, fn. 1), in my discussion of the well-known paper of Clark and Chalmers (1998) and Clark's other works I will be treating them as equivalent. However, later I will be arguing in favor of a version of vehicle externalism that is in opposition to the extended mind hypothesis.

Vehicle externalism is the claim that cognitive architecture (where cognitive architecture refers to the vehicles or mechanisms that allow us to cognize) does not have to be internal to the individual, within neither the head nor even the body of the cognizer. If one accepts that the vehicles of thought or cognition can be external, then it follows that the processes that are based or dependent on those external vehicles or mechanisms are themselves external. Vehicle externalism is primarily opposed to internalism, the view that the mind must be contained within the confines of the brain.

Clark and Chalmers offer a number of examples of vehicle externalism or extended mind (1998: 7ff.). They ask us to imagine the following associated sets of circumstances: an individual is sitting in front of a computer screen and is presented with a series of geometrical shapes that have to be manipulated into predetermined sockets. In the first scenario, the individual must mentally rotate the shapes so as to align them with the sockets. In the second, the individual has the choice to rotate the shape in his head or to rotate it on the screen using the keyboard. In the third scenario, the individual finds herself in some "cyberpunk future" and has received a neural implant whereby she can rotate the images on the screen. We could also imagine that there are speed advantages to the second and third scenarios over the first. According to Clark and Chalmers, all three cases are similar; if we allow that case 3 is on a par with case 1, then "what right do we have to count case 2 as fundamentally different?" (Clark and Chalmers 1998: 7).

Clark and Chalmers also cite a number of other examples in support of their claim for what Clark later called the *parity principle*:

> If, as we confront some task, a part of the world functions as a process which, *were it done in the head*, we would have no hesitation in recognizing as a part of the cognitive process, then that part of the world is (so we claim) part of the cognitive process.
>
> (Clark and Chalmers 1998: 8)

They include the following as examples of vehicle externalism (or what they term "active externalism"): counting on our fingers, an engineer calculating with the aid of a slide rule, using a pocket calculator, a neural implant augmenting a cognitive process, using a Filofax, activities involving language, a notebook used by someone with Alzheimer's, physically manipulating the pieces of a jigsaw puzzle or the Scrabble tiles on a tray, and, based on the findings of Kirsh and Maglio (1994), the physical rotation of shapes in the well-known computer game Tetris to determine whether the shape and slot are compatible. In each of these instances, the internal resources and the external vehicles work together in a coupled system that functions to complete a cognitive task.[3]

Clark and Chalmers work through a number of anticipated counterarguments against the parity principle.[4] The first concerns the view that the cognitive is identified with the conscious and it is therefore not plausible for the cognitive to extend beyond the boundaries of the skull. Clark and Chalmers counter this by pointing out that cognitive processes are not necessarily conscious processes. Another counterargument they deal with concerns the issue of portability of cognitive processes; the issue here is the claim that coupled systems can all too easily be decoupled. If we take it that cognitive processes have to be constantly and directly available, then anything external is merely a temporary add-on. Against this, Clark and Chalmers point out that some parts of our external environment, such as counting on our fingers, are constantly available, and it is always possible in some distant future for various modules to be plugged into our brains to augment some aspect of our cognitive processes, such as memory.

Clark and Chalmers also marshal an example that is intended to demonstrate that the use of a notebook by Otto, an Alzheimer's sufferer, is not functionally different from the use of internal memory by Inga, someone who is not affected by Alzheimer's. The idea is that the notebook takes over the role of normal biological memory; in other words, there is a *functional parity* between the use of the notebook by Otto and the use of normal biological memory. Clark and Chalmers's point is that "what makes some information count as a belief is the role it plays, and there is no reason why the relevant role can be played only from inside the body" (Clark and Chalmers 1998: 14). Of course, none of these examples or illustrations amount to an argument *for* the parity principle as such – they were intended as illustrations and defenses against anticipated counterarguments. As Clark pointed out in a more recent paper, "in the end, [the parity principle] was meant to command rational assent as a means of freeing ourselves from mere bio-chauvinistic prejudices" (Clark 2005: 2).

But the parity principle is based on an argument of sorts, namely that just because the structures underwriting the process are not inside the head (or within the boundaries of the skin), we have no reason to deny that the structures and the processes associated with them are cognitive. As Clark later pointed out:

> The main argument [for the parity principle] takes the form of a challenge: show us why the case of Otto and his notebook (thus elaborated) is not simply that of an unusual realizer: an extended physical vehicle for a set of dispositional beliefs very much like Inga's own.
>
> (Clark 2005: 3)

To claim that, for instance, the physical rotation of jigsaw pieces by an individual in order to anticipate where they might fit is not part of the cognitive process of solving a jigsaw puzzle is Cartesian prejudice, according to this view. But these examples are also intended to illustrate the point about cognitive enhancement I mentioned in the introduction, that the use of structures outside the body often greatly enhance our cognitive abilities, thereby allowing cognitive goals to be achieved that it otherwise would not be possible to achieve (at least not without a large increase in cognitive effort).

But do we have no reason to deny that the external structures and processes associated with cognitive processes are cognitive when those structures are outside the head? Based on the parity principle alone, it appears not. It looks like we can extend the mind to include almost anything in the world. But even Clark advises against excessively extending the mind, against what he calls "cognitive bloat":

> The mind cannot usefully be extended willy-nilly into the world. There would be little value in an analysis that credited me with knowing all the facts in the Encyclopedia Britannica just because I paid the monthly installments and found space in my garage.
>
> (Clark 1997: 217)

In an effort to avoid cognitive bloat and with the case of the neurologically impaired agent (or Alzheimer's sufferer) and his notebook in mind, Clark sets out some features of the "more plausible cases of robust cognitive extension" (Clark 1997: 217). These include the following: availability (in the example, the notebook is always there and not kept at some remote location and rarely consulted), ease of access and use (again, the information in the notebook can be easily accessed and used by the agent), automatic endorsement (the information in the notebook is not subject to critical scrutiny), and trust (the information in the notebook was originally assembled and endorsed by the agent and is therefore trusted).

According to Clark, these conditions may not all be essential and there might be additional conditions that are missing. But his claim is that the extension of the mind requires a "special kind of user/artifact relationship – one in which the artifact is reliably present, frequently used, personally tailored and deeply trusted" (Clark 1997: 217). Elsewhere, where he again cautions against cognitive bloat, he points out that "it is quite proper to restrict the props and aids that can count as part of my mental machinery to those that are, at the very least, reliably available when needed and used (accessed) as automatically as biological processing and memory" (Clark 2001: 156). Although we are far from a set of clear-cut universally applicable conditions, we now at least have something in addition to the parity principle, cognitive enhancement, and the notion of coupled systems, namely a set of features that, according to Clark, can be used, if somewhat imperfectly, to discriminate between proper instances of extended mind and the rest.

Although Clark makes use of the term "artifact" in this context, this does not mean that he intends that only cases involving artifacts can be candidates for vehicle externalism. He and Chalmers do not see, in principle, why there cannot be "socially extended cognition" (Clark and Chalmers 1998: 17); what is meant by this phrase is that some of my mental states could be partly constituted by the states of other thinkers:

For example, the waiter at my favourite restaurant might act as a repository of my beliefs about my favourite meals (this might even be construed as a case of extended desire). In other cases, one's beliefs might be embodied in one's secretary, one's accountant, or one's collaborator.

(Clark and Chalmers 1998:18)

3 Extending the mind into economic activity

If one's secretary, accountant, or waiter can be incorporated into their account of extended mind in this way, then it would appear that Clark and Chalmers would allow that their account can be legitimately extended into the economic and social arena. Clark certainly appears to endorse this in a number of places where he claims that "organizations, factories, offices, institutions, and such are the larger-scale scaffolds of our distinctive cognitive success" (Clark 1997: 186). But his endorsement of the incorporation of vehicle externalism into the economic and social arena could not be clearer than when he compares examples such as using a pen and paper with social and economic institutions:

> Institutions, firms and organizations seem to me to share many of the key properties of pen, paper, and arithmetical practice. . . . Pen and paper provide an external medium in which we behave in ways dictated by the general policy or practice of long multiplication. Most of us do not know the mathematical justification of the procedure. Similarly, firms and organizations provide an external resource in which individuals behave in ways dictated by norms, policies and practices that may even become internalized as mental models.
>
> (Clark 1996: 279)

In the same paper, Clark discusses the view that the traditional theory of rational choice is most powerful in cases where choice is limited and cites Satz and Ferejohn's (1994) explanation that in such cases it is the social and institutional structures in which the chooser is embedded that are doing most of the work and not the individual's cognitions (Clark 1996: 273). My intention here is solely to highlight Clark's willingness for the extended mind hypothesis to encompass social and economic institutional structures, and I will not be engaging with Clark's particular discussion of rational choice theory.

4 Economic example 1: economic transactions that don't tax the mind

If we take on board Clark's acceptance of socially extended cognition and the application of the extended mind hypothesis to economic examples, then economic behavior would appear to contain an abundance of examples of vehicle externalism. To see how this might be, let me first outline a version of the division of labor involving economic exchange. Among the reasons why individuals may be said to engage in certain economic transactions is because they either cannot, or do not want to, go to the effort of producing the required good or service themselves. Although the tasks involved in producing goods and services are often, at least in part, physical tasks, there are many cases where the tasks are (mainly) cognitive. As I will illustrate presently, cognitive enhancement is a feature of such economic transactions. The individual, not wanting to expend effort on a cognitive task (that is possible for her to complete on her own), can save on internal cognitive resources by engaging in an economic transaction. Or, where the cognitive task is impossible for the individual to complete on her own, the economic transaction makes possible the completion of what was otherwise an impossible task.

The central point of the notion of division of labor in economics is that it allows for greater output at lower inputs of labor and this, in addition to other factors, creates a situation whereby, for instance, it is more efficient for me to purchase a computer program from a commercial producer or retailer of programs rather than going to the extraordinary effort of producing it myself. Since producing a computer program is mainly a cognitive task, the savings in such circumstances (purchasing the computer program rather than writing one's own) concern mostly cognitive effort. Or it may be the case that I am not cognitively capable of writing computer programs and therefore engaging in the economic transaction in question allows me to achieve a cognitive goal that I could not achieve on my own. So, economic transactions can be seen, at least in some circumstances, as processes involving external vehicles (in this case producers or retailers of software) that can serve to reduce cognitive effort and sometimes make possible the achievement of cognitive goals that could not otherwise be attained. Such economic transactions therefore cohere with the point about cognitive enhancement.

Economic transactions of this kind are also consistent with the parity principle. In the case of the computer program, there is a functional parity between the economic transaction that provides the person with the computer program and the cognitive process used by the person who produces the program on her own using largely internal resources. In both cases the individual is confronted with the task of coming up with a computer program; in the second case we would have no hesitation in describing the task and the process of writing the computer program as cognitive. In the first case, internal resources are combined with a part of the world, in this case the individual, company, or institution selling the program, in a cognitive process, namely the economic transaction, to complete the task, which is providing the person with the computer program.

This scenario is also in keeping with Clark and Chalmers's notion of a coupled system. According to them, when an individual is linked with an external entity in a two-way interaction, this creates a coupled system "that can be seen as a cognitive system in its own right" (Clark and Chalmers 1998: 8). The external entity is the person or institution that sold the computer program and the economic transaction, a cognitive process, is the process that, in conjunction with an external vehicle or entity, achieves the completion of the cognitive task. Here we have the cognitive enhancement, the functional parity, and the coupled system required for vehicle externalism along the lines set out by Clark and Chalmers.

Although this example strictly follows the letter of Clark and Chalmers's account, it might be claimed that the purchase of the computer program example is not in keeping with the spirit of their account. For instance, it might be argued that the purchaser of the computer program buys it from the owner of the copyright, usually a company, and not the original creators. In Clark and Chalmers's examples, the individual is directly involved in the cognitive task at hand, whereas, in this case, the purchaser is too far removed from the creators. I do not believe that this objection carries weight and nowhere in their account does such an objection arise. In addition, Clark's later endorsement of institutions, firms, and organizations as external vehicles, as I outlined earlier, provides grounds for believing that examples such as the purchase of a computer program are perfectly legitimate. I do not accept that this is a valid objection, but to avoid needless complexity and argument, I will instead invoke a simpler example where Clark and Chalmers's version of vehicle externalism can be applied to an economic transaction, but where the purchaser deals directly with the supplier.

Imagine a situation where I need to complete and file my tax return with the relevant tax authorities. I can accomplish this largely cognitive task on my own, even though it would involve my reading extensive background material, organizing data, performing calculations, and so on. As I am no expert in this area, I am aware that this would take me much time and effort. Instead I can hire a qualified tax accountant to do it for me. In accordance with the division of labor, the accountant can carry out this cognitive task more efficiently, that is, with fewer mistakes and in much less time than I can, because she is trained for this function, has the knowledge required at her fingertips, and, some might argue, a greater aptitude for this sort of work than I. Through contracting an accountant to perform this cognitive task, I am reducing my cognitive effort through reducing the involvement of my internal cognitive resources. This instance clearly exhibits cognitive enhancement.

But I might also want to hire an accountant to formulate my taxes because this task is beyond my cognitive abilities – this could be due to an inability on my part to calculate properly or because I cannot understand the complex instructions involved. Through hiring the accountant I am using a process that will result in my taxes being formulated despite the impossibility of my being able to complete this cognitive task on my own. Therefore this instance also clearly exhibits cognitive enhancement.

What about the parity principle? In this case, following Clark and Chalmers's terminology, a part of the world, namely the accountant, is functioning as a vehicle in the process of calculating my taxes which, were it to go on in my head, we would have no hesitation in accepting as part of the cognitive process involved in completing the cognitive task of formulating my tax return. The accountant in this instance is the external vehicle; Clark and Chalmers allow that persons can be external vehicles, as his waiter example, cited earlier, shows. The cognitive process in question is the economic transaction. While it is not the same cognitive process that occurs when I calculate my own taxes, that is also true in cases acknowledged to be examples of vehicle externalism by Clark and Chalmers; physically manipulating a jigsaw piece with one's fingers is not identical to using one's inner cognitive resources to see how the jigsaw piece might fit. All that is claimed by the parity principle is that there is a parity of function between the two processes.

The accountant and my brain also form a coupled system that is in keeping with Clark and Chalmers's account. First, the individual here is linked with the external entity, the accountant, in a two-way interaction; this creates the coupled system "that can been seen as a cognitive system in its own right" (Clark and Chalmers 1998: 8). Coupled systems are systems where all the components play an active causal role and jointly govern behavior in the same sort of way that internal cognition does. Removal of the external component results in a drop of behavioral competence (Clark and Chalmers 1998: 8–9). Using Clark and Chalmers's terminology, we might say that the accountant plays an active causal role in the formulation of my tax return.[5] And while I could prepare and file my own tax return, the removal of the accountant would greatly reduce my behavioral competence.[6] It might be argued that this is not really a coupled system as it is the accountant who does all the work and I do nothing. It is not entirely true that I do nothing, as I am supposed to discuss my financial affairs with the accountant, provide her with the relevant information in a readable form, check the completed tax return forms, and sign them. In addition, I am involved in the cognitive process of engaging in the economic transaction with the accountant. Also, Clark and Chalmers allow that pocket calculators are external vehicles and therefore involve a coupled system between user and calculator; since pocket calculators only require me to present the calculation to the machine but not actually perform it, I cannot be said to be involved in the calculation process either.

In keeping with the anti-cognitive bloat conditions cited by Clark, the accountant is reliably available when needed. Of course I only need her whenever I need to file a tax return or if ever I were to be audited by the tax authorities. While availability of some kind is necessary for vehicle externalism, it does not have to be a rigid requirement. After all, the examples Clark and Chalmers use are themselves not always available. Pencils and paper are not ready to hand at all times, and Otto's notebook is effectively unavailable to him when he misplaces it or in the absence of a light source.

Turning to some of the other conditions Clark cites against cognitive bloat, the accountant's services are easy to access and use – all I have to do is to provide some financial information. The working of the accountant does not have to be critically scrutinized by me as she has already reached the standards required by her profession and the state. I can therefore trust the work that she does on my behalf.

Although this example is consistent with Clarks and Chalmers's account of extended mind and Clark's other writings on vehicle externalism, I have deep concerns about it. While I am broadly in sympathy with vehicle externalism, I will argue that such examples of economic transactions are not *bone fide* examples of vehicle externalism. First, there is the problem with cognitive bloat. Although Clark provides conditions that are meant to exclude instances that would lead to cognitive bloat, such examples as the economic transactions described above adhere to all of Clark's conditions, including the parity principle, and nevertheless lead to cognitive bloat. If using an accountant to file my taxes is an example of vehicle externalism, then so too is any other economic transaction that involves reducing my cognitive effort or enhancing the efficiency of the outcomes of my cognitive tasks. For instance, all my economic and related interactions with the education sector, the legal profession, the software sector, and those sectors involving intellectual property will make those producers or processes part of my extended mind at any one time. My concern is that such examples are instances of cognitive bloat and we are owed an explanation as to why such economic transactions ought or ought not to be included as instances of vehicle externalism.

Second, if I get an accountant to formulate my taxes instead of doing so myself, although I have managed to avoid the cognitive effort of having to formulate them myself, to what extent can I be said to be cognitively involved at all in the operation? After all, why must it be the case that I am cognitively involved if a part of the world is performing the task for me? Surely that is precisely the point of the economic transaction with my accountant – I don't have to be *cognitively* involved in formulating taxes at all. Similarly, when I purchase a computer program I am doing so because I want to accomplish what it will do without having to write it myself or even because writing computer programs is beyond me. Again, this is an instance where, according to the parity principle, a part of the world functions as a process (writing software or calculating tax returns) which, were it done in the head, we would have no hesitation in recognizing as part of a cognitive process – but why must we go on to claim that such activity is part of the cognitive activity of the purchaser when the scenario is specifically set up by the purchaser so that she does not engage in the relevant cognitive activity at all?

5 Economic example 2: minding money

This second economic example echoes some of the themes contained in Clark (1997), specifically the evolution of coupled systems and the emergence of phenomena that enhance our cognitive abilities. In this example I make use of the standard account of the emergence of money as described by Menger. I then go on to show how money emerges as a response to the cognitive overload of multiple exchange rates between types of goods under conditions of pure barter. As I will demonstrate later, this example coheres not only with the parity principle and the other conditions that Clark puts forward; it is also in keeping with some of the themes in other parts of Clark's work, including the emergence of scaffolding in cognitive systems that mirrors scaffolding in biological systems.[7] According to this account, scaffolding is a common biological feature whereby an organism exploits some feature of its environment so as to increase intake of food or energy but at a reduced expenditure of energy. For instance, the simple sponge orientates itself so as to exploit the existing currents in the sea and therefore reduces the amount of pumping it must do itself so as to feed by filtering food from the water.

Scaffolding in cognitive cases includes all sorts of aid and support from the external world, whether this be from other persons or the structure of the environment itself. For example, the grouping of ingredients in a kitchen takes the form of an external memory aid which the individual can exploit so as to save on cognitive effort. Clark also discusses the occurrence of stigmergic algorithms or procedures in relation to cognitive processes; these are manmade external structures that control or coordinate individual action within certain situations. (He uses the example of a crew navigating a ship without a global plan or script; instead they use stigmergic algorithms of the sort "when condition Y occurs, then do X.") Clark also refers to "stigmergic self-modulation" as "the process by which intelligent brains *actively* structure their own external (physical and social) worlds so as to make for successful actions with less individual computation" (Clark 1997: 191). The emergence of a monetary system and its subsequent improvement strongly reflect these features of Clark's account of scaffolding, as will become clear presently.

The account I present here of money emerging along Mengerian lines begins with conditions of pure barter.[8] By pure barter I mean a situation where money has never been known to exist before, there is no exchange good (a good that is used as a medium of exchange), and no common standard of value.[9] In such circumstances of pure barter, individuals have to value or price each good in terms of all others if they are to participate effectively. No serious cognitive problems arise when there are only a small number of goods available for exchange; for instance, if there are only three goods there will be only three exchange rates, four goods will require six exchange rates, six goods will require fifteen, and ten goods will require forty-five. While forty-five exchange rates might be within the ability of a few (that is, assuming not much fluctuation in the exchange rates), the situation becomes cognitively impossible well before the number of types of goods reaches 100, leading to 4,950 exchange rates – with 1,000 types of goods the number of exchange rates reaches 499,500.[10] Pure barter becomes untenable for most people when the number of types of goods increases beyond a very small number, such as ten. Invariably, some form of common standard would have to be arrived at so as to get around this problem

In addition to this problem of cognitive overload, the absence of money or any medium of exchange implies higher risk, cost, and effort involved in engaging in economic transactions, such as that involved in finding suitable exchange partners. One can imagine traders wandering from town to town in search of other traders who had what they wanted and who in turn wanted what they had to offer. The emergence of regular markets held in specific locations might reduce the effort involved, but without money or an already agreed medium of exchange, going to market would only solve the location problem; it would still not solve the issue of finding someone who wants to sell what you want and wants what you have to sell. The emergence of a stable exchange good (a kind of proto-money or commodity money) would allow possessors of that good to successfully engage in exchange without additional risk or costs.

But of all the goods available on the market, how do we collectively arrive at a stable exchange good? Menger provides us with the mechanism by which, as he claims, certain commodities emerged as commodity money. Stated briefly, Menger's claim is that the commodity that is more saleable than others is likely to become the standard medium of exchange (Menger 1892: 239–55). *Saleableness* is described by Menger as follows:

> A high rate of saleableness in a commodity consists in the fact that it may at every moment be easily and surely disposed of at a price corresponding to, or at least not discrepant from, the general economic situation – at the economic, or approximately economic, price.
>
> (Menger 1892: 245)

High saleableness in a product does not mean that it will have a high exchange value. Products with high saleableness are those that are easily adaptable or divisible for individual customers, easy to transport, durable, and, most important, for which there is a constant demand and supply. To illustrate with a contemporary example, surgical instruments may be very expensive to acquire but are not very saleable in the sense that they are not easy to sell on quickly at their full economic price. On the other hand, cigarettes are highly saleable even though they are relatively cheap.

Menger goes on to explain that, under pure barter conditions, those economic agents who are in possession of highly saleable goods are in a more favorable position when seeking to engage in bartering for other goods. Under conditions of pure barter, if one goes to market with the intention of selling goods of low saleableness and acquiring other goods of low saleableness, immediately seeking out someone who wants approximately what one has and who has approximately what one wants is *not* the best strategy – any attempt to achieve this double coincidence of wants on the part of both parties will involve a high risk of failure. In addition, this assumes that both parties are able to arrive at a mutually agreeable rate of exchange or price. Instead, each party would be better to first exchange their initial endowment of less saleable goods for some highly saleable goods, and then exchange the highly saleable goods for what each actually wants. The point is that it is a lot easier to find an exchange partner if either one is looking for or offering a good which is highly saleable. This is also true for situations where, because of war or some social upheaval, the local currency has collapsed; if one were to try to exchange surgical instruments for petrol in such a scenario, one would be best advised to exchange the surgical instruments for a highly saleable commodity, such as cigarettes, and then use the latter to bargain for the petrol rather than trying to find someone who both requires surgical instruments and wants to sell petrol.

This policy of always exchanging one's less saleable goods for goods that are more saleable is self-reinforcing; as more and more individuals see the benefits and adopt this strategy, one or more highly saleable goods will become even more saleable as they are now demanded as exchange goods, eventually leading to a situation where such goods become more sought after as a medium of exchange than as a good *per se*. In other words, they become more sought after for their exchange-value than their use-value. Precious metals have historically taken on the role of money because they are highly saleable and because they are naturally scarce in relation to the demand for them. Other factors tend to reinforce their acceptance, including that they are not seasonal goods and hence are less likely to fluctuate in value with the seasons, they do not deteriorate, and they are easily portable and divisible. This account of saleableness does not deny that state recognition and regulation have played a role in perfecting and adjusting the social institution of money to the varying needs of commerce; but it is to claim, as Menger does, that "money has not been generated by law" (Menger 1892: 255).

The emergence of money therefore creates a solution to a number of problems: it removes the risks associated with pure barter transactions, it reduces the effort and costs involved in finding an exchange partner, and it reduces the cognitive overload involved in having to remember and compute numerous exchange rates. It might be argued that this is not a representative example of cognition as there are so many other issues involved, such as reduction of risk and effort. But many tasks, such as building a house, are not purely cognitive and yet we would not deny that external vehicles can be used to help complete cognitive tasks associated with building houses. In addition, certain tasks can be completed through either largely cognitive means or physical means. For instance, a jigsaw puzzle can be solved by looking for patterns between pieces and manipulating the pieces to observe the possibilities of fit. Alternatively, the jigsaw could also be solved by largely physical means, namely taking the first piece to hand, attempting to fit it into every other piece, and then performing the same task iteratively with each successive piece.

I now want to show explicitly how this example of money is consistent with Clark and Chalmers's account of vehicle externalism. Cognitive enhancement is clearly present in this example; the emergence of money allows individuals to overcome the cognitive problems associated with the comparison of prices under conditions of pure barter. As we saw, under such conditions the number of exchange rates between goods rises exponentially as more goods become available. Sometimes the emergence of money allows for the completion of the cognitive task of comparing prices so as to arrive at the best value for what one has to offer using fewer internal cognitive resources. But when the number of goods increases, the presence of money allows for the completion of what would have been an impossible cognitive task.

What about the parity principle? Taking the extended mind approach of Clark and Chalmers, money functions as a part of the world in a cognitive process, the process of equating cognitively the market value of each good in terms of all others – in simple terms, comparing prices. Money is therefore the external vehicle.[11] When money emerges, this does not mean that I no longer have to be cognitively involved in the process, as was the case within the tax calculation example; it is still the case that I have to do the simple calculation that if a kilo of wheat is worth $X and a knife is worth $2X, then one knife is priced as equal to two kilos of wheat. If we take it that money is a part of the world that functions in the process of equating market prices and if this process were done in our heads, as it is under pure barter conditions, we would have no hesitation in recognizing it as part of a cognitive process. There is clearly parity of function between the two cases and this example is consistent with Clark and Chalmers's parity principle.

Money, the external vehicle in this example, takes a number of forms, including pieces of paper, coin, checks, and electronic versions. Although money sometimes appears not to require a physical form as such, it does need to have a manifestation that is physical, whether marks on a page or a computer record; otherwise it could not be transferred, counted, or stored. That money does not have to take a physical form, viz. pieces of precious metal, commodities, coins or notes, need not concern us here. Clark is comfortable with instances of external vehicles that do not take physical forms in this sense, as evidenced when he cites institutions, firms, and organizations as external vehicles, as pointed out earlier.

Money (in the form of the prevailing monetary setup or system) and my brain also form a coupled system in the way that Clark and Chalmers describe. The individual is linked with the external vehicle, money, in a two-way interaction in an attempt to arrive at the completion of the cognitive task of obtaining the best value for what she has to offer. In this cognitive task, the individual is constantly comparing goods and services she wishes to sell to monetary amounts, and monetary amounts to goods and services she wishes to purchase, a two-way interaction between the monetary scenario or system and the individual. In accordance with Clark and Chalmers's account, money and brain form a coupled system where all the components play a role and jointly govern behavior in the same sort of way that internal cognition does.

This example is also in keeping with the other conditions that Clark cites in order to avoid cognitive bloat. Money in the form of the prevailing monetary setup is available, easy to use and access, and automatically endorsed and trusted. In fact, history demonstrates that whenever money is no longer available or trusted it ceases to be money. But even though the example of money coheres with Clark's account of vehicle externalism, I am claiming that there are good reasons why we ought not to consider it an example of vehicle externalism. As with the previous economic example, allowing that money is an external vehicle leads to cognitive bloat. Since arriving at the value of money encompasses the sum of all transactions in the market economy, it would appear that our minds must be extended to include the entire market economy. Against this claim, it might be argued that it is not the entire activity of the market that is in question here, but the results of all of that activity. This may be true, but what we are concerned with is the ability of money to measure the values of all of goods and services using one objective measure, and it becomes difficult to even talk about this aspect of money if it is to be shorn of all the transactions that give rise to its fundamental function as a medium of exchange. Because the emergence of money is consistent with Clark and Chalmers's account of vehicle externalism, that account cannot avoid the charge of cognitive bloat.

6 The integration principle: deflating cognitive bloat

In this section I want to deal with two connected problems. First, how do we arrive at a form of vehicle externalism that will avoid cognitive bloat? The simple answer to this question is to drop the parity principle. But this leads to the second issue: if we are to drop the parity principle as a way of deciding what counts as an external vehicle, then how are we to discern external vehicles? I will be suggesting that cognitive integration, as described by Menary (2006a, 2006b), can provide us with the means of overcoming these issues. I will be suggesting that Menary's account of cognitive integration can be extended to provide us with a new principle for discerning external vehicles, which I will call the *integration principle*.

Before discussing this suggested principle, I want to explain the motivations for, and some of the key features of, cognitive integration. As Menary (2006b) demonstrates, the trouble with Clark and Chalmers's version of vehicle externalism, the extended mind hypothesis, is that although it involves the claim that cognition is extended into the world, this is achieved only by comparison with what is already going on in the head. Despite being described by its authors as externalism, the extended mind hypothesis actually gives primacy to the internalist's conception of cognition by making it the starting point of the account of extended mind, and thus incorporates into their own account the very assumptions that Clark and Chalmers originally intended to displace.

How we solve this and other issues related to vehicle externalism, according to Menary, is to reject the parity principle and the extended mind hypothesis in favor of cognitive integration. Cognitive integration is the claim that internal vehicles and processes are integrated with external vehicles and processes in the completion of cognitive tasks, and therefore avoids incorporating internalist conceptions in the way that the extended mind hypothesis does. Menary goes on to set out cognitive integration's commitment to a number of theses. Cognitive agents frequently complete cognitive tasks through the manipulation of vehicles in the environment (the manipulation thesis). Cognition frequently involves the integration of internal vehicles and processes and external vehicles and processes (the hybrid mind thesis). The ability of cognitive agents to complete cognitive tasks can be transformed by learning the practice of manipulating external vehicles (the transformation thesis).

The motivation for cognitive integration arises, in part, out of opposition from some internalists to the extended mind hypothesis. Internalists such as Adams and Aizawa (2001, 2006) and Rupert (2004) have accused extended mind theorists of what they term the "coupling-constitution fallacy," namely that in claiming that an object or process is coupled in some way to some agent, extended mind theorists then infer that the object or process forms a part of cognition. But this assumes a picture of a completely formed agent prior to encountering any external cognitive vehicle, according to Menary. For instance, in the case of Otto, the Alzheimer's patient, and his notebook, "the notebook is coupled to a discrete cognitive agent whereby the notebook becomes part of the memory system of the agent because it is coupled to the agent" (Menary 2006b: 333). According to Menary, we need to get away from this picture because it assumes "a discrete, already formed cognitive agent." Instead, the picture should be one where such cognitive process are hybrid processes and are jointly made up of internal and external processes:

> My *manipulation* of the notebook and my brain processes together constitute a process of remembering. In cases like these, the process of remembering cannot be described exclusively in terms of biological memory or solely in terms of the manipulation of external representations, because it is a hybrid process.
>
> (Menary 2006b: 333)

According to this account, the extended mind hypothesis leads us to make the mistake of thinking that vehicle externalism amounts to merely externalizing what is already inside the head. In other words, the notebook is coupled to the person and becomes part of that person's memory system. But this is to accept internalism as the starting point, to "accept the picture of a cognitive agent as implementing a discrete cognitive system, before they ever encounter an external vehicle" (Menary 2006b: 333). Instead, according to cognitive integrationists, remembering in these instances is the integration of the manipulation of the notebook and brains that together constitute the cognitive process of remembering.

While space does not allow me to enter into an in-depth discussion of cognitive integration, the outline I have provided will help us to understand why the economic examples discussed earlier ought not to be included as instances of external cognitive vehicles. Taking the example of money first, we need to ask ourselves whether money qualifies as an external vehicle in accordance with the cognitive integration account. The question is, is money manipulated as part of an external process and, if so, is that process integrated with internal processes in the completion of a cognitive task? Although money is manipulated (both figuratively through issuing and signing checks, bank transfers, and other financial instruments, as well as physically through handling or counting currency), it is not manipulated as part of an external process that, together with internal resources, forms an integrated cognitive process, and therefore does not qualify as a external vehicle.[12]

So how can we discriminate between proper instances of vehicle externalism and the rest? I argue that this is achieved by examining whether the alleged external vehicle is involved in an external process that is integrated with an internal process or processes in question. This provides us with what I will call the *integration principle*, as follows:

> For something to qualify as an external vehicle, it must be manipulated as part of an external process and that process must be integrated with internal process(es) in the completion of some cognitive task.

We can see that this principle is stricter than the parity principle because it requires the integration of both external and internal processes. The integration principle does not lead to cognitive bloat because it insists on the integration of external processes with internal processes; therefore, the cognitive agent must be always involved in the cognitive process, a condition that the parity principle does not actually stipulate. It is this laxity on the part of the parity principle that gives rise to cognitive bloat.

As has been made clear, money does not qualify as an external vehicle because it is not manipulated as part of an external process that is in turn integrated with internal processes, as set out in the integration principle. This principle also rules out examples involving economic transactions. Taking the instance of the accountant cited earlier, although hiring my accountant allows me not to have to calculate my taxes, the accountant is not manipulated as part of an external cognitive process that is in turn integrated with my internal processes. There are processes going on but these are social (legal and economic) rather than cognitive; I may be bound contractually to my accountant through mutually binding promises, understandings, and commitments, but these are not processes that can be cognitively integrated with my internal processes. To describe economic transactions as cognitive processes would be to confuse the social and legal with the cognitive. When I purchase a computer program, I cannot sensibly or properly be said to be manipulating the seller or producer of the computer program as part of a process that is then integrated with some internal process in the completion of a cognitive task. The integration principle therefore allows us to distinguish between situations where I might use some social or other process to offload cognitive effort or achieve a cognitive goal that are not instances of vehicle externalism from those that truly are. The problem with the parity principle is that it allows something that occurs externally to count as a cognitive process if we would also agree that were it to occur in the head it would be part of a cognitive process. The economic examples demonstrate that the parity principle is too lax in this regard.

But might the integration principle also be too strict? The integration principle covers the examples cited by Clark and Chalmers, such as counting on fingers, calculating with the aid of a slide rule, calculating using a pen and paper, using pocket calculators, manipulating jigsaw pieces, and notebooks used by those with Alzheimer's. (However, it excludes Clark and Chalmers's examples of socially extended cognition, such as the waiter or secretary.) Of course, one must readjust the picture to cohere with the cognitive integration; to use the Otto example, it is his manipulation of the notebook integrated together with his internal processes that constitute, for him, the cognitive process of remembering.

7 Conclusion

In this chapter I have set out Clark and Chalmers's case for their version of vehicle externalism, the extended mind hypothesis. I put forward two types of economic examples that are in keeping with Clark and Chalmers's account of vehicle externalism and are supported by Clark's more recent writings. More specifically, they are consistent with the point about cognitive enhancement, their account of coupled systems, and their parity principle. Even though these economic examples are also in keeping with Clark's additional conditions that are supposed to ward off the possibility of cognitive bloat, I show that they in fact demonstrate how Clark and Chalmers's account inevitably leads to cognitive bloat.

In setting out the first type of example, I demonstrated how certain economic transactions exhibit all the key features of the extended mind; they cohere with the point about cognitive enhancement in that either they allow for the achievement of cognitive goals that otherwise could not be attained or they serve to reduce effort in the form of internal cognitive resources. Using the examples of purchasing a computer program and contracting an accountant to prepare my tax return, I also showed that both instances are coherent with Clark and Chalmers's account of coupled systems and the parity principle.

In addition to the key features of the extended mind hypothesis that economic transactions exhibit, my second economic example, the emergence of money along Mengerian lines, also has the virtue of reflecting some of the themes in Clark's subsequent work on the emergence of scaffolding in cognitive systems. I demonstrated how the emergence of money serves to facilitate the completion of the cognitive task of arriving at the best value for what one has to offer in economic exchange. This example clearly exhibits cognitive enhancement and is consistent with Clark and Chalmers's account of coupled systems and the parity principle. But this example clearly is an instance of cognitive bloat. Because of the coherence of both types of economic examples with Clark and Chalmers's account, by implication that account cannot avoid cognitive bloat.

A significant problem associated with the extended mind hypothesis, as identified by Menary, is that it gives primacy to the internalist's conception of cognition by making it the starting point of that account. Therefore, developing a new account of vehicle externalism that does not fall prey to this problem amounts to an entire change of approach and not merely tinkering with the account by substituting for the parity principle. I advocated the adoption of Menary's account of vehicle externalism, cognitive integration, whereby external vehicles and processes are integrated with internal processes in the completion of cognitive tasks; this account avoids the problem of giving primacy to the internalist conception of cognition associated with the extended mind thesis.

I also advocated extending Menary's account of cognitive integration to include what I call the integration principle. This principle contains the condition that for something to qualify as an external vehicle it must be manipulated as part of an external process, and that process must be integrated with internal processes in the completion of a cognitive task. By insisting on the integration of external and internal processes, this principle is stricter than the parity principle and excludes instances of cognitive bloat that the Clark and Chalmers's account admitted, as is evidenced by the economic examples provided earlier.

But the integration principle is not so strict as to disallow many of the examples cited by Clark and Chalmers. Cognitive integration and the integration principle therefore allow us to eradicate the parity principle without having to relinquish vehicle externalism, at least in the form of cognitive integration. They allow us to avoid cognitive bloat by excluding those instances that were admitted by the parity principle and to prevent the misapplication of vehicle externalism to scenarios where it does not belong.

Notes

1 As will become clear later in the chapter, cognitive enhancement is not a sufficient condition for vehicle externalism.

2 It is possible to accept the parity principle and yet reject vehicle externalism. For instance, Adams and Aizawa bypass the parity principle, allowing that although it is acceptable, it is a matter of contingent fact that "the cognitive processes we find in the real world all happen to be brain bound" (Adams and Aizawa 2001: 46).

3　Clark and Chalmers use the term "coupled system" to refer to cases of active externalism where "the human organism is linked with an external entity in a two-way interaction, creating a coupled system that can be seen as a cognitive system in its own right" (Clark and Chalmers 1998: 8).

4　The following counterexamples and the counterarguments to them are from Clark and Chalmers (1998: 10–18).

5　It is not exactly clear what role the word "causal" plays in Clark and Chalmers's account of coupled systems. If they admit language and social, economic, or institutional structures (or aspects thereof) as vehicles, then their use of causal must be broad enough to include social or psychological causation. It could be argued that in fact some external vehicles play a more normative rather than causal role in cognition – but this is the subject of a separate paper.

6　Risk does not appear in discussions of vehicle externalism. While I might be able to perform some cognitive task, there is a risk of my getting it wrong. My memory does not have to be very bad for me to want make a note of something, especially if the costs to me of forgetting are high. I may want to use an accountant to prepare my taxes because my highest preference is to avoid the risk of making an error.

7　The following biological and cognitive examples of scaffolding are Clark's (1997: 45–46).

8　The account that follows is drawn from Menger (1892).

9　Whether there ever was pure barter of this sort has been contested by a number of contemporary writers (Goodhart 1998; Ingham 2004; Wray 1998, 2004). If the reader shares their qualms, then this example can be taken as a thought experiment.

10　This point and the associated calculations are to be found in Davies (1995: 15). The number of exchange rates is arrived at using the following mathematical formula for deriving mathematical combinations: $^{n}C_{r} = n!/[(n - r)!r!]$. Jevons makes a similar point in his argument for the requirement for money, although in a less well-worked-out fashion (Jevons 1875: 5).

11　Money, qua external vehicle, refers to any form of monetary setup or system, whether that be a form of commodity money or a contemporary advanced currency system.

12　One of the curious aspects of this example is that money does not actually have to currently exist for people to be able to use monetary values. As long as there already has been some form of monetary system in place, this can be used as a "ghost" currency in impure barter, in effect an accounting unit or common standard that can be used to equate the market values of all goods without having to revert to the multitude of exchange rates between types of goods that occurs under pure barter conditions.

References

Adams, F. and Aizawa, K. (2001) "The Bounds of Cognition," *Philosophical Psychology*, 14: 43–64.

—— (2006) "Defending the Bounds of Cognition," in R. Menary (ed.) *The Extended Mind*, Aldershot: Ashgate.

Burge, T. (1979) "Individualism and the Mental," *Midwest Studies in Philosophy*, 4: 73–121.

Clark, A. (1996) "Economic Reason: The Interplay of Individual Learning and External Structure," in J. Drobak and J. Nye (eds.) *The Frontiers Of The New Institutional Economics*, San Diego: Academic Press, 269–90.

—— (1997) *Being There: Putting Brain, Body and World Together Again*, Cambridge, MA: The MIT Press.

—— (2001) *Mindware: An Introduction to the Philosophy of Cognitive Science*, New York: Oxford University Press.

—— (2005) "Intrinsic Content, Active Memory and the Extended Mind," *Analysis*, 65: 1–11.

Clark, A. and Chalmers, D. (1998) "The Extended Mind," *Analysis*, 58: 7–19.

Davies, G. (1995) *A History of Money: From Ancient Times to the Present Day*, Cardiff: University of Wales Press.

Goodhart, C. (1998) "The Two Concepts of Money: Implications for the Analysis of Optimal Currency Areas," *European Journal of Political Economy*, 14: 407–32.

Ingham, G. (2004) *The Nature of Money*, Cambridge: Polity Press.

Jevons, W.S. (1875) *Money and the Mechanism of Exchange*, London: H.S. King and Co.

Kirsh, D. and Maglio, P. (1994) "On Distinguishing Epistemic from Pragmatic Action," *Cognitive Science*, 18: 513–49.

Menary, R. (2006a) *Cognitive Integration: Attacking the Bounds of Cognition*, Basingstoke and London: Palgrave Macmillan.

—— (2006b) "Attacking the Bounds of Cognition," *Philosophical Psychology*, 19: 329-44.

Menger, C. (1892) "On the Origin of Money," *Economic Journal*, 2: 239–55.

Putnam, H. (1975) "The Meaning of 'Meaning,'" in *Mind, Language and Reality: Philosophical Papers, Vol. 2*, Cambridge: Cambridge University Press, 215–71.

Rupert, R. (2004) "Challenges to the Hypothesis of Extended Cognition," *Journal of Philosophy*, 101: 389–428.

Satz, D. and Ferejohn, J. (1994) "Rational Choice and Social Theory," *Journal of Philosophy*, 91: 71–87.

Wray, L.R. (1998) *Understanding Modern Money*, Cheltenham: Edward Elgar.

—— (ed.) (2004) *Credit and State Theories of Money*, Cheltenham: Edward Elgar.

Part 2

Agency, preferences, and reasons

7 There are preferences and then there are preferences

Chrisoula Andreou[1]

1 Introduction

At the heart of this chapter is a distinction between two closely related conceptions of "preference." As will become apparent, the distinction is of great significance relative to a set of interrelated debates in rational choice theory. Here is how the chapter proceeds. I begin by focusing on the following two claims, which are at the core of the standard model of rational agency:

- *The transitive-preferences claim*: A rational agent's preferences are transitive.
- *The preferred-option claim*: In simple cases in which no risk or uncertainty is involved and in which there are only two options, one of which is (all things considered) more preferred, being rational involves choosing the more preferred option over the less preferred option.

Although these claims figure as basic postulates in a great deal of theorizing concerning rational agency, they have not gone unchallenged. Counterexamples (or at least what appear to be counterexamples) to the first claim have been offered; and, as I will explain, counterexamples to the first claim raise a serious difficulty for the second claim as well. I argue, however, that what appear to be irresistible counterexamples to the first claim, and so problem cases for the second, are not genuine counterexamples. This undertaking involves showing that the conception of preference that is in play in the apparent counterexamples differs subtly but importantly from the conception of preference that is in play in both the transitive-preferences claim and the preferred-option claim (assuming the claims are charitably interpreted). The difference between the two conceptions is subtle in that *both* conceptions fit the following description: an agent's preferences can be conceived of as a system of rankings that can be traced to the agent but that need not invariably be revealed in choice and need not (even if the agent is an individual rather than a collective) invariably reflect the vivacity of the agent's felt desires. After distinguishing the two relevant conceptions of preference, I conclude by using the distinction to show that although Condorcet's paradox and Arrow's related Impossibility Theorem seem to imply that there is a rational defect inherent in democratic collectives, appearances are, once again, deceiving.

2 The transitive-preferences claim and the money-pump argument

One's preferences are transitive if they satisfy the following condition: for all x, y, and z, if one prefers x to y, and y to z, then one also prefers x to z.[2] It is tempting to think that a clear-headed individual must have transitive preferences. For example, can we really imagine a clear-headed individual who, given her current situation, prefers owning an apple to owning a banana, and owning a banana to owning an orange, and yet also prefers owning an orange to owning an apple? And even if we can imagine such an individual, is it not clear that such preferences conflict with rational agency? For, as is suggested by the famous money-pump argument, given the right circumstances, nontransitive preferences can lead an agent to voluntarily accept a series of trade offers that leaves her worse off, relative to her preferences, than when she started.

To see this, suppose Ann is an agent with the nontransitive fruit preferences just described. Suppose further that Ann has an orange and a dollar of spending money (in pennies). Finally, suppose that there is some small amount of money, say a penny, such that she prefers (1) owning a banana and one less penny of spending money over owning an orange, (2) owning an apple and one less penny of spending money over owning a banana, and (3) owning an orange and one less penny of spending money over owning an apple. Given an unanticipated opportunity to trade her orange and a penny for a banana, Ann will be led by her preferences to trade. Once she has the banana, she will, given an unanticipated opportunity to trade her banana and a penny for an apple, be led by her preferences to make a second trade. If she then encounters an unanticipated opportunity to trade her apple and a penny for an orange, her preferences will prompt her to trade yet again. But this leaves her with an orange, which is the fruit she had to begin with, and only 97 pennies. And if unexpected trading opportunities keep popping up, things will only get worse. Though she values her spending money, preferring more to less, her preferences seem to ensure that she can serve as a money pump. (Note that if the trades are with a series of acquaintances looking for a better snack, rather than, say, with a coalition of entrepreneurs out to exploit poor Ann, the term *money sieve* rather than *money pump* might be more appropriate.)[3]

3 The money-pump argument, the puzzle of the self-torturer, and the preferred-option claim

But the money-pump argument need not be seen as supporting the transitive-preferences claim. For, it is arguable that what the money-pump argument suggests is that *either* a rational agent's preferences are transitive *or* a rational agent does not always allow herself to be led by her preferences. As such, someone who thinks there is good reason to reject the transitive-preferences claim can see the money-pump argument as supporting the second disjunct. The money-pump argument can thus be seen as undermining the preferred-option claim, rather than as supporting the transitive-preferences claim. So the question is: is there good reason to reject the transitive-preferences claim? Given the money-pump argument, a solid counterexample to the transitive-preferences claim means trouble for the preferred-option claim as well.

Toward seeing that there might be a problem with the transitive-preferences claim, consider Warren Quinn's famous puzzle of the self-torturer.[4] Quinn's puzzle features an agent with nontransitive preferences, and, as Quinn suggests, given the situation it seems dogmatic to dismiss the agent's preferences as irrational. Here is the situation: Someone, call him the self-torturer, has a special electric device attached to him. The device has 1,001 settings: 0, 1, 2, 3 . . . 1,000. Increasing the device's setting increases the amount of electric current applied to the self-torturer's body. Although the increments in current are so tiny that the self-torturer cannot tell the difference between adjacent settings, the self-torturer can tell the difference between settings that are far apart from one another. In particular, there are settings that would take the self-torturer to a state of excruciating pain. The self-torturer is faced with the following choice situation. Once a week he has the opportunity to compare all the different settings and then, if he so chooses, to move up one setting. Moving up a setting gets him $10,000; but once he moves up a setting he can never permanently return to a lower setting. The self-torturer is concerned with increasing his fortune, but he also cares about feeling good. Given his concerns, he finds himself with the following preferences: For any two settings s and $s + 1$, the self-torturer prefers (all things considered) stopping at $s + 1$ to stopping at s. This is perfectly understandable, since the self-torturer cannot feel any difference in comfort between adjacent settings but gets $10,000 at each advance. But, understandably, the self-torturer also prefers stopping at a low setting (such as 0) over stopping at a high, excruciatingly painful setting (such as 1,000).

Were the self-torturer's pair-wise preferences between consecutive settings transitive, he would prefer stopping at setting 1,000 to stopping at setting 0. For, he prefers stopping at setting 1 to stopping at setting 0 and also prefers stopping at setting 2 to stopping at setting 1, so he would, if his preferences were transitive, prefer stopping at setting 2 to stopping at setting 0. But he also prefers stopping at setting 3 to stopping at setting 2, so he would, if his preferences were transitive, prefer stopping at setting 3 to stopping at setting 0. Continuing with this line of reasoning leads to the conclusion that if the self-torturer's preferences were transitive he would prefer stopping at setting 1,000 to stopping at setting 0. But the self-torturer does not prefer stopping at setting 1,000 to stopping at setting 0, so his preferences are not transitive.

Because it seems dogmatic to dismiss the self-torturer's preferences as irrational, Quinn questions the preferred-option claim instead.[5]

The self-torturer's case is in some ways very odd. Yet, as Quinn points out,

> the self-torturer is not alone in his predicament. Most of us are like him in one way or another. We like to eat but also care about our appearance. Just one more bite will give us pleasure and won't make us look fatter; but very many bites will.
>
> (Quinn 1993: 199)

Similarly, many of us want our philosophical work to be well researched, but also want to publish our philosophical contributions promptly. Reading just one more hot-off-the-press book before finalizing one's work for publication will improve one's grasp of the literature and won't interfere with one's goal of promptly publishing one's contributions; but reading very many hot-off-the-press books before finalizing one's work will. So, although Quinn's use of science fiction makes for a starker example, science fiction is not necessary to defend the idea that changes can add up in a way that makes nontransitive preferences perfectly rational.

Moreover, once this is recognized, even a simple case like the following might suggest itself as a solid counterexample to the transitive-preferences claim: suppose someone, call her Megan, is qualified for each of three jobs. Job A is not very stimulating at all, but will support a high standard of living. Job B is fairly stimulating and will support an average standard of living. Job C is highly stimulating, but will support only a low standard of living. Suppose further that though Megan prefers having a high standard of living to having an average standard of living she, overall, prefers job B to job A, because the difference between a high standard of living and an average standard of living is not big enough to make passing up a stimulating job attractive to Megan. Similarly, though Megan prefers having an average standard of living to having a low standard of living she, overall, prefers job C to job B, because the difference between an average standard of living and a low standard of living is not big enough to make passing up a highly stimulating job attractive to Megan. And yet, Megan prefers job A to job C because the difference between a high standard of living and a low standard of living *is* big enough to make passing up even a highly stimulating job attractive to Megan. Should Megan's preferences be dismissed as irrational? A prior commitment to the transitive-preferences claim or the preferred-option claim would prompt one to answer yes.[6] But if these claims are not taken for granted, Megan's case can be plausibly described as one of those cases in which changes add up in a way that makes nontransitive preferences perfectly rational.

There are, in addition to Quinn's case of the self-torturer, several other cases that have been offered as counterexamples to the transitive-preferences claim.[7] I have focused on Quinn's case because it is, I think, the most forceful. Still, Quinn's case is not a genuine counterexample. For, as with the other cases that have been offered, Quinn's case relates to a conception of preference that, as I will argue, differs subtly but importantly from the conception of preference that is in play in both the transitive-preferences claim and the preferred-option claim.

4 Preferences

In light of Quinn's case, should we conclude that a rational agent's preferences can be nontransitive and therefore a rational agent will not necessarily choose in accordance with her preferences? The answer to this question depends on what conception of preference is assumed. Given the conception of preference that is in play in Quinn's case, and in other purported problem cases for the transitive-preferences claim and the preferred-option claim, the answer is yes. In this familiar sense of preference, an agent can just find herself with certain preferences. But there is another conception of preference that, as I will argue, can accommodate both the transitive-preferences claim and the preferred-option claim while taking care of the purported problem cases. According to this second conception of preference, an agent's preferences can be conceived of as a system of rankings that the agent *commits to* in light of her preferences in the first sense and her choice situation.[8]

I will refer to an agent's preferences in the first sense as her *given preferences* and to an agent's preferences in the second sense as her *chosen preferences*. What these two senses of preference have in common is that, in both senses, an agent's preferences can be conceived of as a system of rankings that can be traced to the agent. Relatedly, in both senses, to prefer x to y is to rank x over y. While in some cases the system of rankings that an agent commits to will be identical to the system of rankings that captures her given preferences, in other cases the systems will, for good reason, differ.[9]

Before showing how the distinction between given preferences and chosen preferences can be used in defense of the transitive-preferences claim and the preferred-option claim, I will say a little bit more about both sorts of preferences. Note first that given preferences and chosen preferences need not be tied to a single mind or be revealed in choice. A collective might, for example, employ a democratic method, such as majority rule, in order to determine its given preferences. In such a case, the collective's given preferences are not tied to a single mind but rather to a set of minds united by a preference-determination procedure. Furthermore, the collective's given preferences over a particular pair of options need not be revealed in choice since the collective might never implement any plan for realizing its preferred option. This may be due to poor organization or to negligence on the part of certain members of the collective, but there can be other reasons as well. If, for example, the collective finds itself with nontransitive given preferences – which can happen even if the given preferences of its members are transitive[10] – it might favor committing to a system of rankings that differs from its given preferences. As with its given preferences, a collective's chosen preferences need not be tied to a single mind. Furthermore, its chosen preferences over a particular pair of options need not be revealed in choice since the collective might never implement any plan for realizing its preferred option. (What is revealed in choice may be yet a third system of rankings.)

Note also that, as is perhaps particularly clear when the agent is a collective, it must not be assumed that given preferences over a specific set of options relevant to a specific choice situation exist prior to the agent's considering the options. It would be odd, for example, to suppose that prior to embarking on its search for a new faculty member, an academic department already had given preferences over the candidates that are now under consideration and that the department's preference-determination procedure, which might be applied after extensive discussion, is simply revealing the preferences that were there all along. In the case of individuals, the suggestion that preferences are not simply there to be discovered is supported by experimental results that indicate that the preferences individuals find themselves with are at least sometimes determined in part by how the individuals framed the available options during the framing phase preceding evaluation.[11]

Note finally that, given time and mental energy constraints, it is to be expected that, for both given preferences and chosen preferences, an agent's preferences will often be arrived at as needed for choice. Take, for example, the self-torturer. After he considers his predicament and finds himself preferring, for each setting, stopping at that setting to stopping at the previous setting, while also preferring stopping at some very low setting to stopping at some relatively high setting, he will presumably not waste his mental energy reflecting carefully on his situation at setting 789 and on his situation at setting 999 in order to determine his given preference with respect to stopping at 789 versus stopping at 999. Furthermore, if, in dealing with his predicament, he commits to a system of rankings that directs him to advance at settings 0 and 1 but to stop at setting 2 – if, in other words, his *chosen* preferences are such that stopping at setting 1 is ranked higher than stopping at setting 0, stopping at setting 2 is ranked higher than stopping at setting 1, but stopping at setting 3 is ranked lower than stopping at setting 2 – he will presumably not waste his mental energy expanding his system of chosen preferences by ranking additional pairs of settings.

Now let us return to the issues of whether a rational agent's preferences will necessarily be transitive and whether a rational agent will necessarily choose in accordance with her preferences. Given Quinn's example of the self-torturer, it seems quite sensible to resist the idea that a rational agent's *given* preferences will necessarily be transitive. But if a rational agent's given preferences are not necessarily transitive, then the money-pump argument suggests that a rational agent will not always allow herself to be led by her given preferences. For, if an agent's given preferences are nontransitive and she consistently allows herself to be led by her given preferences, then she can (given the possibility of unanticipated trade opportunities) be used as a money pump.

Still, there is room for the following plausible interpretations of the transitive-preferences claim and the preferred-option claim: a rational agent's *chosen* preferences will necessarily be transitive; and a rational agent will necessarily act in accordance with her *chosen* preferences. Indeed, it is quite plausible to suppose that, even if one's given preferences are not transitive, a rational agent will, in order to avoid serving as a money pump, make sure that any system of rankings she commits to is a set of transitive chosen preferences. Furthermore, given that an agent's chosen preferences are committed to in light of her given preferences and her choice situation, it is quite plausible to suppose that a rational agent will necessarily act in accordance with her chosen preferences (which can, of course, be altered or expanded if the agent realizes that some alteration or expansion is in order).

At this point it might be objected that if the transitive-preferences claim and the preferred-option claim are interpreted as concerning chosen preferences rather than given preferences, the requirements of rationality that they capture become too easy to satisfy. There are at least two things to say in response to this. First, the requirements of rationality captured by the claims are far from vacuous – there is no shortage of cases in which disorganization, negligence, or temptation leads to violations. Second, I have not claimed that, put together, the transitive-preferences claim and the preferred-option claim capture *all* there is to being rational; so if one finds the requirements of rationality captured by these claims too easy to satisfy, one can always defend additional rational requirements. I myself believe that there are additional rational requirements. Indeed, the idea that an agent's chosen preferences are committed to in light of her given preferences and her choice situation itself suggests that an agent's chosen preferences must not only be transitive, but must also take into account (and be pragmatically justifiable in relation to) the combination of her given preferences and her choice situation. Even when one's given preferences are nontransitive, and so one's chosen preferences cannot just duplicate one's given preferences, it cannot be assumed that the only rational constraint on one's chosen preferences is that they be transitive. Consider, for example, the case of the self-torturer. Intuitively, the self-torturer would, in light of his given preferences, be irrational if he committed to a system of rankings that directed him to advance to and then stop at some high setting that he finds intolerable (as opposed to some low setting that he finds perfectly acceptable). I am thus happy to grant that the transitive-preferences claim and the preferred-option claim do not capture all there is to being rational; there are, I allow, additional rational requirements, including requirements related to the pragmatic justifiability of one's chosen preferences in relation to one's given preferences and one's choice situation. And though I will not (and need not, given the aims of this chapter) attempt to work out these requirements here, the task is obviously of great theoretical and practical significance.

My conclusion is that there is no need to abandon the transitive-preferences claim and the preferred-option claim in light of purported problem cases, such as the case of the self-torturer. Both claims can be interpreted in a way that saves them from what appear as irresistible counterexamples, and gives them a level of plausibility that makes sense of the fact that they figure as basic postulates in a great deal of theorizing concerning rational agency. Furthermore, as far as I can tell, chosen preferences do not differ from given preferences in any ways that make them a less suitable focus for rational choice theory.

5 Given preferences, chosen preferences, and Condorcet's paradox

In this section, I will use the distinction between given preferences and chosen preferences to show that although Condorcet's paradox and Arrow's related Impossibility Theorem seem to imply that there is a rational defect inherent in democratic collectives, this conclusion does not actually follow.[12]

Let D be a democratic preference-determination procedure that takes as inputs the preferences of the members of a collective, and that generates a system of collective preferences. And suppose that D satisfies the following principle:

> P: If everyone in the collective ranks x above y, then x will be ranked above y in the preference system that is generated by the collective's preference-determination procedure.

Given a few additional basic assumptions about D that we need not get into here, it follows from Condorcet's paradox and from Arrow's theorem, which builds on Condorcet's paradox, that a collective using D can find itself with a system of nontransitive preferences even if the preferences of its members are transitive. Given the transitive-preferences claim, this result seems to reveal a special problem for democratic collectives. Consider the following line of reasoning:

1   As per the transitive-preferences claim, a rational agent's preferences are transitive.
2   As per Condorcet's paradox, a collective using D can find itself with nontransitive preferences even if the preferences of its members are transitive.
3   So D is a rationally defective preference-determination procedure.

Though this line of reasoning might seem quite compelling, it is problematic. The premises do not support dismissing D as a rationally defective preference-determination procedure if D is being used to determine the collective's *given* preferences. For, as is suggested by my discussion in the previous sections, the transitive-preferences claim, which figures as the first premise, is most plausibly interpreted as concerning chosen preferences rather than given preferences. So a collective can use D to determine its given preferences and then determine its chosen preferences in light of its given preferences and its choice situation. If the collective's given preferences are transitive, then the collective can simply commit to its given preferences. If, however, the collective's given preferences are nontransitive, then employing the simple identity mapping to get from its given preferences to its chosen preferences will not be a rationally available course of action. Having arrived at a single system of given preferences using D, the collective will have to take a further non-trivial step to arrive at a distinct system of chosen preferences. As I have indicated in relation to the case of the self-torturer, although rationality may leave quite a bit of leeway with respect to the process of arriving at chosen preferences, the demand that chosen preferences be pragmatically justifiable in relation to the agent's given preferences and choice situation arguably imposes at least some constraints on the process.

The key point is that to show that a certain type of collective preference-determination procedure will sometimes yield collective preferences that are nontransitive (as Condorcet's paradox does) is not to show that procedures of that type are rationally defective. The procedures can be just fine, so long as they are used to determine given preferences, not chosen preferences. For, as we have seen, charitably interpreted (so that it is not threatened by apparent counterexamples), the transitive-preferences claim allows that given preferences may fail to be transitive. It is only chosen preferences that are required to be transitive.

Since rational agents can have nontransitive given preferences, individuals, dictatorial collectives, and democratic collectives *all* need some way of getting from a single system of nontransitive given preferences to a single system of transitive chosen preferences. One thing that we know for certain and that is immediately apparent in the case of individuals and dictatorial collectives, where there is by hypothesis only one determining voice, is that the process of getting from a single system of nontransitive given preferences to a single system of transitive chosen preferences *cannot* satisfy the following principle:

P*: If unanimity among everyone with a voice results in x being ranked above y in the preference system that is fed into the process, then x will be ranked above y in the preference system that is generated by the process. Similarly, if unanimity among everyone with a voice results in x being ranked as equal to y in the preference system that is fed into the process, then x will be ranked as equal to y in the preference system that is generated by the process.

Where there is only one determining voice, all the rankings in the given preference system will (trivially) be unanimous. If, therefore, the resulting system of chosen preferences is to be transitive, at least one of the unanimously supported rankings in the nontransitive given preference system will not be carried over. An important implication for my purposes is that democratic collectives do not face any special problem if they too are unable, in at least some cases of getting from given preferences to chosen preferences, to satisfy P*.

In short, individuals, dictatorial collectives, and democratic collectives can all, without fault, have nontransitive given preferences. They therefore all need some way of getting from a single system of nontransitive given preferences to a single system of transitive chosen preferences. And in no case can the process invariably preserve unanimously accepted rankings.

6 Conclusion

Using my distinction between given preferences and chosen preferences, I have defended the transitive-preferences claim and the preferred-option claim against apparent counterexamples. While these apparent counterexamples assume that the claims are to be interpreted as concerned with given preferences, the claims are actually best interpreted as concerned with chosen preferences. It is chosen preferences, not given preferences, that must be transitive; relatedly, it is her chosen preferences, not her given preferences, that the rational agent invariably follows. As I argued in the preceding section, the idea that given preferences need not be transitive has important implications concerning the interpretation of Condorcet's paradox and Arrow's related Impossibility Theorem. In particular, my argument contests the idea that these two results imply that there is a rational defect inherent in democratic collectives.

If my reasoning in this chapter in correct, then cases like that of the self-torturer should not be seen as undermining the basic postulates of the standard model of rational agency. Nor should they be dismissed as cases in which the agent's preferences are irrational. Rather, they should be seen as cases that, like this chapter, invite reflection on the challenging process of getting from a single system of given preferences to a single system of chosen preferences when the obvious and natural choice of committing to one's given preferences is not rationally permissible because these preferences are nontransitive. Relatedly, if successful, this chapter resolves the conflict between those sympathetic with the standard model of rational agency and those sympathetic with cases like that of the self-torturer, and prompts inquiry into an issue that both groups can recognize as pertinent.

Notes

1 My thanks to George Ainslie, Kenneth Arrow, Luc Bovens, Donald Bruckner, Ben Eggleston, Stephen Gardiner, Edward McClennen, Elijah Millgram, Barbara Montero, Don Ross, Mariam Thalos, Peter Vallentyne, Mark D. White, Mike White, and audience members of the Economics and Philosophy of Mind session at the 2005 Eastern Economic Association meeting for their valuable feedback on earlier drafts of this chapter. I am also grateful to Idil Boran for

comments on a related paper; her comments on that paper influenced the shape of this chapter as well.

2 Note that this condition need not be interpreted as presupposing that all pair-wise rankings are menu independent. (An agent's ranking of two options is menu independent if it does not depend on what other options, if any, are available.) Rather than presupposing that all rankings are menu independent, the transitivity condition can be interpreted as concerning menu-independent rankings, as well as rankings that do not vary over the series of option-sets the agent faces. Note that in the simple cases that I am concerned with, in which the agent is invariably choosing between just two options, the agent never faces the same pair of options in two different option-sets, and so the agent's pair-wise rankings do not vary over the series of option-sets the agent faces. Still, the agent's preferences can be nontransitive. The issue in this chapter is whether they can be nontransitive even if the agent is rational.

3 The original presentation of the money-pump argument appears in Davidson et al. (1955). Note that although Edward McClennen (1990) has forcefully argued that a "sophisticated planner" is not vulnerable to being pumped if she foresees her trade opportunities, a series of trade opportunities can be unexpected, and so even if Ann is a sophisticated planner, she can end up worse off, relative to her preferences, than when she started. Robin Cubitt and Robert Sugden (2001) show that an agent can avoid being money pumped via inconsistencies that can survive economic selection; the issue of whether these inconsistencies are rationally permissible is, however, left unsettled.

4 A few bits of my discussion of the self-torturer are borrowed from Andreou (2005b; 2006).

5 There are others who have done the same. See, for example, Bratman (1999) and Nozick (1993). Note that, as I have pointed out in previous work (for example Andreou 2006), although the self-torturer's pain situation is characterized by vagueness, Quinn's reasoning does not incorporate the sort of sophistical reasoning that figures in constructing sorites paradoxes. Indeed, Quinn denies the soritical inference that if a tiny increment in current cannot take one from a state in which one is not in excruciating pain to a state in which one is in excruciating pain, then the self-torturer will not be in excruciating pain no matter how many increments in electric current are applied.

6 In their presentation of the money-pump argument, Davidson *et al.* (1955) consider a case with the same structure as Megan's case and then introduce the money-pump argument to show that the agent's preferences are irrational. But, as I have explained, if there is no independent reason to think that the agent's preferences are irrational, the money-pump argument can be interpreted as undermining the preferred-option claim rather than as supporting the transitive-preferences claim.

7 See, for example, Graham Loomes and Robert Sugden's (1982, 1984) case of the reasoner with regret aversion and John Broome's (1991) case of the reasoner with cowardice aversion. Note that Broome ultimately ends up arguing that his apparent counterexample is not really a counterexample after all.

8 I appeal to essentially the same conception of preference in Andreou (2005a), where I defend the assumption in rational choice theory that a rational agent's preferences are complete. Note that, unlike promising to act in accordance with a system of rankings, committing to a system of rankings is – at least as I mean it to be understood – an intra-agent rather than an inter-agent accomplishment.

9 Of course, it might be that our psychology, as individuals, is such that our given preferences tend to adjust themselves to our chosen preferences whenever there is any difference. Nothing I will say hangs on whether or not any such alteration on the part of our given preferences tends to take place.

10 This is proved by Condorcet's paradox, which I will turn to shortly.

11 See Tversky and Kahneman (1986). It may, of course, still be true that when a *rational* agent considers a set of options and arrives at a system of given preferences, these preferences are not even in part determined by the way the options were framed. Note that how the framing phase proceeds is a highly contingent matter that is affected by priming. Relatedly, the phase can range from an active process of information (re)organization to a relatively passive acceptance of an externally supplied frame.

12 My discussion of Condorcet's paradox and Arrow's theorem will be very rough and quick. In-depth discussions are readily available in the extensive literature on both results.

References

Andreou, C. (2005a) "Incommensurable Alternatives and Rational Choice," *Ratio*, 18: 249–61.

—— (2005b) "Going from Bad (or Not So Bad) to Worse: On Harmful Addictions and Habits," *American Philosophical Quarterly*, 42: 323–31.

—— (2006) "Environmental Damage and the Puzzle of the Self-Torturer," *Philosophy & Public Affairs*, 34: 95–108.

Bratman, M. (1999) "Toxin, Temptation, and the Stability of Intention," in *Faces of Intention*, Cambridge: Cambridge University Press.

Broome, J. (1991) *Weighing Goods*, Oxford: Basil Blackwell.

Cubitt, R. and Sugden, R. (2001) "On Money Pumps," *Games and Economic Behavior*, 37: 121–60.

Davidson, D., McKinsey, J., and Suppes, P. (1955) "Outlines of a Formal Theory of Value," *Philosophy of Science*, 22: 140–60.

Loomes, G. and Sugden, R. (1982) "Regret Theory: An Alternative Theory of Rational Choice under Uncertainty," *Economic Journal*, 92: 805–24.

—— (1984) "Regret Theory and Information: A Reply," *Economic Journal*, 94: 649–50.

McClennen, E. (1990) *Rationality and Dynamic Choice*, Cambridge: Cambridge University Press.

Nozick, R. (1993) *The Nature of Rationality*, Princeton, NJ: Princeton University Press.

Quinn, W. (1993) "The Puzzle of the Self-Torturer," in *Morality and Action*, Cambridge: Cambridge University Press.

Tversky, A. and Kahneman, D. (1986) "Rational Choice and the Framing of Decisions," *Journal of Business*, 59: S251–78.

8 Freedom from choice

Reconsidering Sen's case for maximizing opportunities

David George

1 Introduction

The attempts by Amartya Sen to replace the neoclassical economist's criteria for measuring human well-being with a model that is richer in content and more eclectic in its theoretical underpinnings has been both impressive to academics and influential in the policy-making realm. Sen has not been hesitant to present ideas that he himself appears to realize are neither complete nor immune from criticism, and the critical response to his "capabilities and functionings" approach to assessing well-being is extensive indeed.[1]

A recurrent thread through Sen's writings has been concern about the near-total neglect by standard neoclassical theorists of the intrinsic valuation that agents place on freedom. As he repeatedly notes, the valuation placed on a choice set, according to received theory, is determined strictly by the most preferred alternative within this set. If A is chosen when A, B, and C are available, then, according to this way of thinking, the absence of alternatives B and C would have been of no consequence. In other words, having A, B, and C as possibilities and choosing A is rated as normatively equivalent to having only A available (and chosen).

In what follows, my primary objective will be to reveal a serious shortcoming in Sen's critique of neutrality toward the size of the choice set. I will agree with Sen that neutrality toward the size of the choice set represents a shortcoming. However, I will attempt to demonstrate that Sen's conclusions are incorrect for one important class of occurrences. While I will agree with Sen that limiting choice should not be treated as inconsequential just because the preferred element is not one of the items eliminated, I will be focusing on instances where such restrictions are beneficial rather than costly for the agent.

The remainder of the chapter will be divided into four sections. In the next section I will describe two conditions specified by Sen – content independence and context independence – that freedom is argued to require. The third section will summarize the main features of metapreferences or second-order preferences and the primary conclusions that I have reached in my previous work. The fourth section will contrast Sen's examples of content-dependent and context-dependent preferences with different examples that are illustrative of the possibility that such dependence can be a necessary byproduct of the agent's expression of a free will. In the fifth section I will argue that the insistence of Mahatma Gandhi that his legendary fast occur with food within his grasp attests not to the well-being that freedom creates but to its potential to worsen the agent's well-being. In the final section the greater controversy of "metafreedom" – the freedom to decide on the extent of one's freedom – will be briefly considered.

2 Content- and context-independent preferences

Sen's views on freedom have mainly been offered in the broader context of his extensive writings on a capabilities and functionings approach to the assessment of human well-being. In what follows, I will be summarizing Sen's claims while using the more conventional tools of constraints and preferences. While Sen's interpretation of – "capabilities" – and the related concept – "functionings" – was intended to offer a rich substitution for "choice sets" and "items comprising the choice set," respectively, Sen himself has, in his numerous writings over the years, acknowledged that a strong connection remains. Writing in 1985, he states that "a person's capability set can be defined as the set of functioning vectors within his or her reach" (Sen 1985b: 200–01). Writing fourteen years later, he offers this definition:

> a person's "capability" refers to the alternative combinations of functionings that are feasible for her to achieve. Capability is thus a kind of freedom: the substantive freedom to achieve alternative functioning combinations (or, less formally stated, the freedom to achieve various lifestyles).
>
> (Sen 1999: 75)

There has been extensive confusion over the difference between functionings and capabilities, but, as these passages indicate, one decides what one's functionings will be from a larger set of potential functionings.[2] For the purposes of what follows, nothing of substance will be lost by substituting "bundle" for "chosen functionings" and "choice set" for "capabilities."

As Philip Pettit has demonstrated, for Sen, "freedom on a given issue requires the agent's preference between options to be decisive in a content-independent way" (Pettit 2001: 5). Consider what this is saying: let there be two items, A and B, but suppose that only B is within the agent's choice set. Suppose that the agent selects the sole opportunity available – B – and would further indicate if asked that he prefers B to the unavailable bundle A. Sen would not take the lack of any true choice between alternatives in this situation to be a reason for questioning its decisiveness. In Pettit's words, such decisiveness for Sen "requires only indirect control or indirect freedom;

if the exercise of choice does not determine what happens, how the person would have chosen does" (Pettit 2001: 3).

Now suppose that A is allowed into the choice set, and suppose further that in this instance the agent chooses A. For Sen, the agent was not originally free with respect to A and B since his preference was clearly content dependent. Only if A was *not* a possibility did the agent experience a preference for B, and hence this could be described as a content-dependent freedom that does not reflect true freedom to choose.

I have chosen to introduce content dependence through an abstract format because there are examples that tend to bias one's reaction to the reasonableness of such a stipulation in quite opposite ways. For Martha Nussbaum (2001), the typical example of a content-dependent preference was that experienced by a woman living in a less economically developed, patriarchal society who has learned to accept as inevitable her second-class status. In such a case it is indeed unsettling to describe as "free" a woman who prefers being a second-class citizen over the prospect of being an engaged citizen equal to a man in status. Her preference is, on the face of it, content dependent, and might be understood as a strategy for being at peace with the constraints that she faces and is unable to alter.

Consider now a different sort of example, namely that of a smoker who finds herself increasingly in settings where smoking is prohibited. If she announces that in such settings she prefers to do without a cigarette rather than have one, is there something about the situation that should cause us to question how free she really is? If allowing her to smoke would change her preference in favor of smoking, do we want to insist that in this latter situation she is free but in the former she was not?

Before seeking answers to these questions, it needs to be noted that Pettit also sees Sen's specification of decisive preferences as requiring that they be context independent. Again quoting Pettit, context-dependent preferences are "decisive only so far as the person enjoys the gratuitous favour of certain others – the sort of favour that can be bestowed or withdrawn at the pleasure of the giver" (Pettit 2001: 6). A context-dependent preference differs from a content-dependent one only in that the former has the same options within the choice set at all times. Returning to the example of the smoker, there are numerous situations in which one is in an environment in which smoking is formally an option (for example while walking on a city street) but in which those in the vicinity would feel harmed by the exposure to smoke. The potential smoker finds herself preferring not to smoke, but this is only because of the milieu in which she finds herself. Were she alone in her walk, the preference to smoke would arise and she would light up a cigarette. Again, do we wish to see her free in the context-independent case but unfree when her social milieu causes her preference to change? Before confronting the questions of the agreeableness of content independence and context independence as criteria for freedom in more depth, a detour into a consideration of metapreferences is necessary.

3 Reasoned scrutiny and metapreferences: a neglected connection

The type of preference ranking that I shall be interested in here is variously known as a metapreference ranking, or second-order preference ranking or higher-order preference ranking. I have chosen to include "ranking" in each of these descriptions in order to minimize ambiguity. To illustrate, consider the agent summarized in Figure 8.1. Line 1 is the metapreference ranking, with the items that are ranked being preferences over bundles. Line 2 is the preference over bundles that is currently experienced by the agent.[3] Line 3 is the agent's choice in light of line 2. As I have argued at length elsewhere, to have a preference for A over B is to say that the agent will choose A when both A and B are available.[4] This particular constellation of metapreference ranking, preference ranking, and chosen bundle thus captures a particular sort of internal conflict, namely an agent who is freely choosing but is nonetheless "in conflict" with himself. He wishes he had a preference for B relative to A, happens to have a preference for A relative to B, and thus chooses A.

The weakness of informal language has proven to be a barrier in communicating this relatively simple structure of a complex, self-reflective agent. Casual use of "preference" often applies to both lines 2 and 3; that is, preference is used both to describe the thing preferred and the preference ranking itself. Similarly, metapreference is used to apply to line 1 but has also been used to apply to what the agent would wish to see appearing in line 2. There is thus the danger of treating the agent's experienced preference as what line 2 actually is and metapreference as what one wishes that it were. That is, one might specify the experienced preference as (A pref B) and the metapreference as (B pref A).

To fall into such a discursive convention is unfortunate, for it amounts to negating exactly the feature of the metapreference approach to internal conflict that sets it apart from the two-selves or multiple-selves approaches.[5] For such approaches, the agent can violate a basic core assumption of transitivity in the preference relationship. A preference for A is supposed to rule out a simultaneous preference for B. The correct use of "metapreference" allows the preservation of this core assumption. The conflicted agent does indeed prefer A to B and most definitely does not prefer B to A. That is to say, while (A pref B) is true and [(B pref A) pref (A pref B)] is simultaneously true, (B pref A) is not true. For a two-selves approach, in contrast, it can be

$$(B \text{ pref } A) \text{ pref } (A \text{ pref } B) \qquad\qquad (1)$$

$$(A \text{ pref } B) \qquad\qquad (2)$$

$$A \qquad\qquad (3)$$

Figure 8.1 A conflicted agent's metapreference, preference, and choice.

simultaneously true that (A pref B) and (B pref A). But as surely as the statement that John is taller than Bill is assumed to rule out the possibility that Bill is also taller than John, (A pref B) should preclude (B pref A) if the intended meaning of a preference is to be preserved.

According to the philosopher Harry Frankfurt (1971), the ability to experience metapreferences is the characteristic of human beings that sets them apart from other sentient creatures. As Frankfurt emphasizes (and as economists would agree), animals have preferences as surely as do humans. They regularly and predictably choose some possibilities over others. But only humans, by Frankfurt's account, are capable of reflecting on their preferences and either valuing them as being what they want them to be or wishing that they were different. Frankfurt offers an unconventional definition of what it means to have a free will. To act in accord with one's experienced preference (which, it should be kept in mind, both humans and nonhuman animals can do) is to act according to the will that one has. Distinct from this, according to Frankfurt, is the ability to select the preference ranking that one would like to have. To have the preference ranking that one most values is, by such an argument, to exercise a free will, a quite different capacity than simply acting on the will that one happens to be experiencing.[6]

Two seminal articles by Sen (1974, 1977) are generally cited as the first to make extensive use of the idea of metapreferences. It is thus ironic that my aim in the present chapter is to demonstrate that Sen's neglect of metapreferences seriously compromises his specification of the conditions for freedom. But, again ironically, the specific conditions of the scenario presented by Sen may have detracted attention from the more interesting instances of internal conflict that metapreferences allow us to model.[7]

In Figure 8.2 is shown the simple prisoner's dilemma. The numbers in each box specify the payoff to the two players, with the number on the left representing the utility payoff to player 1 and the number on the right the payoff to player 2. Given the assumption that for each player it is true that (4 pref 3 pref 2 pref 1), and assuming no utility interdependence, each player would, of course, be inclined to choose dominant strategy B and the result would be a payoff of just 2 for each player. Sen's introduction of metapreferences was in the context of offering a solution to the dilemma. He asked us to imagine a meta-ranking of the payoffs for each agent of [(3 pref 4 pref 1 pref 2) pref (4 pref 3 pref 2 pref 1)], and went on to explain that if the agent could simply act "as if" it were indeed the case that (3 pref 4 pref 1 pref 2), then each player would become better off *in terms of the preference ranking each in fact has*. In other words, were both agents to choose strategy A – the dominant strategy if the preferred ranking was to prevail – then each would realize a payoff of 3 rather than 2, a net gain regardless of whether the preferred or unpreferred preference ranking is experienced by the agent. In this special case, one does best in terms of one's extant preference ranking by acting as if his ranking were different than it actually is.

Player 2

		A	B
	A	3,3	1,4
Player 1			
	B	4,1	2,2

Figure 8.2 The prisoner's dilemma.

Sen's use of the metapreference ranking in this particular context was indeed a powerful one and has likely been most influential in isolating a case when an agent is clearly best off doing other than what she prefers. An unfortunate side effect, however, has been this model's likely contribution to the misconception that rationality *always* dictates doing that which one prefers to prefer. This is not true in the more typical case when outcomes are not the consequence of the combination of individual decisions. In my earlier example, it would have made no sense for the agent who preferred A to B to choose B, even though he wished that he had a preference for B. Assuming otherwise would weaken the power of the metapreference model. It would no longer explain internal conflict since the sudden existence of a metapreference contrary to the agent's experienced preference would be no different, for all practical purposes, than a shift in the experienced preference itself. There would be no rationale for freely undertaken behaviors which the agent at the same time regrets. Whether Sen himself failed to see the more interesting (and infinitely more numerous) cases in which it was not rational to act as if one's preferred preference prevailed unless it indeed *did* prevail is not at issue. But that it may have unintentionally steered attention away from the more typical and intransigent cases of conflicts seems likely.

While this is an error of omission on Sen's part, there is a more serious error of commission worth considering. As already noted, for Harry Frankfurt it is the capability of having preferences about one's preferences that distinguishes humans from animals, and the capacity to shape one's preferences accordingly that constitutes the exercise of a free will. For Sen, in contrast, second-order preferences enter not at all into his attempts to describe what sets humans apart. In rejecting the claim that rationality requires self-interest, Sen argues that this "repudiates the most profound capacity of the human self which distinguishes us, in many different ways, from the rest of the animal kingdom, namely our ability to reason and to undertake reasoned scrutiny" (Sen 2002: 46).

I agree with Sen that "rationality . . . demand[s] that . . . one's goals . . . should be supportable through careful assessment and scrutiny" (Sen 2002: 41), but reject the implication that such "reasoned scrutiny" would necessarily suffice to alter one's preferences as one believes they ought to be altered. Consider two different cases of reasoned scrutiny. Suppose that an agent is about to drink a colorful, sweet-smelling liquid that she has been led to believe will quench her thirst while having no ill side effects. Suppose that with further reasoned scrutiny she uncovers some facts about the person offering the drink that reveal him to be a pathological murderer who has poisoned before, and that the agent thus elects to forego the offer of a drink (and vacate the premises as soon as possible). In such an instance, the exercise of the human capacity for reasoned scrutiny has managed to change both her metapreference and her experienced preference. Prior to discovering the terrifying revelation about her host, she preferred drinking to not drinking and preferred having this particular preference. After her discovery, it is safe to say that both her metapreference and experienced preference changed.

But consider now a second case. Suppose that an agent is about to settle down with a bowl of Pub Mix snack, described on its label as "a savory blend of crunchy snacks," and that, having no sense whatsoever about possible harmful effects that this product might in the long run have on his health, this agent not only prefers the snack relative to other uses of his time but prefers having this preference as well. Further suppose that a sudden urge for "informed consumption" leads this agent to engage in some reasoned scrutiny prior to consuming the product by carefully reading the nutritional information attached to the package. After discovering that a serving contains 130 calories (and that his definition of a serving is twice the seller's definition) and that close to one-third of these calories are fat, what changes might be anticipated?

Such information might of course alter both the agent's metapreference and preference and thus cause him to reject consuming the snack. But not to be ruled out is a different effect, namely a change in the agent's second-order preference without any change in the experienced preference simultaneously occurring. Our metapreferences are not visceral in quite the way that some of our experienced preferences can be. The intellectual project of scrutinizing one's possible choices and re-evaluating them when necessary would thus appear to have more effect on the former than on the latter. I would not dispute Sen's claim that reasoned scrutiny might be specified as a necessary condition for the exercise of a free will. While not explicitly stated by Frankfurt, the very act of having preferences about one's preferences presupposes some reasoned scrutiny. However, all the reasoned scrutiny imaginable is not necessarily sufficient to alter one's preferences. In short, while on the one hand a pioneer in the introduction of metapreferences to the economic literature, Sen's specification of reasoned scrutiny manages to leave out the significance of exactly such preferences from the discussion, and is all the weaker as a consequence.

If reasoned scrutiny is judged to be insufficient to assure the exercise of a free will (and, operationally, an improvement in one's preferences), what other paths might be possible? In the section that follows I will be arguing that the deliberate restriction of one's choice set can in certain instances serve precisely this end.[8] I will show that the freedom to restrict one's choices can serve as a means, to paraphrase Frankfurt, of exercising a free will. And not only will this be intended to replace reasoned scrutiny as a sufficient condition for the exercise of freedom; it will require sacrificing Sen's requirement that preferences be content independent and context independent if we are to regard them as expressions of freedom.

4 Content dependence as a necessary byproduct of free will

A slightly more formal work-up of the snack food example just noted will assist in clarifying the dynamics of self-paternalistic action and will at the same time require the rejection of Sen's content-independence criterion for judging an action as free. In Figure 8.3 appear two combinations of metapreference, preference, and choice. Let P stand for "Pub Mix" and N for "not having Pub Mix." As with the previous example, line 1 shows the agent's metapreference, line 2 the regular preference, and line 3 the action chosen.

In both of the scenarios shown, this agent would prefer to have a preference to abstain from the Pub Mix snack. In scenario 1, however, he experiences a preference for the snack and thus chooses to consume the snack. In scenario 2, in contrast, the preference that he experiences is to not consume the snack and, as a consequence, he chooses not to. That scenario 2 is superior to scenario 1 only requires the self-evident axiom that having the preference one prefers having, and acting on it, is a better state of affairs than having one's unpreferred preference (and acting on it).

The question becomes what, if anything, can an agent experiencing scenario 1 do to bring about scenario 2? Simply choosing N will not represent an improvement. At first consideration, it might appear that this indeed leaves the agent better off, since the choice, if not the preference itself, would conform with the overall preferred state of affairs. However, it is by definition the case that selecting what one prefers (whether the preference is preferred or not) is better for the agent than choosing what is not preferred. Although he would prefer having a preference to not have the Pub Mix and would act on

Scenario 1	Scenario 2	
(N pref P) pref (P pref N)	(N pref P) pref (P pref N)	(1)
P pref N	N pref P	(2)
P	N	(3)

Figure 8.3 From internal conflict to internal harmony.

this preference by abstaining in such a case, it is unfortunately not the preference that he experiences in this case. Given that he is saddled with the unpreferred preference, to abstain would make him worse off than would indulging in the snack.[9] It follows that an improvement from scenario 1 requires that something change the preference that the agent experiences. And as I have argued previously (George 1998; 2001: ch. 2), one device commonly employed to achieve exactly this is the elimination of possibilities from one's choice set. For me, and, I assume, for most people, a strategy for "not wanting" something is to tamper with the menu that I face by eliminating the item that I want not to want. When the Pub Mix is absent from my house (and at the rate I'm going it soon will be gone), I no longer can choose to consume the mix, and, more significantly, will find myself not wanting it.

Accepting the above casts serious doubt on Sen's condition of content independence as a necessary condition for the existence of freedom. Sen would declare that the content-dependent nature of my preference casts doubt upon the whole picture and that I am not truly exercising freedom over the set of P and N. But consider how, by Frankfurt's account, I would be said to be using exactly such content restriction to exercise the very highest freedom, namely the freedom to shape my will. Only in virtue of banishing P from my choice set can my preference for N emerge. The content dependence of this preference speaks not to its illegitimacy, but to the very special nature of my human capability to shape my tastes.[10]

The earlier discussed condition of context independence becomes equally problematic. I find myself in many situations where the eating of Pub Mix is feasible but socially disadvantageous. Suppose I am in front of a class and that I have a bag of Pub Mix resting in my pocket. Never for a moment would I entertain the possibility of opening the bag and popping an occasional treat into my mouth during the class. I could do so, but the context of a room full of students who would find this odd is enough to keep me from even considering such an action. This is clearly a context-dependent preference. If the opprobrium of the students could be eliminated, say by my gaining the ability to indulge in the snack in a way that is completely undetectable by those in the room, I would likely indeed prefer to snack. It is only the context in which I find myself that has caused my preference to be otherwise. Yet, all things considered, I do not consider my freedom violated by this social dynamic. Qualities of my social context serve to alter my preferences from what they might be in the complete absence of third-party awareness of my acts. More often than not, the direction of the shift in my preferences is favorable if my metapreferences are allowed to serve as the final arbiter. My reasons for wanting to not want the snack mix have nothing to do with social approval, and it so happens that social opprobrium (in this case from a college-age segment of the population not known for the rigidity of their demands) shapes my preferences in a way that I find desirable. Still again, I do not feel unfree as a consequence, but more truly free in seeing my preferences shaped for the better.[11]

There is one clear difference between the context-dependent example I have constructed and the content-dependent preference discussed earlier. In the earlier case, it was the agent who freely gave up some of his freedom. He deliberately acted so as to not have the snack mix as a possibility at a later time. In contrast to this, the context-dependent preference I've described was shaped by a context which the agent had no immediate role in shaping. One might argue that the act of agreeing to belong to a society that is partly defined by its context-shaping properties represents a choice or, alternatively, one might argue that the democratic characteristics of the society lend a representative imprimatur to such context-shaping tendencies. Regardless, however, the tendency of the context to shape preferences in the direction favored by the agent is enough to speak of freedom-enhancing constraints.

5 Freedom as Gandhi's means to deepen his sacrifice

This now brings us to a compelling story that Sen has offered at several points to illustrate the value that freedom has from a deontological, non-consequentialist perspective:

> Sometimes the value of what is chosen relates integrally to what is rejected. For example, "fasting" is possible not just through starving, but through starving *out of choice*, by deliberately rejecting the option of eating. Removing the option of eating for a person who wants to fast to make a political point (for example, as Mahatma Gandhi did while protesting the British rule) would be a real loss for him, even though eating is not his best option, nor the one he would actually choose.
>
> (Sen 2002: 18)

The case being described here bears some similarities with the earlier example of my attempt to counter my passion for Pub Mix, but the differences are quite pronounced as well. In setting up the analytics of this case, I will contrast Gandhi's situation with the situation facing an agent who would follow a strict diet regimen regardless of whether tempting foods were or were not within her choice set, but who nonetheless elects to deprive herself of the option to indulge in these foods.

Beginning with the considerably more mundane case of the creative dieter, let there be three possible states that the agent ranks (her experienced preference) and a metapreference ranking of three of the six possible experienced preference rankings. The left side of Figure 8.4 shows the agent's abbreviated metapreference ranking, preference ranking, and choice when she has full freedom of choice over the three states.[12] The right side summarizes the situation when steps have been taken to free her from some choices by removing all junk food from her immediate surroundings.

Freedom of choice   **Freedom from choice**

(B > A > C) pref (A > B > C) pref (C > B > A)   (B > A > C) pref (A > B > C) pref (C > B > A)

                   B > A > C   B > A > C

                        A   B

Where:

A	Foregoing all proscribed food while suffering pain	
B	Foregoing all proscribed food while suffering less pain	
C	Indulging in proscribed food	

Figure 8.4 Restricting choice as a welfare-improving action.

When this agent has freedom to choose to consume or forego the junk food, the option B becomes unavailable since foregoing this food results in "pain" rather than "less pain." Thus, though the agent has the preference that she prefers having, her preferred element B is simply unavailable and she thus chooses A. She is succeeding in *eating* what she prefers to prefer but unfortunately must bear some psychological pain in the process of achieving this objective. When the agent is able to remove the junk food from her choice set, her well-being improves, as indicated on the right side of Figure 8.4. Having the junk food out of sight causes it to be out of mind as well, and the act of doing without this food is less onerous.

Figure 8.5 is similar to Figure 8.4 except that (1) the word "proscribed" has been dropped since the goal is to forego *all* food, not just junk food; and (2) the preferred preference is now "A > B > C" instead of "B > A > C," since by assumption Gandhi prefers to prefer having a more costly sort of fast (one with suffering) rather than a painless fast; and (3) the preference actually experienced is A > B > C instead of B > A > C.

I am assuming that Gandhi preferred to forego food and to do so at a cost of some suffering to better communicate to the British the depth of his devotion to his cause. Somewhat paradoxically, in this particular case the act of ridding himself of all opportunities to eat, because it would remove the subjective displeasure of fasting, would leave Gandhi worse off. Rather than being able to achieve A, as freedom to choose allows him to do on the left, the act of liberating himself from the continual option of eating would

Freedom of choice   **Freedom from choice**

(A > B > C) pref (B > A > C) pref (C > B > A)   (A > B > C) pref (B > A > C) pref (C > B > A)

                  A > B > C   A > B > C

                       A   B

Where:

A	Foregoing all food while suffering pain	
B	Foregoing all food while suffering less pain	
C	Indulging in food	

Figure 8.5 Preserving free choice as a means of expressing sacrifice.

necessitate his having to settle for B, the act of foregoing food while suffering less pain than he might. My way of summarizing the situation suggests the very opposite of what Sen has suggested, namely that the valuation placed on freedom to choose by Gandhi did not signal an inherent valuation of freedom, but a valuation of freedom in this particular case because of the displeasure it could cause. We seem to have here an odd sort of testimony indeed to the advantages that freedom can provide!

6 Concluding considerations

The major analytical tool that has been used here to cast doubt upon Sen's integration of freedom into any assessment of the well-being of agents is the metapreference construct, that human characteristic of being able to rank the different potential preference rankings that one might expect to experience at a future moment in time. The freedom to act has been enriched by the recognition of metafreedom, understandable as the freedom to preserve or to sacrifice specific future freedoms.

The ethical implications of choosing one's preferences could be complex but as an empirical fact are usually not. The literature has generally assumed that the preference ranking that an agent would prefer having relative to what he happens to be experiencing would, if anything, have beneficial rather than harmful effects on other members of society compared with the extant ranking. In cases offered in this chapter, the preferred preference was usually superior from a prudential standpoint, but common also have been cases when agents experienced regret at the negative impact of their expressed preferences on others and wished to improve these preferences accordingly. While it is formally possible for an agent to prefer to be nice to others while simultaneously preferring to prefer to be sadistic, such conflicts are rare and the shaping of one's preferences is thus not something that society has occasion to discourage.

With respect to metafreedom – the freedom to preserve or to give up one's freedom to act – matters are more complex. Clearly instances exist where societies expressly forbid the exercise of metafreedom to be less free. The law does not permit a person to contractually agree to relinquish his freedom and become another's slave one year from the time of agreement, even if that person is motivated to do so by a hefty payment that would allow luxurious living for his remaining year of freedom. Similarly, one cannot enjoy the freedom to give up one's right to vote. The inalienability of rights can be thus understood as one means to guard against the exercise of specific metafreedoms to be less free.

While it is necessary to acknowledge that the freedom to give up freedoms such as these can be problematic, the examples I have used here illustrate that there need be nothing morally complex in many instances of seeking to shape one's tastes. In the cases that have served as illustrations in this chapter, there was no formal ceding of freedom, but rather actions taken that would make impossible (or very expensive) the fulfillment of the unpreferred preference at a later time. Yet it is worth noting that governments do outlaw certain activities that might serve as inexpensive ways to shape our tastes through limiting our freedoms. So, for example, as David Laibson has noted, one who is seeking to give up, say, smoking cannot enter into a binding contract with a willing party wherein the smoker would agree to pay a certain amount if he indulges in the habit that he prefers to not prefer (Laibson 1997: 448). Since the other party would suffer no material loss (there is no "consideration") if the unhappy smoker were to smoke and then refuse to pay the agreed-upon amount, court actions for breach of contract would not be possible. Clearly, the law (at least in the U.S.) is failing to encourage a potentially simple way that people might call upon to facilitate the shaping of their tastes.

Amartya Sen's capability approach may have the potential to better judge the advances of those attempting to put behind them the oppressive state brought on by poverty and politically repressive regimes. This same approach, however, unfortunately ignores the onerous "consumptionism" that prevails in more economically advanced nations and further risks putting in motion forces that will cause developing nations to evolve precisely into such societies. As Des Gasper asks, "how sufficient would be a conception of freedom that ranks highly an educated, well-paid . . . person habituated, perhaps even addicted, to 30–40 hours of television and video-viewing per week?" (Gasper 2002: 455). And, as I would add, how sufficient would such a conception be if such an agent preferred that his preferences were different but lacked the social supports that would help him to change?

Notes

1 For the development of Sen's capabilities and functioning approaches, see, in particular, Sen (1985a, 1985b, 1987, 1988, 1993, 1999, 2002). For critical responses to this work, see Carter (1996), Cohen (1993, 1994), Gasper (2002, 2005), and Pettit (2001). For attempts to link the capabilities approach with the literature on happiness, see Comim (2005) and Teschl and Comim (2005).

2 A particularly rich deconstruction of the many different potential interpretations of Sen's capability approach appears in Gasper (2002).

3 Preferences about one's preferences will always be referred to as metapreferences in what follows. The traditional preference ranking of bundles will be referred to as simply "preferences" or "experienced preferences." The use of "experienced" is meant to draw attention to the immediacy of such preferences in determining the agent's choices. It is a less than ideal adjective since one experiences one's metapreference as well, but is, I believe, a useful way to distinguish the two sorts of preferences at an intuitive level.

4 A defense of the tautological sense of preference rests on defining preferences as "overall" in scope rather than "intrinsic." For further development of this distinction, see George (1993; 2001: ch. 2).

5 Major early contributors to the multiple-selves tradition include Schelling (1978, 1980), Elster (1979, 1983), Thaler and Shefrin (1981), and Cowen (1991, 1993).

6 As I have argued, Frankfurt was too categorical in his definition of a free will. Having precisely those preferences that one would most prefer having is likely to

lie outside one's range of choice. I have hence spoken of the freedom of will in a comparative sense. One has more freedom of will if one can take actions that result in one's preferences improving, even if they are in no sense the most preferred imaginable preferences.

7　The primary intent of my previous work on metapreferences was to demonstrate that markets are inefficient in their role as shapers of our tastes (George 1984, 1993, 1998, 2001). From the non-problematic assumption that sellers can influence experienced preferences and the assumption that they do not shape our metapreferences (a more heroic assumption that eases the demonstration of my conclusions but is not critical), I have shown that, absent enforceable property rights in preferences or well-specified social conventions about the appropriateness of persuasion, sellers will too often change preferences for the worse and too seldom change them for the better.

8　Sen does offer one circumstance in which restraint of options can leave the agent better off. As he notes, "you may prefer mangoes to apples, but refuse to pick the last mango from a fruit basket, and yet be very pleased if someone else were to 'force' that last mango on you" (Sen 2002: 161), the point being that one would look bad in choosing the last of anything. This is a different consideration, and, I think, much more of a special case than what will be described in the section that follows. For a psychologist's treatment of the benefits that can come from limiting one's choice set, see Barry Schwartz (2004).

9　It will be easier to summarize this conclusion by the specification of "complex elements," each of which shall consist of a preference ranking and a bundle. For economy of presentation, let complex element (AB and A) denote "a preference for A over B and the possession of A." To say that that an agent has a metapreference or second-order preference for A can be taken to require that (AB and A) is preferred to (BA and B). In words, having one's preferred preference and acting on it is preferred to having the unpreferred preference and acting on it. Having the unpreferred preference and acting counter to it – (BA and A) – would necessarily be ranked as worse still. Thus, these complex elements can be ranked (AB and A) preferred to (BA and B) preferred to (BA and A). For more on this, see George (2001: 79–89).

10　Sen uses "menu dependence" to describe situations in which one's preferences depend on what is available. Jon Elster (1983) separates such dependence into two categories. "Sour grapes" refers to those situations in which the removal of the preferred item from the choice set causes one to no longer prefer it, while "grass is greener" describes those situations when the removal of an unpreferred item causes one to suddenly prefer it. The language chosen by Elster is certainly colorful but has the unfortunate effect of trivializing such reactions. As a strategy for preference change, removal of, say, cigarettes from the choice set should not imply that the changed preference is somehow illegitimate. Within the more explicitly behavioral economics literature, the expression used to describe preferences that change as options change is "adaptive preferences." For a review of this literature, see Teschl and Comim (2005).

11　A similar bias appears in the title of Timur Kuran's otherwise excellent book, Private Truths, Public Lies (1995). Beginning with the observation that what one says about a matter in public often differs from what one might say about the matter if no one were present, Kuran goes on to give legitimacy and moral authority to the latter, private utterance. Speaking for myself, reflection indicates that while my public utterances are indeed often context dependent I usually identify more with them than with certain thoughtless private utterances that I might make in the absence of a social context. Such private utterances might have a greater spontaneity but can often be less civil, as one who has ever experienced blind refereeing or been a blind referee can usually attest.

12 To permit an economical presentation in Figures 8.4 and 8.5, the "pref" appearing between the elements of the experienced preference ranking has been replaced by the ">" symbol.

References

Carter, I. (1996) "The Concept of Freedom in the Work of Amartya Sen," *Politeia*, 12(7): 7–29.

Cohen, G.A. (1993) "Equality of What? On Welfare, Goods, and Capabilities," in M.C. Nussbaum and A. Sen (eds.) *The Quality of Life*, Oxford: Oxford University Press, 9–29.

—— (1994) "Amartya Sen's Unequal World," *New Left Review*, 203: 117–29.

Comim, F. (2005) "Capabilities and Happiness: Potential Synergies," *Review of Social Economy*, 63: 161–76.

Cowen, T. (1991) "Self-Constraint versus Self-Liberation," *Ethics*, 101: 360–73.

—— (1993) "The Scope and Limits of Preference Sovereignty," *Economics and Philosophy*, 9: 253–69.

Elster, J. (1979) *Ulysses and the Sirens: Studies in Rationality and Irrationality*, Cambridge: Cambridge University Press.

—— (1983) *Sour Grapes: Studies in the Subversion of Rationality*, Cambridge: Cambridge University Press.

Frankfurt, H.G. (1971) "Freedom of the Will and the Concept of a Person," *Journal of Philosophy*, 68: 5–20.

Gasper, D. (2002) "Is Sen's Capability Approach an Adequate Basis for Considering Human Development?" *Review of Political Economy*, 14: 435–61.

—— (2005) "Subjective and Objective Well-Being in Relation to Economic Inputs: Puzzles and Responses," *Review of Social Economy*, 63: 177–206.

George, D. (1984) "Metapreferences: Reconsidering Contemporary Notions of Free Choice," *International Journal of Social Economics*, 11(3–4): 92–107.

—— (1993) "Does the Market Create Preferred Preferences?," *Review of Social Economy*, 51: 323–46.

—— (1998) "Coping Rationally with Unpreferred Preferences," *Eastern Economic Journal*, 24(2): 181–94.

—— (2001) *Preference Pollution: How Markets Create the Desires We Dislike*, Ann Arbor, MI: University of Michigan Press.

Kuran, T. (1995) *Private Truths, Public Lies: The Social Consequences of Preference Falsification*, Cambridge, MA: Harvard University Press.

Laibson, D. (1997) "Golden Eggs and Hyperbolic Discounting," *Quarterly Journal of Economics*, 112: 443–77.

Nussbaum, M.C. (2001) "Symposium on Amartya Sen's Philosophy 5: Adaptive Preferences and Women's Options," *Economics and Philosophy*, 17: 67–88.

Pettit, P. (2001) "Symposium on Amartya Sen's Philosophy, 1: Capability and Freedom: A Defence of Sen," *Economics and Philosophy*, 17: 1–20.

Schelling, T.C. (1978) "Ergonomics, or the Art of Self-Management," *American Economic Review: Papers and Proceedings*, 68(2): 290–94.

—— (1980) "The Intimate Contest for Self-Command," *Public Interest*, 60: 94–118.

Schwartz, B. (2004) *The Paradox of Choice: Why More Is Less*, New York: Harper-Collins Publishers, Inc.

Sen, A.K. (1974) "Choice, Orderings, and Morality," in S. Kroner (ed.) *Practical Reason*, Oxford: Blackwell, 54–67.

—— (1977) "Rational Fools: A Critique of the Behavioural Foundations of Economic Theory," *Philosophy and Public Affairs*, 6: 317–44.

—— (1985a) *Commodities and Capabilities,* New York: Elsevier Science Publishers.

—— (1985b) "Well-Being, Agency and Freedom: The Dewey Lectures 1984," *Journal of Philosophy*, 82:169–221.

—— (1987) *On Ethics & Economics,* Cambridge, MA: Basil Blackwell, Inc.

—— (1988) "Freedom of Choice: Concept and Content," *European Economic Review*, 32: 269–254.

—— (1993) "Capability and Well-Being," in M.C. Nussbaum and A. Sen (eds.) *The Quality of Life*, Oxford: Oxford University Press, 30–53.

—— (1999) *Development and Freedom,* Oxford: Oxford University Press.

—— (2002) *Rationality and Freedom,* Cambridge, MA: The Belknap Press of Harvard University Press.

Teschl, M. and Comim, F. (2005) "Adaptive Preferences and Capabilities: Some Preliminary Conceptual Explorations," *Review of Social Economy*, 63: 229–47.

Thaler, R.H. and Shefrin, N.M. (1981) "An Economic Theory of Self-Control," *Journal of Political Economy*, 89: 392–406.

.

9 Does *Homo economicus* have a will?

Mark D. White[1]

1 Introduction

Economics is often described as the science of choice, but the typical economic agent in fact has no choice – his decisions are made for him by his preferences and constraints. This may be sufficient for normative purposes, demonstrating how agents "should" make choices if they want to adhere to the economic conception of instrumental rationality and maximize their utility or degree of preference satisfaction. But it has little connection to how real persons make decisions, for we like to believe that, given all of the information at our disposal, we have true, free choice. We can make the "right" choice, or we can make the "wrong" one. We can let principles and commitments reign over our most intensely felt preferences, sometimes choosing to endure great sacrifice for our beliefs, or we can succumb to our basest temptations, even ones that our judgment clearly counsels against.

To support such free choice, some would say that each of us has a *will*, a distinct faculty of choice that operates between judgment and action, and can either follow the dictates of one's best judgment or not. In this chapter I will suggest a way to incorporate a meaningful conception of the will into the economic model of decision-making, relying on recent work by philosophers such as John Searle and R. Jay Wallace, who themselves question the standard models of choice in philosophy. I further develop a basic model that I introduced in several other papers that can help understand fallibility in choice, such as succumbing to temptation, as well as resisting it. I offer a description of how one's character or strength of will changes as temptations are confronted (successfully or not). I compare my approach to others offered in the literature, and I conclude with suggestions for future applications of my basic framework.

2 Agency and choice in economics and philosophy

The standard view of economic decision-making, embodied in the metaphorical figure of *Homo economicus*, is that agents choose options to maximize utility based on stable, given preferences within constraints usually provided by the market (prices and income). This model is applied most straightfor-wardly to consumer choice, in which a consumer divides his income between various goods and services at various prices, and rationally purchases the bundle of goods that provides him the highest level of "utility" (understood simply as an index of preference satisfaction) within the opportunity set defined by his income and the vector of market prices he faces.

Of course, the economic model of choice has been extended far beyond the simple example of consumer purchases. Formal preferences may be defined over any options, based on the consequences thereof, including char-itable giving, characteristics of a romantic partner, or the happiness (or misery, as it were) of a friend or family member. Understood as mere rank-ings, not necessarily based on any particular psychological foundation such as desire, preferences can include anything that can be ranked or is commen-surable with other options. Likewise, constraints may be extended to include other scarce resources (such as time, most obviously), and the budget constraint can be partially endogenized by modeling income as a function of human capital formation and effort (though perhaps ultimately based on inherent talents, or just a bit of luck). Even ethical choices have been modeled in this framework: as John Broome (1992) writes, any system of personal ethics with a teleological component can be embodied in preferences. Duty-based systems of ethics can also be handled by including moral prohibitions and prescriptions among an agent's constraints and preferences (Sen 1977; Dowell *et al.* 1998; Minkler 1999; White 2004).

But even assuming this level of inclusiveness and generality in the content of his preferences and constraints, the typical economic agent is assumed always to choose the most preferred option available within his constraints. This is essentially the traditional view of action theory in philosophy, that desires (preferences) and beliefs (information) determine the decision made and the action taken. Among the most famous proponents of this view is Donald Davidson (1980), who wrote that desires and beliefs together completely determine and cause an action.[2] In a simple way, the desire/belief model seems eminently rational, and, indeed, if the agent's preferences are consistent (and fulfill other technical considerations, especially in cases of uncertainty), this process defines rationality as far as economists and most decision theorists are concerned.

This may be sufficient for a prescriptive model of rational choice, albeit one of a somewhat tautological nature: *if* persons are concerned solely with satisfying their given preferences, *then* they should choose the most preferred option available. But does it suffice as a positive description of choice? Do agents always and everywhere, reliably and without fail, choose the most preferred option available? Of course, there are many critics of simple rational choice models that would say no, based on theories of bounded rationality (Simon 1955) and cognitive biases (Kahneman and Tversky 1979). While acknowledging their validity and importance, I am neither making nor disputing those arguments here; indeed, everything I will say here is compatible with such ideas, though I set them aside for the purposes of this discussion.

I am not questioning whether individuals consistently come to the best decisions given their ability to acquire and process information, but whether or not they always follow through on that decision when the time comes to act on it. The essential problem on which I focus is that economic models make no distinction between decision (or judgment) and action. (In fact, neither do most philosophers in the field of action theory, as we will see.) Once an agent comes to her decision based on her best judgment, of course she acts on it – why wouldn't she? The action is seen as little more than an afterthought, the physical manifestation of her choice, the acting out of a formed intention. This is one reason that most economists and philosophers have had so much trouble explaining cases of weakness of will or *akrasia*, in which a person acts against his best judgment. In the traditional view of choice, this is paradoxical: if the agent decides that doing A is the best option available, why would he then choose to do something other than A? It seems nonsensical, and in this simplistic view of choice it certainly is.[3]

Economists have had little to say about this; as psychiatrist George Ainslie has written, "the straightforward simplicity of utility theory seems to have put it out of business as an explanation for irrational behavior" (Ainslie 2001: 17), which would include making choices against one's better judgment. Social economist Mark Lutz laments the fact that "economic choice takes the real choice out of economics" (Lutz 1999: 155), and quotes G.L.S. Shackle to the same effect: "conventional economics is not about choice, but about acting according to necessity" (Shackle 1961: 272).

There has been more criticism from philosophers, albeit aimed at traditional action theory in general (rather than economic models of choice). John Searle criticizes what he calls the "Classical Model" in his book *Rationality in Action*, writing that "it represents human rationality as a more complex version of ape rationality" (Searle 2001: 5). R. Jay Wallace refers to the standard model of choice in action theory as the "hydraulic conception," which "pictures desires as vectors of force to which persons are subject, where the force of such desires in turn determines causally the actions the persons perform" (Wallace 1999a: 432). Wallace links this conception with psychological determinism, which "leaves no room for genuine deliberative agency. Action is traced to the operation of forces within us, with respect to which we as agents are ultimately passive, and in a picture of this kind *real agency seems to drop out of view*" (Wallace 1999a: 434, emphasis added). J. David Velleman also maintains that "the [standard] story fails to include an agent," and that in this story "reasons cause an intention, and an intention causes bodily movements, but nobody – that is, no person – *does* anything" (Velleman 1992: 461, emphasis in original). He adds:

> what makes us agents rather than mere subjects of behavior – in our conception of ourselves, at least, if not in reality – is our perceived

capacity to interpose ourselves into the course of events in such a way that the behavioural outcome is traceable directly to us.

(Velleman 1992: 465–66)[4]

To look at it in a slightly different way, what has been missing (in both philosophy and economics) is the realization that deciding to do something (based on one's judgment) and actually doing it are two different things, and the connection between them is not trivial, not direct, and not easily modeled. Economist Timothy Brennan asks in what sense choices are *ever* voluntary in the economic model of choice: "the problem is . . . that it presupposes the possibility of a dichotomy between what a person does and what they want to do" (Brennan 1990: 114). John Searle writes of "gaps" in the decision-making process, one in particular between judgment and action, and in this gap lies the seat of agency, true free choice, in which the agent decides whether or not to act on her best judgment:

We presuppose that there is a gap between the "causes" of the action in the form of beliefs and desires and the "effect" in the form of an action. This gap has a traditional name. It is called "the freedom of the will."

(Searle 2001: 13)

Despite the tenets of traditional action theory, Searle holds that actions do not result directly and deterministically from antecedent causes such as desires (or preferences) and beliefs. These undoubtedly have an effect, of course, and in many cases (even most cases) the eventual action taken can be linked to those causes, giving the impression that they truly determined the actions. But often agents do not follow their best judgment or decision based on these desires and beliefs, when for some reason they act differently: your "decision is not causally sufficient to produce the action. There comes the point, after you have made up your mind, when you actually have to do it. And once again, you cannot let the decision cause the action" without an act of true choice (Searle 2001: 14).

This choice occurs in the gap mentioned previously, and the operation of the will within this gap is inexplicable, for this is where free choice occurs.[5] Searle also holds that this gap is a necessary condition for true rationality. Actions taken as a direct result of antecedent causes are no more sophisticated than actions taken by animals or computers (hence the "ape rationality" comment); it is humans' ability to choose to act on our beliefs and desires – or not to – that defines our rationality, much differently from the standard definition of strictly following one's judgment based on desires and beliefs.[6]

3 Introducing the will

Criticisms such as these lead some to postulate a distinct faculty of will, the true seat of choice which operates separately from, and possibly contrary to, one's judgment based on desires and beliefs.[7] Discussion of the will as a distinct faculty has been rare in recent action theory and philosophy in general, most scholars following the position of Gilbert Ryle, who declared the notion of a separate will "an inevitable extension of the myth of the ghost in the machine," his characterization of the more general idea of Cartesian dualism (Ryle 1949: 63), and Donald Davidson, who wrote of "mysterious acts of the will" (Davidson 1980: 83). More recently, economist/ philosopher Don Ross discusses the implications of cognitive science for the idea of an autonomous will, concluding that "the very idea of a will as a specific causal engine is not a very helpful idea" (Ross 2005: 257). And, of course, the term "will" is often used in different senses; for instance, Harry Frankfurt discusses will in his famous work "Freedom of the Will and the Concept of a Person" (1971), but in the context of being able to follow one's higher-order preference, not a faculty of choice once those preferences are recognized.[8] George Ainslie, well known to economists for his exposition of hyperbolic discounting and the consequent development of picoeconomics (Ainslie 1992), questions the existence of a separate faculty named the will (as does Ross), and instead uses the term to summarize his theory of choice arising out of intrapersonal bargaining between subsequent "selves" to overcome the temporary preferences resulting from hyperbolic discounting: "I argue that this intertemporal bargaining situation *is* your will" (Ainslie 2001: 104, emphasis in original).

Understandably, perhaps, the will has received much less attention in the economics literature, being rarely mentioned even in the relatively sizable literature on self-control.[9] Besides the works by Lutz and Brennan already mentioned, a paper by Robert Cooter (1991), subtitled "Towards an Economic Theory of the Will," seems to be the most explicit discussion of the will in economics (specifically, law and economics). Cooter's model bears some superficial likeness to the one presented below, particularly in his use of a probability distribution (over risk aversion), but ultimately it still models choice in a deterministic fashion.

But in recent decades there has been a renewed discussion of the will as a "psychological phenomenal something whose existence philosophers have in recent years tended to deny" (O'Shaughnessy 1980: 30). R. Jay Wallace is a strong proponent of this view, naming his theory the "volitionist conception of rational agency":

> On the volitionist conception, there is an important class of motivational states that are directly subject to our immediate control. Familiar examples from this class of motivations are such phenomena as decision and choice. Ordinarily we think of decisions and choices not merely as states to which we happen to be subject. Rather they are states for which we are ourselves directly responsible, primitive examples of the phenomenon of agency itself. It is most often in our power to determine what we are going to do, by deciding one way or another. Furthermore, when we exercise our power of self-determination by actually making a

decision, the result is something we have done, not something that merely happens to us.

(Wallace 1999b: 236–37)

Elsewhere, Wallace writes that "rational agents are equipped with a capacity for active self-determination that goes beyond the mere susceptibility to desires and beliefs" (Wallace 2001: 2). Richard Holton holds that "the agent's decision is determined not just by the relative strength of the conative inputs, the desires and the intentions. Rather, there is a separate faculty of will-power which plays an independent contributory role" (Holton 2003: 40), and which takes effort to exert, leading into a discussion of strength and weakness of will.

4   A model of choice incorporating the will

While mine is not to contribute to the philosophical debate on the will, I do take the position that there is a separate faculty of decision which can be called the will, distinct from the deliberative faculty of reason. The way I have chosen to incorporate the will into the economic choice model is to use a multiple utility framework, in which the single preference ranking or utility function normally assumed in choice models is replaced by a system of two or more such rankings.[10] Multiple utilities allow for qualitatively different or incommensurable motivations to be separated, either in parallel or hierarchically, in the decision-making process. A common application of this technique is to model ethically motivated behavior, so rankings based on self-interest and ethics can co-exist but operate separately.[11] While I have argued elsewhere (White 2006) against the use of multiple utilities to model ethical behavior, or any deterministic choices, they can be very useful to represent the nature and role of the will in a framework of true, free choice.

For the simplest case, we assume two qualitatively different rankings, representing two "paths" the agent can follow, or two "aspects" of his personality.[12] Examples of dual rankings include self-interest versus ethical concerns; John Stuart Mill's distinction between "high" and "low" pleasures; and short-term versus long-term goals. In each case, I will assume there is a "preferred" ranking, a set of options we would rather choose from if we had such a choice (sometimes known as a metapreference). Usually, we would rather behave altruistically or ethically, pursue "higher" pleasures, or focus on long-term goals (though the particular choice of preferred path is not important). But the opposite in each pair has its own unique pull as well: thinking only of yourself, indulging in "base" pleasures, or living for the moment (to the detriment of future plans). Because of this force, we do not always follow these "preferred" paths, and explicit inclusion of the concept of will in the economic choice model will help explain this.

I understand a person of stronger will or character to be one more likely to follow his preferred path. A stronger will does not guarantee this choice, however: even the strongest among us fails to do the "right" or "better" thing in every instance. This likelihood can be represented by a simple probability distribution, with probability p^H placed on following the "better" ranking and p^L (=1 - p^H) on following the "worse" one.[13] A stronger will would be associated with a higher p^H, and vice versa, reflecting the observation that, as strong as a person may be, she occasionally fails to pursue the better plan. (In other words, p^H never equals 1, though it can approach it.) Note that the decision-maker does not maximize utility over this probability distribution, as he would in standard cases of uncertainty about states of the world (such as a firm maximizing profit by setting a price when facing uncertain market demand). His particular choice situation confronts him after the draw from the probability distribution is made: with a probability of p^H he will make a decision along the higher or better path, and vice versa.

To the outside observer, the choice made by the agent appears to be a truly random event; however, it is not random, but, rather, merely inexplicable. Following Searle, true choice occurs in a gap in the rational process, after all deliberation has taken place and all reasons are weighed against each other, but before action is actually taken. The chosen action has no necessary psychological antecedents, which makes it essentially impossible to model as a rational process.[14] The likelihood that someone will make a certain decision is represented by our probability distribution, but this does not mean the choice is truly random, as held by those who attempt to model free will along the lines of quantum mechanics.[15] Consider a coin flip: we treat it as random, but the outcome can be predicted if all of the forces acting on the coin are perfectly known. In other words, the coin is not free, but is instead a passive non-agent reacting to the forces surrounding it, according to physical determinism. But free choice may not be completely explained or predicted even if an agent's desires and beliefs are known, which denies psychological determinism.[16]

Now we examine the probabilities themselves: what can affect them and how do they change over time? An example may be the best way to demonstrate the properties of the probability distribution. Let's suppose Bill has resolved not to eat donuts for health reasons though he craves them regularly. Let's say that Bill has a p^H of 75 per cent (and p^L of 25 per cent), implying that when tempted to eat donuts, he chooses not to three times out of four, but succumbs to temptation one time out of four. When faced by this temptation, he has a strong reason not to eat donuts (his health) and a weaker reason to eat them (immediate gratification). His best judgment is to abstain, and if his will were perfectly strong he would always follow the stronger reason and successfully abstain 100 per cent of the time. But his will is not perfectly strong, and he turns down the donuts only 75 per cent of the time.

As Ainslie and others would advise, in an attempt to reinforce his better judgment he may engage in a meta-strategy not to be in situations in which he would be tempted (such as being near a donut shop). Following such a strategy is no less a matter of will, thereby falling under the probability distribution: he successfully chooses to avoid donut shops 75 per cent of the time, but wanders into them the other 25 per cent, in which cases he buys donuts one quarter of the time. Such a self-restraining strategy would cut his incidence of donut-eating down to 25 per cent of 25 per cent, or 6.25 per cent. (This is where a behaviorist will misinterpret Bill's character; it is not that his p^H is 92.75 per cent, but that he takes measures to compensate for his true p^H of only 75 per cent.) An important point to be remembered is that taking such preventive measures is just as much an act of will as the choice at the time of immediate temptation, though, due to hyperbolic discounting, the degree of temptation may be much less at the earlier time. As Elster writes, "to take cold showers in order to develop the strength of will to stop smoking is not a very good strategy if stepping under the cold shower requires the very will-power it is supposed to develop" (Elster 1979: 44).

This example leads us to elaborate on this basic framework, stemming from the realization that people may have more resolve in some situations than others. One can easily imagine a person who would never think of embezzling money from his employer but may be tempted to have an extramarital affair with a co-worker (or the other way around). With regards to the law, in which respect for the law may be tied to character, some drivers would never run a red light, but exceed the speed limit with impunity.[17] For such situations, we would posit various probability distributions, one for each type of situation. In the example given earlier, Bill may have a stronger resolve to avoid donut shops altogether and very little resolve to resist once in one, making his strategic planning more important.[18] Nor must all decisions be binary in nature; a person may choose between staying sober, indulging in a beer (mild intoxicant), or imbibing hard liquor (heavy intoxicant). However descriptively accurate such a model may be, this formulation would sacrifice the resolve/temptation dichotomy that I believe is more intuitive. (This decision could easily be represented as choosing whether or not to drink, and then, if drinking is chosen, choosing what to drink, retaining binary choice in a sequential setting.)

5 Modeling character change

How might an agent's character-based probability distribution change? We can imagine that Bill's 75/25 per cent split holds for "normal" temptations, and as long as only normal temptations are faced (and he resists them 75 per cent of the time) his probability distribution will remain fairly constant. We would also expect him naturally to succumb more often when faced with relatively great temptations (a fresh batch of his favorite donuts left on his desk) and to resist relatively minor ones (a stale, half-eaten donut sitting on the top of the trash bin). But what if the opposite happens: Bill resists the fresh donuts on his desk, or raids the garbage can for the stale one? We can call these "extraordinary" temptations (in the literal sense of "unusual," not "large"), and some would say that extraordinary temptations are the true test of our character. Therefore, succumbing or resisting extraordinary temptations would imply a change in character, and this would be reflected in one's p^H and p^L.

If Bill succumbs to a relatively insignificant temptation, that indicates a lapse in character, or weakening of will, and his probability distribution would be revised to reflect this: his p^H would fall (and, by implication, his p^L would rise), perhaps to 70 per cent (and 30 per cent). This implies that after such a significant lapse he is more likely to give in to normal temptations in the future. But if he were to resist the unusually high temptation, that would mean his character has improved or his will has strengthened, and his new probability distribution would reflect that, with p^H rising, perhaps to 80 per cent, and p^L falling to 20 per cent. This corresponds to Holton's (2003) analogy of willpower to a muscle: the more it is exercised, the stronger it becomes, which in our model is reflected in the probabilities.[19]

How exactly would the probabilities change – linearly, proportionally, exponentially, or randomly? It seems plausible that if someone starts with high p^H, succumbing to the first extraordinary temptation she faces would not affect her probabilities much, and she may even return to her original probabilities after some time. But repeated lapses would be reflected in increasing declines in her p^H (and increases in her p^L). This can be captured by assuming that changes in p^H (or p^L) are inversely proportionate to p^H (or p^L) itself: when p^H is large, changes in it from succumbing will be small at first, but as p^H shrinks, the changes grow. Looking at it from the other direction, a person with high p^L who successfully resists an extraordinary temptation would not likely experience a large change in her probabilities. This conception is similar to regarding will as having a sort of inertia, so one's probabilities remain fairly constant until the person reverses character continuously for a period of time (a process similar to Bayesian updating).

But one can easily think that the process may also work the other way: think of a proudly resolute person, who suddenly succumbs to what would normally be a very small temptation. One could imagine that this transgression would have significant effects on her character, as it may imply that her strength of will was exaggerated.[20] Along the same lines, a person who is very weak-willed may, upon resisting a significant temptation, experience a significant improvement in her character, and see her probabilities change accordingly. Rather than displaying inertia, this conception seems to lead toward a equilibrium state between extreme strength and weakness of will, with people at each extreme of the character "spectrum" eventually heading toward the middle after succumbing to or resisting extraordinary temptations.

Does character or strength of will display inertia regardless of its strength, or does it tend toward a central equilibrium in most people? Perhaps each conception applies to some persons and not others, or to some situations and not others. This question remains open, but I think both ideas have attractive points.

Looking at the broader literature, this analysis of the change in probability distributions relates to similar attempts to model resistance to temptation and the dynamic effects on character of repeated resistance or submission. In one such model, George Ainslie characterizes the will as a recursive process of self-evaluation: "the will is created by the perception of impulse-related choices as precedents for similar choices in the future" (Ainslie 1992: 161).[21] This idea has come under criticism from scholars such as Michael Bratman (1996) and Robert Nozick (1993), who also link present and future actions, but in different ways. However, both scholars point out the need for a causal link or rational mechanism to connect present action with future ones. In response to Ainslie's grounding will on precedent, Bratman compares the situation to Newcomb's paradox and wonders why one's past decision should have any impact on one's future choices. He then suggests an answer in the form of his theory of intention as planning (in which an entire sequence of events is planned and committed to from the beginning). Responding to the same issue, Nozick offers symbolic utility as an answer (in which the current action assumes the utility of the correlated future actions).[22]

The model I have presented provides a third answer, wherein present choices affect future choices through their effect on one's will or character. What ties all of the previous theories together – Ainslie's strategic behavior, Nozick's principles, Bratman's plan-forming intentions – is that they all neglect the role of the will by trying to compensate for it. One way to look at these theories is that they make it easier for a will of given strength to stick to long-term, higher goals. But these strategies are only necessary for those lacking a strong will in the first place.[23] Similar to economic theories of self-control, they focus on changing the psychological determinants of actions instead of emphasizing the role of the will or character in decision-making. Elster recognizes but minimizes this possibility: "I would not deny that some degree of self-control can be achieved simply by pulling yourself up by the bootstraps, but ... more durable results are achieved by acting on the environment" (Elster 1979: 37). But if the actions taken on the environment are not themselves durable, their effect on one's choice is not likely to be durable either, while internal changes to one's character are more likely to last throughout changes in the external environment.

Wallace refers to Ainslie's self-control strategy specifically as the "cold shower paradigm," and he writes that "we achieve control by devising strategies to influence causally the motivational strength of the desires to which we are subject." However,

> to suppose that self-control must always conform to the cold shower paradigm turns us into passive bystanders at the scene of our own actions. We don't really determine which actions we perform directly, rather we attempt to manipulate the psychological influences to which

we are subject, in the hope that *they* will eventually bring it about that we do what we judge to be best.

(Wallace 1999a: 436)

Wallace points out the recursive problem with this idea, that the strategic manipulation must have been an act of the will, unless it *too* was a result of manipulation at a higher level, and so on. (It is at this point in his paper that Wallace introduces volition to solve this problem.)

6 Conclusion

In this chapter I discussed incorporating an explicit and meaningful conception of the will into a formal model of economic decision-making, inspired by the criticisms of traditional theories of choice and action offered by philosophers John Searle and R. Jay Wallace (with precedents reaching back to Immanuel Kant and Thomas Reid). In these alternative conceptions of choice, actions do not derive logically from an agent's desires and beliefs, but instead from her free choice, which operates in what Searle terms a "gap" in the typical process of rationality. This choice cannot be modeled, as it is an act of free will, and thus appears as random to the outside observer. Accordingly, I represent the likelihood of a given choice with a probability distribution representing character or strength of will, and discuss possible ways that this probability distribution can change over time. This chapter should be understood as merely an introduction, as many components of the model have yet to be worked out in detail, and there are many interesting applications yet to be analyzed.

One topic in particular to which this model may be usefully applied is the connection between addiction and rationality, the discussion of which can be traced primarily to the work of economists Gary Becker and Kevin Murphy (1988). This paper has spawned a significant literature elaborating on, and criticizing, the model and analysis therein.[24] Addiction has many aspects in common with weakness of will (Wallace 1999a; Elster 1999: ch. 5), and many of the same scholars who have written on weakness of will and rationality, such as Jon Elster and George Ainslie, have also written on addiction and rationality. The collection edited by Elster and Ole-Jørgen Skog (1999) is particularly useful, and in his contribution to it Ainslie writes that "conventional utility theory ... does not explain an addict's internal conflict, as evidenced in the extreme case by attempts to restrict his own future freedom of choice" (Ainslie 1999: 66).[25] The model of character change developed herein may help to explain this conflict, as well as some dynamic aspects of addiction, such as descent into and ascent out of addiction, and the relapses that are all too common for recovering addicts. It would also emphasize that just as becoming addicted may be a rational choice (according to Becker and Murphy), breaking out of an addiction is also a rational choice, but one that takes a strong will to accomplish.

Notes

1 For insightful comments and criticisms I thank George Ainslie, Chrisoula Andreou, Bob Chiles, John Davis, Dan Kramer, Barbara Montero, and Don Ross, as well as participants in both the International Network for Economic Method/Allied Social Science Associations meetings in January 2005 and the Philosophy Forum at the College of Staten Island in March 2005, at which early versions of this work were presented. All errors and omissions are my own, and the acknowledgements above should not be taken to imply agreement with anything written herein.

2 This general perspective on the nature of choice is sometimes traced back to David Hume, for whom, famously, reason was slave to the passions; see Searle (2001: 5). Roderick Chisholm traces it rather to Hobbes: "according to Hobbism, if we know, of some man, what his beliefs and desires happen to be and how strong they are . . . then we may deduce, logically, just what is it that we will do." He contrasts this view with the "Kantian approach" (with which Chisholm agrees), in which "there is no logical connection between wanting and doing, nor need there even be a causal connection" (Chisholm 1964: 34–35, emphasis in original). This of course refers to Kantian autonomy; see White (2006), which relates Kantian autonomy to the model elaborated upon later in this chapter, as well as note 4 below (regarding Kant and Thomas Reid).

3 See the introductory chapter in Stroud and Tappolet (2003) for a summary of research on weakness of will; and White (2006) for a discussion of weakness of will in the context of the model described later in this chapter.

4 This mode of thought has precedents, of course, such as the writings of Thomas Reid and Immanuel Kant (as mentioned in note 2), who both held that freedom of action is characterized by independence from external and internal influences. "By 'freedom' Kant means our ability to act in *complete* independence of any prior or concurrent causes other than our own will" (Sullivan 1989: 46, emphasis in original); and, referring to Reid, "if some action of ours is free then our decision or act of will to do that action cannot have been causally necessitated by any prior events, whether they be internal or external" (Rowe 1987: 157). For the original statements, see Kant (1993 [1785]) and Reid (1969 [1788]).

5 In their book on humanistic economics, Mark Lutz and Kenneth Lux agree with Searle that truly free choice "has no antecedents, no determining principles, and no maximization. We have no way of 'explaining' free choice precisely because it is free" (Lutz and Lux 1988: 117).

6 Searle writes of three gaps ("at least"), "the gap between the reasons for the decision and the decision, second the gap between the decision and the initiation of the action, and third there is a gap between starting the task and its continuation to completion" (Searle 2001: 14–15). I focus here primarily on the second gap, though some of my introductory comments refer to the first as well. (I thank Chrisoula Andreou for pointing this out.)

7 This discussion does not presuppose the existence of free will in the metaphysical sense. Agents' decisions may ultimately be consistent with physical determinism, but this occurs without their conscious knowledge. The agent has the distinct experience of making a choice, one that does not necessarily follow directly from her beliefs and desires, which renders it inconsistent with psychological determinism, though not necessarily with physical determinism (see Wallace 1999a: 238, n.31). Therefore, I do not discuss "agent causation," which in its strongest form holds that an agent is "a prime mover unmoved" (Chisholm 1964).

8 David George (2001: ch.2) recasts Frankfurt's framework in terms of preferences (before suggesting an alternative theory); see also Chapter 8 in this volume.

9 See, for instance, Schelling (1984a, 1984b) and Thaler and Shefrin (1981).
10 Sen (1977) is considered the seminal statement on multiple utilities in economics. An exchange within the journal *Economics and Philosophy* is particularly enlightening: see Etzioni (1986), Brennan (1989), Lutz (1993), and Brennan (1993).
11 See Margolis (1982) and Etzioni (1987, 1988), among others.
12 In this way the model resembles that of Steedman and Krause (1986), but the similarity ends here (see White 2006). This part of the model may also resemble Ainslie's conflicting interests, but unlike Ainslie I do not impute any agency to the aspects or paths.
13 The terms "better" and "worse," or "higher" and "lower," are used for convenience only, and do not imply any normative judgment of someone's chosen path or action. (I thank Dan Kramer for pointing out this likely inference.)
14 As mentioned before, this does not rule out physiological or neurological explanations, just psychological ones.
15 See Searle (2004: 230–34) for a discussion and refutation of the quantum mechanics argument for free will.
16 Another analogy may be drawn to game theorists' concept of trembles, "unpredictable lapses of reason, accidental mistakes, [or] tiny errors of judgment" (Hargreaves Heap and Varoufakis 2004: 81). Usually, such trembles are assumed to occur with infinitesimal probability, and are used to refine Nash equilibria, but the idea of unpredictability parallels the discussion here. (I thank Don Ross for suggesting this analogy.)
17 See White (2005) for further discussion of this model with respect to criminal behavior, respect for the law, and the economics of crime.
18 It is difficult to imagine the opposite, having more resolve at the donut shop than before, given the phenomenon of hyperbolic discounting.
19 There is also evidence (cited and discussed in Holton 2003) that exertion of willpower to achieve self-control in one area will lessen it in another, implying an opportunity cost from extraordinary willing (in contrast to the advantage of enhanced willpower in the future, at least in that area).
20 This way of looking at character change suggests deviation of self-perception from true character: an agent may think herself stronger or weaker than she actually is. I leave this possibility for later work (but see note 22 for more on self-perception).
21 Ainslie proceeds to represent willpower as intrapersonal bargaining between present and future selves, but the model described herein requires no such elaborate technique. See Bratman (1996: 47–50) for a critique of this modeling strategy, and Chapter 2 in this volume for further commentary.
22 Another question posed by both Bratman and Nozick is: does present choice affect future choices, or just our perception of our own character (which may itself affect future choices)? I think Nozick's discussion of principles affecting the probability of repeated action as well as one's estimate of that probability is close to my model, though, again, more work remains in exploring any connection.
23 At a recent conference, Roger McCain spoke of how his father, when quitting smoking, would always keep a pack of cigarettes in his pocket to ensure that he really had quit, and had not simply "strategized" his way (temporarily) out of the habit by keeping cigarettes out of his grasp. (I thank Roger for permission to repeat this account.)
24 In particular, Skog (1999) provides a very helpful simplification and explanation of the Becker–Murphy model, as well as insightful criticisms.
25 See also Chapter 8 in the present volume regarding limiting one's future freedoms.

References

Ainslie, G. (1992) *Picoeconomics: The Strategic Interaction of Successive Motivational States within the Person*, Cambridge: Cambridge University Press.
—— (1999) "The Dangers of Willpower," in J. Elster and O.-J. Skog (eds.) *Getting Hooked: Rationality and Addiction*, Cambridge: Cambridge University Press, 65–92.
—— (2001) *Breakdown of Will*, Cambridge: Cambridge University Press.
Becker, G. and Murphy, K. (1988) "A Theory of Rational Addiction," *Journal of Political Economy*, 96: 675–700.
Bratman, M. (1996) "Planning and Temptation," reprinted in (1999) *Faces of Intention: Selected Essays on Intention and Agency*, Cambridge: Cambridge University Press, 35–57.
Brennan, T.J. (1989) "A Methodological Assessment of Multiple Utility Frameworks," *Economics and Philosophy*, 5: 189–208.
—— (1990) "Voluntary Exchange and Economic Claims," in W.J. Samuels (ed.) *Research in the History of Economic Thought and Methodology*, vol. 7, Greenwich, CT: JSI Press, Inc., 105–24.
—— (1993) "The Futility of Multiple Utility," *Economics and Philosophy*, 9: 155–64.
Broome, J. (1992) "Deontology and Economics," *Economics and Philosophy*, 8: 269–82.
Chisholm, R.M. (1964) "Human Freedom and the Self," reprinted in G. Watson (ed.) (2003) *Free Will*, 2nd edn., Oxford: Oxford University Press, 26–37.
Cooter, R.D. (1991) "Lapses, Conflict, and Akrasia in Torts and Crimes: Towards an Economic Theory of the Will," *International Review of Law and Economics*, 11: 149–64.
Davidson, D. (1980) *Essays on Actions and Events*, Oxford: Oxford University Press.
Dowell, R.S., Goldfarb, R.S., and Griffith, W.B. (1998) "Economic Man as a Moral Individual," *Economic Inquiry*, 36: 645–53.
Elster, J. (1979) *Ulysses and the Sirens: Studies in Rationality and Irrationality*, Cambridge: Cambridge University Press.
—— (1999) *Strong Feelings: Emotion, Addiction, and Human Behavior*, Cambridge, MA: MIT Press.
Elster, J. and Skog, O.-J. (eds.) (1999) *Getting Hooked: Rationality and Addiction*, Cambridge: Cambridge University Press.
Etzioni, A. (1986) "The Case for a Multiple Utility Conception," *Economics and Philosophy*, 2: 159–83.
—— (1987) "Toward a Kantian Socio-Economics," reprinted in C.K. Wilber (ed.) (1998) *Economics, Ethics, and Public Policy*, Lanham, MD: Rowman & Littlefield, 139–49.
—— (1988) *The Moral Dimension: Toward a New Economics*, New York: The Free Press.
Frankfurt, H.G. (1971) "Freedom of the Will and the Concept of a Person," *Journal of Philosophy*, 68: 5–20.
George, D. (2001) *Preference Pollution: How Markets Create the Desires We Dislike*, Ann Arbor, MI: University of Michigan Press.
Hargreaves Heap, S.P. and Varoufakis, Y. (2004) *Game Theory: A Critical Text*, 2nd edn, London: Routledge.
Holton, R. (2003) "How Is Strength of Will Possible?," in S. Stroud and C. Tappolet (eds.) *Weakness of Will and Practical Irrationality*, Oxford: Oxford University Press, 39–67.
Kahneman, D. and Tversky, A. (1979) "Prospect Theory: An Analysis of Decision under Risk," *Econometrica*, 47: 263–91.
Kant, I. (1993 [1785]) *Grounding for the Metaphysics of Morals*, trans. J.W. Ellington, Indianapolis: Hackett Publishing Co., Inc.

Lutz, M.A. (1993) "The Utility of Multiple Utility: A Comment on Brennan," *Economics and Philosophy*, 9: 145–54.

—— (1999) *Economics for the Common Good: Two Centuries of Social Economic Thought in the Humanistic Tradition*, London: Routledge.

Lutz, M.A. and Lux, K. (1988) *Humanistic Economics: The New Challenge*, New York: The Bootstrap Press.

Margolis, H. (1982) *Selfishness, Altruism, and Rationality*, Cambridge, MA: Harvard University Press.

Minkler, L. (1999) "The Problem with Utility: Toward a Non-Consequentialist/ Utility Theory Synthesis," *Review of Social Economy*, 57: 4–24.

Nozick, R. (1993) *The Nature of Rationality*, Princeton, NJ: Princeton University Press.

O'Shaughnessy, B. (1980) *The Will: A Dual Aspect Theory*, vol. 1, Cambridge: Cambridge University Press.

Reid, T. (1969 [1788]) *Essays on the Active Powers of Man*, Cambridge, MA: MIT Press.

Ross, D. (2005) *Economic Theory and Cognitive Science: Microexplanation*, Cambridge, MA: MIT Press.

Rowe, W.L. (1987) "Two Concepts of Freedom," reprinted in T. O'Connor (ed.) (1995) *Agents, Causes, and Events*, Oxford: Oxford University Press, 151–71.

Ryle, G. (1949) *The Concept of Mind*, Chicago: University of Chicago Press.

Schelling, T.C. (1984a) *Choice and Consequence*, Cambridge, MA: Harvard University Press.

—— (1984b) "Self-Command in Practice, in Policy, and in a Theory of Rational Choice," *American Economic Review Papers and Proceedings*, 74(2): 1–11.

Searle, J. (2001) *Rationality in Action*, Cambridge, MA: MIT Press.

—— (2004) *Mind: A Brief Introduction*, Oxford: Oxford University Press.

Sen, A.K. (1977) "Rational Fools: A Critique of the Behavioural Foundations of Economic Theory," *Philosophy and Public Affairs*, 6: 317–44.

Shackle, G.L.S. (1961) *Decision Order and Time in Human Affairs*, Cambridge: Cambridge University Press.

Simon, H.A. (1955) "A Behavioral Model of Rational Choice," *Quarterly Journal of Economics*, 69: 99–118.

Skog, O.-J. (1999) "Rationality, Irrationality, and Addiction – Notes on Becker's and Murphy's Theory of Addiction," in J. Elster and O.-J. Skog (eds.) *Getting Hooked: Rationality and Addiction*, Cambridge: Cambridge University Press, 173–207.

Steedman, I. and Krause, U. (1986) "Goethe's *Faust*, Arrow's Possibility Theorem and the Individual Decision-Taker," in J. Elster (ed,) *The Multiple Self*, Cambridge: Cambridge University Press, 197–231.

Stroud, S. and Tappolet, C. (eds.) (2003) *Weakness of Will and Practical Irrationality*, Oxford: Oxford University Press.

Sullivan, R.J. (1989) *Immanuel Kant's Moral Theory*, Cambridge: Cambridge University Press.

Thaler, R. and Shefrin, M. (1981) "An Economic Theory of Self-Control," *Journal of Political Economy*, 89: 392–406.

Velleman, J.D. (1992) "What Happens When Someone Acts?," *Mind*, 101: 461–81.

Wallace, R.J. (1999a) "Addiction as Defect of the Will: Some Philosophical Reflections," reprinted in G. Watson (ed.) (2003) *Free Will*, 2nd edn., Oxford: Oxford University Press, 424–52.

—— (1999b) "Three Conceptions of Rational Agency," *Ethical Theory and Moral Practice*, 2: 217–42.

—— (2001) "Normativity, Commitment, and Instrumental Reason," *Philosopher's Imprint*, 1(3) (http://www.philosophersimprint.org/001003).

White, M.D. (2004) "Can *Homo Economicus* Follow Kant's Categorical Imperative?," *Journal of Socio-Economics*, 33: 89–106.

—— (2005) "A Social Economics of Crime (Based on Kantian Ethics)," in M. Oppenheimer and N. Mercuro (eds.) *Law & Economics: Alternative Economic Approaches to Legal and Regulatory Issues*, Armonk, NY: M.E. Sharpe, 351–73.

—— (2006) "Multiple Selves and Weakness of Will: A Kantian Perspective," *Review of Social Economy*, 64: 1–20.

10 Rationalizing coordination

Towards a strong conception of collective intentionality

Hans Bernhard Schmid[1]

1 Introduction

With very few exceptions, philosophy of mind has exclusively been concerned with *individual* intentions. Not all intentionality, however, is of the form *ego cogito*. There are intentional states of the form *nos cogitamus*, too. Among the most exciting recent developments in the philosophy of mind is the turn to a systematic analysis of the structure and role of *collective intentions and beliefs*. Philosophers such as Raimo Tuomela, Margaret Gilbert, John Searle, and Michael Bratman have put the analysis of shared intentionality on the map of philosophical thinking. Even though no consensus concerning the structure of collective intentionality has emerged as yet, this movement has substantially widened our view of the mind.

The aim of this chapter is twofold. First, an especially conspicuous example for the importance of this development to the social sciences in general and economic theory in particular shall be given, that is, the theory of *coordination* (Sections 2–4). Coordination problems differ from *cooperation* problems in that, intuitively speaking, rational participants aim at "matching" their individual choices among the available alternatives, so that there is no incentive for unilateral defection. Whereas the structure of cooperation (as exemplified by the prisoner's dilemma) has been at the very center of much thorough philosophical analysis – as well as of experimental work in economics – over the last half-century, the structure of *coordination* has not received nearly as much attention. One reason for this is that in most real-life cases coordination problems are easily solved by means of *conventions*. In line with some recent literature on the topic, I will claim that, because of its individualistic limitations, the standard economic model of human behavior fails to explain how conventions make coordination among rational agents possible.

In the second part of the chapter (Sections 5–7), it is argued that even though the existing accounts of collective intentionality point the way towards an adequate account of coordination, a stronger conception of collective intentionality than the ones to be found in the existing literature is needed. In a discussion of Robert Sugden's theory of team thinking, Michael

Bratman's account of shared cooperative activity, and John Searle's theory of collective intentionality, three features of an adequate account of collective intentionality are introduced. The chapter concludes by addressing an objection that is often raised against stronger conceptions of collective intentionality, that is, the problem of the group mind.

2 The trouble with deconditionalization

For all of its blatant absurdity, the following fictional story might serve as an introduction to the problem. On a sunny afternoon, the police are called to the site of an accident. A look at the scene immediately makes clear what has happened. On a winding street, a car has come into the oncoming traffic's way, resulting in a frontal collision. Luckily, no one is seriously hurt. The police question the culpable driver. Why did he come into the other driver's way? Did he lose control of his car, did he experience any technical difficulties prior to the accident, or was he inattentive or somehow distracted? The driver answers no: he had become aware of the oncoming car early enough, he was in full control of his car at all times, and he knows the traffic rules that were in no way violated by the other driver. He has no suicidal or otherwise destructive impulses or desires, nor any reason to assume the other driver had such preferences. So why did he end up on the wrong side of the street? He answers with a stern expression on his face: "I just couldn't see why I should keep to my own side of the street rather than swerve to the other's in order to avoid a collision."

For a moment, the police officer in charge loses his straight face in disbelief, and a disparaging remark concerning the driver's state of mind slips from his mouth. Now it is our driver's turn to lose his calm. Angrily and firmly, he asserts that he knows perfectly well that he is the guilty party in terms of the law, and he will accept all charges in terms of legal accountability, but he rejects any accusations of irrationality. He explains that, in hindsight, he knows very well that he would have better chosen to stay on the right side of the street. But that does not mean, he claims, that his decision to swerve to the other side was *irrational* at the time it was made. For when the oncoming car approached, he had to decide between the two strategies "right" and "left." As opposed to right, left is illegal and therefore is connected with the risk of getting fined by the police. At the same time, however, it would be plainly irrational *not* to commit a minor traffic violation such as choosing "left" if it is the only way to avoid an accident.

"Thus I knew," our driver concludes, "that if the other driver had decided to swerve to the left, it would have been rational for me to swerve to the left, too. And since all of this is common knowledge, and since the other driver is a rational being too, I assumed that he must be having the same thoughts, thinking that I have them too, and so on and so forth. It dawned on me that, however deep my (and his) analysis of the situation would dig, the *rational* thing to do in our respective shoes would always remain *hypothetical*. In such situations, you can say what's rational only *if* you have some expectation concerning the other's decision. But, at the same time, you know that the other's decision in turn depends on his expectation concerning your own choice. Thus, in my reasoning I got stuck in a circle of 'ifs,' and when we finally reached the point where each of us had to make his final decision over our strategies, I saw there was no way to derive from all that what was *in fact* rational for the other driver and for me to do. You can't say the other driver's choosing right was rational and my choosing left irrational. For, as it turned out, his decision to stick to the rules turned out to be wrong, too, since he could easily have avoided getting stuck in this car accident by swerving to the left!"

Of course there is something wrong with this claim. This whole way of reasoning is profoundly mistaken. From a commonsensical understanding of rationality at least, we should take the police officer's side for once and admit that he is probably right when he doubts our driver's rationality. To the pre-theoretical eye, it is obvious that it is *plainly irrational* not to keep to the right where the right-side rule applies, if one assumes that the rules as well as the absence of suicidal preferences are common knowledge. But is this strong (and presumably reasonable) pre-theoretical intuition backed by our standard theory of rationality in action, such as is implied in the economic model of behavior? Can our driver be proven wrong within the theoretical framework of individual expected utility maximization?

Our driver is, of course, well aware that there are not only two coordination equilibria in the game at hand (right/right and left/left), but also a convention. In David Lewis's (1969) terms, right/right is salient or, in Thomas Schelling's (1960) terms, a focal point, which makes, in a sense, right the obvious choice for each. Our driver does not ignore the existence of the right-side traffic rule, or deny that this rule is common knowledge among the participants. Also, he might easily grant that it is clear from previous experience that the probability of the strategy "right" being chosen by the drivers in a given population is extremely high. What he is getting at is that mere objective behavioral regularities and the existence of precedents do not provide a reason for a rational choice. Our driver's point is that he could not form any prior expectation concerning the other's behavior because he knew that as a rational being the other driver would have to base his decision on his expectation concerning our driver's behavior, and not just blindly follow some behavioral pattern. And indeed it's hard to see why it should be rational not to treat the other as a rational being, but as some sort of compulsive salience seeker (we will come back to this later). If, however, the other party is treated as a rational being, it is clear that it is rational for him to conform to the general pattern only if he expects that the same will hold true for our driver himself, which sets off the infinite regress of interdependent expectations.[2] In Raimo Tuomela's words, what our driver is getting at is the "deconditionalization problem" in the theory of coordination (Tuomela 2002: 388). "Deconditionalization" here means getting rid of the condition deriving from which "right" is the rational choice, that is, the big if: "right" is the rational choice if one has no reason to expect the other to choose "left." It seems impossible, however, to derive from the hypothetical (or "conditional") rationality of "right" that, given common knowledge of the right-side traffic rule and the absence of suicidal preferences, "right" is in fact the rational choice.[3]

Deconditionalization can be a real-life problem in situations where there are no conventions, and no salient solution or focal points (as in the case of two pedestrians colliding on the sidewalk because of a mismatch of the chosen strategies). Where there are commonly known conventions (such as in the case of motorized traffic), however, these problems do not empirically occur. It seems that in these latter examples deconditionalization is easily achieved. We do not experience serious difficulties in deciding whether or not to stick to the traffic rules in order to avoid a collision, where the rules and the absence of suicidal preferences are common knowledge. Our pre-theoretical intuition is that, in a very basic sense, this is simply a matter of *rationality* in terms of straight reasoning. One of the philosophical questions behind this is the following: How precisely do salience and the existence of conventions provide us with reasons? Why is it rational to choose the salient strategy in pure coordination games, when apparently the existence of conventions, focal points, or salient solutions do not *per se* solve the deconditionalization problem? Or, put negatively: what precisely is wrong about our driver's claim that, right-side traffic rule or not, any attempt to base a rational decision on salience is immediately drawn back into the infinite regress of interdependent expectations?

3 The principle of coordination

In his very influential paper on the topic, David Gauthier (1975) addressed this question. Going beyond Lewis and Schelling, his brilliant move was to draw attention to the role of the *description* under which the players perceive their available strategies.[4] For drivers who do not know any conventions, the alternatives at hand are simply "right" and "left."

The situation might look like Figure 10.1. For rational players ("rational" in terms of individual expected utility maximization), it is clear that,

	left	right
left	0/0	–1/–1
right	–1/–1	0/0

Figure 10.1 Pure coordination.

	choose salience	*ignore salience*
choose salience	0/0	−0.5/−0.5
ignore salience	−0.5/−0.5	−0.5/−0.5

Figure 10.2 Coordination, relabeled strategies.

according to the "principle of insufficient reason," they will choose randomly between the two strategies, which makes all four possible outcomes equally probable. If, however, "right" is salient, each player's choice is now a different one: it is between the alternatives "choose salience" (that is, choose right) and "ignore salience" (that is, choose randomly). This choice has a single coordination equilibrium, viz. both choose salience.

After the "relabeling" of the available strategies, the situation looks like Figure 10.2. By means of salience, a game with two equally good coordination equilibria is miraculously transformed into a game with only one best coordination equilibrium, which makes it rational to choose the according strategy, that is, to stay on one's own side of the street. All of a sudden, the deconditionalizing problem seems to disappear. However, this transformation is too good to be true, and our driver will have no hard time proving Gauthier wrong (cf. Provis 1977; Miller 1991; Gilbert 1989b; Goyal and Janssen 1996). For Gauthier simply ignored that in the transformed version of the game the choice is not between two, but between three strategies. The options open to the players are not just either to observe salience (that is, choose right) or to ignore salience (that is, choose randomly); the third option is to choose the non-salient (that is, choose "left").[5] In other words, in a derivative sense, the existence of salience makes the non-salient strategy salient (one might speak of secondary or derivative salience). This third strategy, however, has another equally good coordination equilibrium (both choose the non-salient), which throws us right back into the initial deconditionalizing problem. The "relabeled" situation is shown in Figure 10.3.

Another line of argument in Gauthier's paper goes as follows. The drivers could get by each other either by both choosing right or by both choosing

	observe salience	*ignore salience*	*choose the non-salient*
observe salience	0/0	−0.5/−0.5	−1/−1
ignore salience	−0.5/−0.5	−0.5/−0.5	−0.5/−0.5
choose the non-salient	−1/−1	−0.5/−0.5	0/0

Figure 10.3 Coordination, relabeled, complete set of strategies.

left. However, right/right is not only the *salient* solution. It is also *payoff dominant*, that is, better for both, for by choosing left both drivers run the risk of getting fined for violation of the traffic regulations even if they manage to get by each other collision free. (The risk of getting caught in the act is low, but it rises to certainty when a collision results, for then the police will be called in and the culpable driver will be fined.) Thus the two coordination equilibria in the initial game are not equally good after all, which means that right is *weakly dominant* for both.

Thus a more adequate description might reveal an asymmetry between the two coordination equilibria in the original situation, as shown in Figure 10.4. Compared to right/right, left/left is Pareto inferior. As Gauthier states in his famous "Principle of Coordination," this makes it rational to choose the superior strategy:

> In a situation with one and only one outcome which is . . . a best equilibrium, if each person takes every person to be rational and to share a common conception of the situation, it is rational for each person to perform that action which has the best equilibrium as one of its possible outcomes.
>
> (Gauthier 1975: 201)

However, it is not as obvious as it might first appear that the principle of coordination is a *rational* principle, and indeed it seems that what our driver is getting at is that it is not. In spite of the fact that left/left is Pareto inferior, it is still an equilibrium, that is, it is rational to choose left if one expects the other to choose left also. Thus it appears that, just as in the case with two equally good equilibria, both strategies are *hypothetically* rational. Or, in other words, it is rational for the single participants to adopt Gauthier's Principle of Coordination only if they expect it to be adopted by the other participant, too. Thus, once more, the participants see themselves confronted with the deconditionalizing problem. From the participants' perspective, the question "Why does rationality require *me* to follow this principle?" remains open (Hollis and Sugden 1993: 11).

This, however, did not slip Gauthier's notice. Against possible objections of this type, he argues that because of the coincidence of the individual

	right	left
right	0/0	–1/–2
left	–2/–1	–0.1/–0.1

Figure 10.4 Coordination, unequal equilibria.

payoffs in both equilibria the participating individuals can identify their respective individual choice over the two possible strategies (right and left) with a collective choice over the two equilibria. Since right/right is better for both than left/left, it seems clear that right is the rational individual choice. In a much similar vein, Maarten C. Janssen has argued that right is the rational choice since whoever so chooses chooses the "better plan" (Janssen 2001a, 2001b).

Will that finally convince our driver? There is reason for doubt. That left/left is Pareto-inferior as compared to right/right did by no means escape his notice. Thus he will grant that right/right is the better plan. What he points out, however, is the fact that when the oncoming car approached he had to make an *individual* decision, not a common decision. It had nothing to do with a decision over plans; it was a decision between strategies. In his view, this difference is a decisive one, for it is all that his reasoning was about: the strategic interdependence of decisions in the given situation. It is simply impossible to derive from the fact that right/right is the "best plan" in terms of the optimal outcome which would be rationally chosen in a *common* decision that right is the rational *individual* decision for either driver in the given situation. Whether or not there is a single best equilibrium, as long as there are multiple coordination equilibria the basic deconditionalizing problem remains the same.

For all that remains for a more detailed analysis of the problem at hand, it might have become apparent how stunningly little there is to say against our driver within the framework of the standard theory of rationality in action. If this should turn out to be true, it seems that what we have here is an open conflict between theory and common sense. If the foregoing is right, this tension is not just an *apparent* tension; there is something wrong either with our pre-theoretical intuition or with the theory.

4 The irrationalist position

So what is at fault here – common sense or the standard theory? This is by no means a rhetorical question. Not all philosophers who believe that the standard theory of rationality in action cannot be reconciled with the commonsensical intuition concerning the rationality of coordination hold that the theory is at fault. Quite to the contrary: some philosophers state that we should let go of our pre-theoretical intuition rather than revising the standard theory. Famously, Thomas Schelling seems to be vaguely pointing in this general direction when he states that success in pure coordination games "depend[s] on imagination more than on logic" (Schelling 1960: 57).

It appears, however, that once we start saying that focal points or salience do not provide a reason for a rational decision in pure coordination games, we end up having to grant our driver that he was right after all in saying that there was ultimately no *rational* decision in his particular situation. Such a concession not only ruffles the feathers of our common sense; it also gives rise to the question: how do we reliably manage to coordinate along the guidelines of the traffic rules if it is not outright *rational* to stick to those rules? Is this system of conventions on which we rely so much in our everyday dealings really built on mere *imagination*?

Those philosophers who take the *irrationalist* position in the current debate on the structure of coordination usually quote some non-rational impulse (for example, Thalos 1999), some psychological propensities, or "blind" behavior (cf. Gilbert 1989b). In this view, our driver was by no means *irrational* when he failed to choose right; he just happened not to act on the usual kind of impulse.

Is this irrationalist position right? I do not think that we have to go much deeper into the details to encounter some of the difficulties into which this line of argument seems to run. It is obvious that non-rational impulses (including habits, psychological propensities, or some such) are neither a *sufficient* nor a *necessary* condition for human coordinative behavior. Any student driver who knows the rules, and knows that the rules are common knowledge, will stick to them, even though she has not yet acquired any corresponding habits or extra-rational propensities and impulses. It is not the corresponding impulses that make it rational to choose the salient strategy; rather, it is because it is rational to choose the salient strategy that we acquire the corresponding impulses and habits. In other words, the irrationalist position puts the cart before the horse.

This becomes even clearer when we consider those (admittedly rare) cases where it is not by acting on impulses but by *suppressing* them that coordination is achieved. As any continental European or American who has ever made the experience of driving a car in Great Britain or Australia will confirm, it is possible to coordinate along the lines of the left-hand traffic rule in spite of persisting impulses to the contrary. In the case of the people coming from continental Europe driving off the car ferry in Dover, a great deal of impulse suppression is required. It seems plausible that this is only possible because under normal circumstances (that is, where common knowledge of those rules and the absence of suicidal preference can be assumed) people such as student drivers and foreigners find it perfectly *rational* to stick to the traffic regulations in order to avoid collisions.

Against this, an irrationalist philosopher of coordination might argue the following: the fact that under special and unusual circumstances such as learning to drive (or driving according to unfamiliar rules) coordination is achieved rationally without appropriate impulses (or even by suppressing them) does not disprove the fundamental role of impulses in coordination, because it is the *other drivers'* impulses to which it is rational to adapt one's own behavior. Thus it still seems to hold that any sound reasoning about what equilibrium to aim at in coordination games ultimately bottoms out in mere impulses. However, this defense of the irrationalist position does not stand up to closer scrutiny. It is not necessary either to act on impulses or to count on the other's appropriate impulses to achieve coordination. Coordination can even be achieved where both parties act against their impulses, and where this is common knowledge.

The following example may serve as an illustration. The island of Jersey, the largest of the Channel Islands, is popular with tourists, many of whom come over from the continent, since Jersey is only some fourteen miles off the French coast. There is public transportation on the island, but in order to avoid the crowd and to reach the most beautiful places many tourists either rent a car on the island, or have their own car brought over by ferry. There are many narrow roads with no separated lanes on Jersey; in order to avoid the branches sticking out of the hedges on both sides, most cars drive in the middle of the road, moving aside (often without reducing their considerable speed) only to let oncoming cars pass by. Because the states of Jersey are part of the United Kingdom, this is done by both swerving to their left. Drivers who come from the continent have to suppress their impulses in order to adapt to the left-side traffic rule. What flies directly in the face of the irrationalist position, however, is this: even drivers who are clearly recognizable to each other as coming from the continent by their number plates and by the location of the driver's seat in their cars coordinate without any difficulty by keeping to their left.

From an irrationalist viewpoint, this must appear like a small miracle. For, clearly, these drivers neither act on impulse nor rely on the impulses of the other drivers (since it is common knowledge between them that both drivers are from the continent). But if it is true that in this particular situation there are indeed no appropriate impulses, habits, psychological propensities and such, how then is coordination possible? The obvious answer is very simple: contrary to what the irrationalists say, common sense is correct. Given common knowledge of the rules and of the absence of suicidal preferences, sticking to the basic traffic rules is simply the *rational* thing to do.

It is true that, as experienced drivers in our everyday world, we do not *think* about whether or not we should stick to the rules; we just do it "blindly." This, however, does not mean that rationality is not involved here, or that it comes second to our habits and impulses. For if we let ourselves "blindly" be guided by the rules, we do this precisely because we think that this is the rational thing to do. And how could this belief be so pervasive if it is wrong?

5 Team thinking

If the foregoing is right – that is, if we can neither accommodate our pre-theoretic intuitions in our standard theory of rationality in action (Section 3), nor let go of our pre-theoretic convictions concerning the rationality of coordination (Section 4) – it seems that the correct position will be the only one that is left: to do something about the theory in order to make it fit our deeply engrained pre-theoretic conviction. If so little can be said against our driver from within the conceptual framework of our standard theoretic understanding of rationality in action, we will have to revise this framework. Obviously, there is something more to rationality in coordination than mere individual expected utility maximization in the sense discussed above.

There are several theories that point out the way to go. In their *General Theory of Equilibrium Selection in Games*, John Harsanyi and Robert Selten claim that the principle of coordination – their term is "payoff dominance" – cannot be derived from individual rationality, but implies an altogether different concept, a *collective* concept of rationality:

> Our theory uses two independent, and ostensibly very different, criteria of rationality. One of them, risk dominance, is based on *individual* rationality: it is an extension of Bayesian rationality from one-person decisions to n-person games involving strategic interaction among n players, each of them guided by Bayesian rationality. . . . In contrast, payoff dominance is based on *collective* rationality: it is based on the assumption that in the absence of special reasons to the contrary, rational players will choose an equilibrium point yielding all of them higher payoffs, rather than one yielding them lower payoffs. That is to say, it is based on the assumption that rational individuals will cooperate in pursuing their common interest if the conditions permit them to do so.
>
> (Harsanyi and Selten 1988: 365)[6]

Picking up on Harsanyi and Selten's insight, Robert Sugden has developed his theory of *team thinking* (Sugden 1993, 1996, 2000, 2003). Very roughly, the basic idea of Sugden's theory, as well as Michael Bacharach's (1998) somewhat related account seems to be the following. The problem with the standard theory is that it conceptually restricts the "units of agency" to single individuals. This leads to an inadequate account of those situations, where we do not reason and act as single isolated individuals, but as *members of teams* instead. "Team membership" is basically meant in the sense of participation in collective action. To understand the structure of team thinking, it is important to see the situation at hand as one of *shared intentionality*.

Here, the recent turn to collective intentionality comes into play. Whereas "classical" philosophy of mind focused exclusively on the analysis of *individual* intentionality, it has become increasingly clear over the last two decades that in order to account for the social dimension of human action and cognition, the analysis has to be extended to *shared* intentional states. Based on seminal contributions dating from the 1980s, the analysis of *collective intentionality* has gradually evolved into a distinct field of research. The most important theories of collective intentionality are those by Raimo Tuomela (1995; Tuomela and Miller 1988), Margaret Gilbert (1989a), John Searle (1995), and Michael Bratman (1999), all of which differ in fundamental ways. Tuomela's account rests on individuals' intentions to do their part, together with a structure of mutual belief. Searle criticizes Tuomela and claims that collective intentions are irreducible to sets of individual intentions. Searle's account rests on intentions of the form "we intend . . . " in the individual minds of the participants. Bratman, for his part, gives an account of collective intentions in terms of interrelations of individual intentions of the form "I intend that we . . . ." Gilbert again follows an altogether different line by making *collective commitments* the center of her account of collective intentions. These differences notwithstanding, the importance of collective intentionality analysis for our understanding of both the mind and the social world has been widely recognized in philosophy, as well as in many neighboring disciplines.

Can collective intentionality analysis indeed help to understand the rationality of coordination? With regard to the example of our drivers, this might seem rather unlikely at first. For obvious reasons, the paradigmatic cases of shared intention are cooperatively loaded cases such as Searle's (1990: 400ff.) example of the joint intention to cook a sauce hollandaise, Gilbert's (1990) example of the joint intention to go for a walk, or Tuomela's (1995: 137f.) example of a group of people joining forces to push a broken-down car. By comparison to such intensely communal endeavors, it might seem that there is nothing genuinely collective or social about our driver's intention to avoid bumping into another driver whom he does not even know by sticking to the right-side traffic rule.

The theory of team thinking, however, points out the hidden element of sharedness that is implicit in these cases. If "avoiding a collision" is seen as something the two drivers desire individually, the deconditionalizing problem appears to be insoluble. If we conceive of the participating individuals as acting on their individual desire to get by the other collision free, we immediately find ourselves caught up in the regress of interdependent expectations that our driver pointed out. This is not the case, however, for drivers who are seen as basically sharing the aim to get by each other collision free. Given the fact that what we together intend to do is to get by each other, what is rational for me is to perform my share of what maximizes our shared desire. Thus "right" is not rational because it immediately yields a better outcome (which it does only conditionally – if the other driver were to choose left, my choosing left would be in the best interest not only of myself, but of the team also). It is rational for me to choose right because it is my part in what we should be doing.[7] The fact that individuals can be team members has consequences for what it is rational for them to do. For "one of us," the decision to move left is plainly irrational. Thus the deconditionalizing problem is solved.

The theory of team thinking requires a theory of rationality, intentionality, and action that is richer than the one that is implicitly adopted in the standard economic model of behavior, because it allows for a sense in which *teams* can be said to have preferences (or even make choices) which are, in a certain sense, *irreducible* to simple individual preferences (or choices) (cf.

Sugden 2000). In this view, not all preferences, goals, desires, and other intentional states are individual goals and intentional states. In the case of the driver's coordination problem, there are not two separate individual goals not to collide; the participants act on a *shared* goal instead (cf. Schmid 2005a). Getting by each other collision free is not anything the single individual drivers want. It is something they want *together*. This desire is *irreducible* in the sense that it is not the case that the drivers share their desire (have a preference for right/right) because they have the appropriate individual desires (that is, an individual preference for right); rather, their individual "contributive" intentions or preferences are *derived* from the shared intention or preference.

Thus in this situation the drivers do not appear as distinct units of agency, but as members of a whole that in a sense appears to be capable of thinking and acting. To capture this trait of team thinking, Sugden invokes a rather strong concept of collectivity. It seems that there are not only individuals at the basic level of explanation of social phenomena, but also teams, to which, following Sugden, the participating individuals are members "in something like the old sense in which arms and legs are members of the body" (Sugden 1993: 86).

The idea of some irreducible sense of collectivity goes much against the individualistic grain of current social theory and social science. It might even appear that in the theory of team thinking some somber group mind raises its head. Indeed it seems that Sugden himself loses some of his anti-individualistic courage when getting sight of these possible ontological consequences of his theory. What could possibly save us from ending up in a collectivist group mind conception once we start loosening the individualistic restriction of the classical account? Sugden resorts to the following solution. In a rather harsh contrast to his strong concept of membership, he hastens to assert that the existence of the collective depends on the participating individuals thinking of themselves in terms of team members, which conforms to the classical, individualistic, Weber-style view of the social, in which collectivities are "real" only as parts of the contents of the intentional states of individuals.[8]

In a much similar vein, Michael Bacharach based his theory of *team reasoning* on some "group identification," in which individuals come to take themselves to be members of a team: "in certain circumstances, individuals tend to identify themselves with a group; and a group identification leads them to team-reason" (Bacharach 1998: 132). Besides these two important philosophers, there are other attempts to reconcile the acknowledgement of the role of some kind of "team reasoning" with an individualistic ontology of action. Thus Janssen puts forth an even weaker version of the role of collectivity in coordination, replacing "collective rationality" with what he calls "individual team member rationality." Again, the ontological line behind this is stoutly individualistic: "where there is enough information and knowledge about each other, players can consider themselves as a team and think individually what is best for the team and its members" (Janssen 2000: 13).

There are at least two reasons, however, to reject the view that team thinking (by any name mentioned above: collective rationality, team reasoning, or individual team member rationality) depends on some "taking oneself to be a member of the team" from the side of the individual members (or some reflective "group identification" or some such). First, this view seems rather absurd if we consider cases such as our driver. We obviously do not have to "take ourselves to be members of a team" to find it rational to stick to the traffic regulations in order to avoid accidents. If team thinking is at work in these cases (and I believe that it is), the element of collectivity involved here is obviously not a matter of some reflective attitude or belief about oneself, for it seems that, phenomenologically speaking, there are no such attitudes whatsoever involved here. Team thinking does not require that the participating individuals take themselves to be members of the team.[9] Reflective awareness of one's status as a team member is neither a sufficient nor a necessary condition of team thinking. It is not sufficient, because one can mistakenly identify oneself as a team member, and it is not necessary, because one can be a member of a team without reflectively identifying oneself as such. In this sense, team thinking is pre-reflective. This also means that if we do correctly think of ourselves as members of some team, this is because we are a team, and not the other way around, as Sugden and those subscribing to a similar view of the role of collectivity in coordination seem to believe.

The second reason is the following. Consider again the driver's coordination problem. From the viewpoint of the standard theories of team thinking, whether or not "right" is rational ultimately depends on *who one takes oneself to be*. If I take myself to be "one of us" ("the other driver and me") – that is, a member of a team – right is the rational choice, because right/right is what *we* intend to achieve, and my choosing right is my individual contribution to our shared goal. Whereas for somebody who exclusively optimizes her or his individual desires right is just as hypothetically rational as left. It all depends on one's identity in terms of one's reflective understanding of oneself. Identity, one could say, is a matter of self-categorization, and it is prior to rationality.

Thus these theories of team thinking seem to offer a kind of a compromise between our driver's way of reasoning on the one hand and common sense on the other, in that they hold on to the commonsensical view that it is rational to choose right, while at the same time some tacit assumption that is accepted throughout the debate is jettisoned. Why should it be necessary to be able to prove our driver wrong if one claims that right would have been the rational choice? Sugden, Bacharach, and Janssen seem to maintain the commonsensical claim to rationality without having to bear the burden of proof against our driver. "Right" is the rational choice – but from the perspective of a team member, not from the perspective of an isolated individual. What it is rational to do depends on who one takes oneself to be.[10]

As convincing as this relativizing move might seem with respect to the trouble with the rational fool of our initial example, there are some serious doubts left. Let us again take the pre-theoretical, commonsensical perspective. If in our everyday understanding we take "right" to be the rational choice, we take it to be the rational choice, full stop. We do not mean something like right is the rational choice "for people who take themselves to form a spontaneous team together with the oncoming drivers," or "for people who do not only individually prefer to avoid a collision, but team-prefer to get by the other." If we call our driver irrational given all he says about the circumstances of his decision, we do not mean something like "irrational as a team member, but rational from the perspective of an atomistic individual." Once again, we mean irrational, full stop. Thus it seems that if indeed team thinking is involved in coordinative behavior of this kind, and if we are right in holding on to the commonsensical view concerning the rationality of such behavior, a more robust conception of the collectivity of team thinking than the one put forth by Sugden is needed. No matter what our self-image might be, we simply are team members in these situations, and as such we share our intentions and goals. What makes our driver irrational is that he is not aware of who he is: he is not an isolated individual, but one of us.[11] The individualistic social ontology to which these theorists subscribe must be dropped.

This, however, is not easily done. For, as we shall see in the next section, it seems that dropping individualism about intentionality is tantamount to endorsing collectivism: the group mind raises its ugly head. Fear of the group mind is so pervasive in the current debate, and plays such an important role in the individualistic setting that most philosophers of collective intentionality endorse, that I think it is justified to spend the last section of this chapter trying to address these worries. This is not only to postpone the burdensome task of delineating a more adequate (that is, less individualistic) account to future explorations of the issue. Rather, it is in the light of these considerations that two further basic features of a more robust conception of collective intentionality are revealed. Collective intentionality is not just pre-reflective. It is also, as will be argued in the following section, both *irreducible* and *relational*.

6 Who's afraid of the group mind?

What seems unfortunate in the theories of team thinking is that the existence of the team is made a matter of its members taking themselves to be its members. However, it was only with the seemingly honorable aim of avoiding some collectivist conception of group mind that theories of team thinking resorted to basing the existence of the team on some reflective individual attitude in the first place. Thus the decisive question is: Does a stronger account of collective intentionality imply endorsing some collectivist macro-subject or group mind?

This is a question that is of great importance to the current larger debate on collective intentionality, in which the issue of the group mind is ubiquitous. Its prominent role in this debate seems to stem from a rather innocent-looking assumption. Where there is intentionality, it is said, there has to be somebody who "has" it – the subject. Now if it is claimed that there is such a thing as *collective* intentionality, and that collective intentionality has to be distinguished from *individual* intentionality, the conclusion seems to force itself on us that it has to be not the single individuals, but the collectives themselves that "have it." And for collectives to have intentions, some sort of a collective mind or group mind seems to be required, something hovering over and above the minds of the individuals involved.

This apparent implication of the very concept of collective intentionality does not look very appealing. Even though there is no consensus concerning the structure of collective intentionality, all philosophers of collective intentionality agree that there is no mind over and above the minds of individuals. While the general question of whether or not (and, if so, in what sense) collectives can act remains to some degree controversial, it seems obvious that it is unacceptable to treat collectives as "subjects" of intentions and actions in the ordinary sense in which individuals are the bearers of their intentional states. Even if the notion of the collective subject is stripped of its mentalistic content, it still does not quite appeal to us because it is vaguely associated with collectivistic (or even totalitarian) notions of the social. If the collective "has" intentionality, the individual seems to be no more than an organ – that is, merely an instrument – which flies in the face of our idea of individual intentional autarchy or autonomy (cf. Pettit 1996: 117ff.).

Thus it seems quite understandable that all philosophers of collective intentionality set themselves the task to show that collective intentionality is possible without there being a group mind involved. The specter of the group mind (or collective subject) has to be exorcised, and one can identify two different ways in which this is done. The softer way is the one chosen by Gilbert (1989a) and Tuomela (1995: 231). Some sort of collective subject is admitted to the theory (in Gilbert's case the "plural subject"), but it is domesticated so as to be consistent with an otherwise thoroughly individualistic conceptual framework. The collective subject is solidly founded in the intentional autonomy of individuals by reducing the collective subject either to sets of individual intentions (Tuomela 1995) or to the reflective self-understanding of the single participating individuals as members of the team (cf. Gilbert 1989a: ch. 4). The tougher way of dealing with the group mind is simply to treat it as an absurd collectivist idea that has to be banished from the theory of collective intentionality straightaway; Searle sometimes speaks of "a perfectly dreadful metaphysical excrescence" (Searle 1998: 150; cf. also Searle 1990: 406).[12]

On this "hard" line against the collective subject, the group mind is avoided in two different ways involving two different kinds of individualism, subjective and formal individualism, one of which is rejected while the other is endorsed. Searle makes a bold move beyond formal individualism by claiming that collective intentionality is *irreducible* to individual intentionality. Collective intentionality consists of intentions of the form "We intend . . . ." In order to avoid the group mind, however, he endorses subjective individualism by emphasizing that collective intentionality is exclusively *in the minds of individuals* and independent of anything external (Searle 1990: 406f.).

Interestingly, Bratman seems to make the opposite move. Going beyond *subjective* individualism, Bratman emphasizes the *relational* character of shared intentionality. As "interlocking webs" (Bratman 1999: 9) of the participant individuals' intentions, shared intentionality is structurally dependent on entities external to the individual mind of each single participant. At the same time, however, and in a certain tension with this bold interrelationalistic move beyond subjective individualism, Bratman banishes the group mind by stressing that his account is thoroughly "reductive in spirit" (Bratman 1999: 108) and endorsing formal individualism.[13]

Looking from afar at how the group mind is dealt with, it might appear that the theory of collective intentionality is caught in a dilemma, or, rather, stuck in some kind of double bind. On the one hand, the aim is to break with individualism in the sense of the orthodox concentration on purely individual intentionality. On the other hand, individualism (in the broad sense of an emphasis on the role of the individual) seems to be the only effective means against the group mind. And this is what causes the most difficulties in these two influential accounts of collective intentionality. Searle has been rightly criticized for his subjective individualism, while the focus of critique in the debate that followed Bratman's account is on his formal individualism (cf. Schmid 2003b for a detailed discussion).

I do not have the space to present the arguments here, but the upshot of this is that an adequate account of collective intentionality should not depart from *either* subjective *or* formal individualism. Rather, it should depart from *both* versions of individualism. Instead of arguing directly for a non-individualistic account of collective intentionality, let me turn to the most obvious objection any such account will have to face instead. If both formal and subjective individualism are left behind, what, then, about the group mind? How can a robust conception of collective intentionality avoid flying into the face of our intuitive notion of individual intentional autarchy?

I believe that the answer is rather simple. The whole trouble with the group mind arises from the attempt to assign collective intentionality to *one* individual source or bearer. It arises from the attempt to give some acceptable answer to the question: Who is it that *has* collective intentions? Who is it that *does* the team thinking? And this question, innocent as it might look, is heavily loaded with historical ballast that we should simply jettison and leave behind. Only in the last decades, we have successfully managed to get rid of Descartes's quest for absolute certainty in philosophy. However, the Cartesian preoccupation with the individual subject still persists. It is still a deeply rooted idea that where there is intentionality, there has to be *one* somebody who "has" it as its owner, source, or bearer – if not an individual human being, than some group mind. It is the fact that most philosophers of collective intentionality hold on to this assumption that gives rise to the fear that, by moving too far away from individualism, we are running the risk of getting stuck with the group mind.

Collective intentions, however, are not intentions of the kind anybody *has* for herself – not single individuals, and not some group mind. Rather, it is something individuals *share*. Indeed, there is all the less reason to resort to individualism in order to avoid the group mind as the latter is clearly itself an individualistic concept. The group mind arises from the conceptual compulsion to assign a single subject to collective intentions. Collective intentions, however, do not have a *single* subject. They have many. Thus the group mind is nothing we should be afraid of. It is merely a distorted individualistic image of a non-individualistic, holistic concept of the mind.

7 Conclusion

In this chapter, I have argued that collective intentionality permeates human interaction down to its very basic modes. It is our capacity for collective intentionality that deconditionalizes rational decision-making where coordination among agents is required. Where there is no incentive for unilateral defection, rational agents will think and act as a team. In order to account for this, however, it is necessary to depart from individualistic assumptions such as those implied in the standard economic standard model of behavior, and to widen the perspective to collective intentionality.

Second, I have argued that a stronger conception than the one to be found in the received literature is necessary in order to develop an adequate account of collective intentionality. I have introduced the following three features of a strong conception (though only the first feature is developed in some detail above):

1   Collective intentionality is *pre-reflective*. It is not a matter of some reflective attitude of the participating individual (that is, the individual's taking herself to be a member of a team), or "self-categorization."
2   Collective intentionality is *irreducible* to individual intentionality; that is, it does not consist in some set of intentions of the form "I intend . . . ." An adequate account is incompatible with *formal* individualism.
3   Collective intentionality is *relational*. An adequate account is incompatible with *subjective* individualism.

In the last section of the chapter, I have claimed that widespread fears that a more robust conception of collective intentionality will get stuck with the group mind are mistaken.

What are the consequences of collective intentionality analysis for economic theory? The widening of perspective implied in collective intentionality analysis directly affects the notion of the agent. This meets with other tendencies in "heterodox" economic theory. As John Davis has pointed out in his book on the theory of the individual in economics (Davis 2003: 130–49), collective intentionality analysis seems to mesh seamlessly with an increasing unease with the "atomistic" standard model of the agent. In this vein, collective intentionality analysis is particularly attractive because it opens a perspective on social identity and human embeddedness that does not hinge on adventitious stigmata such as birth and destiny. There is a tendency in the received literature to conceive of social identities as fixed entities. As Amartya Sen (2004) has convincingly argued, however, social identities are *made* rather than *discovered*; they are a matter of what we *do* rather than a matter of *what we are*. For all of the work that needs to be done in this relatively new field of research, collective intentionality analysis seems to be a promising candidate to be able to show how these identities come about.[14] If the argument developed in this chapter is right, it seems that some very rudimentary forms of "social identity" – that is, shared goals pursued by a team – are at play even in the most transient of our interactions, such as the one of two drivers successfully passing by each other on the highway.

Notes

1 This chapter was originally presented as a paper at the 12th International Congress of Logic, Methodology, and Philosophy of Science in Oviedo, Spain, on August 11, 2003. Parts of the argument developed here first appeared in Schmid (2003a), and some passages of Section 6 are taken from Schmid (2003b). I am very grateful to Barbara Montero and Mark D. White for sharp comments on earlier versions of this chapter.
2 For a very clear formulation of the problem, compare Parsons and Shils (1951: 105).
3 "An agent cannot rationally . . . form and satisfy his action intention without a circular reference to the other agent's intention. Hence, he cannot, so to speak, finitarily infer or compute the satisfaction value of statements like 'I will do X if you will do X' in the kind of coordination situation on the basis of independently assignable satisfaction values of 'I will do X' and 'you will do X,' because there simply are no such satisfaction values" (Tuomela 2002: 390).
4 For a more detailed account of Gauthier's approach, compare Sugden (1995).
5 Provis has a convincing explanation of why this obvious weakness of his transformation argument could have slipped Gauthier's notice: the existence of the third option "is obscured because Gauthier introduces his suggested alternatives as being choosing the salient option and ignoring salience. That phraseology diverts attention from the fact that one way of not ignoring salience on an option is by performing the non-salient option qua non-salient option" (Provis 1977: 509).

6 Raimo Tuomela seems to adopt a similar view on the deconditionalization problem. He says that deconditionalization is not a "fully 'r-rational'" procedure (Tuomela 2002: 395f.), where "r-rational" is something like individual instrumental rationality. However, he distinguishes r-rationality from a wider everyday sense of rationality, which seems to include the possibility of rational deconditionalization.

7 In Susan Hurley's (1989: 145ff.) view, "right" is rational not because of its causal consequences, but because of its constitutive consequences, that is, because our individual choosing right constitutes the action that is best for both of us. I am somewhat uncomfortable with Hurley's way of rationalizing coordination, because it seems obvious that it renders unanswerable the question "should I do what constitutes my part in what constitutes the best collective choice, or should I rather do my part in what constitutes the second-best collective choice." Obviously, it is rational to choose the latter alternative if one expects the other to choose that alternative too. In other words, Hurley's constitutive rationality does not solve the deconditionalizing problem.

8 "A team exists to the extent that its members take themselves to be members of it" (Sugden 2000: 192).

9 This is obscured in Sugden's account because of his preoccupation with more cooperatively loaded cases such as his footballer's coordination problem (Sugden 2000, 2003).

10 For a clear statement of this, compare Elizabeth Anderson's "Priority of Identity to Rational Principle": "what principle of choice it is rational to act on depends on a prior determination of personal identity, of who one is. The validity of the principle of expected utility (maximizing the satisfaction of one's personal preferences) is conditional on regarding oneself as an isolated individual, not a member of any collective agency" (Anderson 2001: 30).

11 As argued earlier, this does not mean that we have to be reflectively aware of our "true" nature as social beings in order to avoid collisions in everyday life. Indeed the fact that even individuals who take themselves to be atomistic homines oeconomici can successfully coordinate in real life shows how far our reflective self-image can depart from our pre-reflective way of reasoning.

12 For Bratman's view on the collective subject, see Bratman (1999: 111; 122f.).

13 Compare Bratman's conceptual analysis in Bratman (1999: 105).

14 For an interpretation of Sen's influential criticism of orthodox economic theory in terms of collective intentionality analysis, see Anderson (2001) and Schmid (2005a). For a discussion of the importance of collective intentionality analysis for experimental economics, compare Schmid (2005b).

References

Anderson, E. (2001) "Unstrapping the Straitjacket of 'Preference': A Comment on Amartya Sen's Contributions to Philosophy and Economics," *Economics and Philosophy*, 17: 21–38.

Bacharach, M. (1998) "Interactive Team-Reasoning: A Contribution to the Theory of Cooperation," *Research in Economics*, 58: 117–47.

Bratman, M.E. (1999) *Faces of Intention: Selected Essays on Intention and Agency*, Cambridge: Cambridge University Press.

Davis, J.B. (2003) *The Theory of the Individual in Economics*, London: Routledge.

Gauthier, D. (1975) "Coordination," *Dialogue*, 14: 195–221.

Gilbert, M. (1989a) *On Social Facts*, Princeton, NJ: Princeton University Press (1992 reprint).

—— (1989b) "Rationality and Salience," reprinted in *Living Together: Rationality, Sociality, and Obligation* (1996), Lanham, MD: Rowman and Littlefield, 23–37.

—— (1990) "Walking Together," reprinted in *Living Together: Rationality, Sociality, and Obligation* (1996), Lanham, MD: Rowman and Littlefield, 177-94.

Goyal, S. and Janssen, M.C. (1996) "Can We Rationally Learn to Coordinate?," *Theory and Decision*, 40: 29–40.

Harsanyi, J.C. and Selten, R. (1988) *A General Theory of Equilibrium Selection in Games*, Cambridge, MA: MIT Press.

Hollis, M. and Sugden, R. (1993) "Rationality in Action," *Mind*, 102: 1–35.

Hurley, S. (1989) *Natural Reasons: Personality and Polity*, Oxford: Oxford University Press.

Janssen, M.C.W. (2000) "Towards a Justification of the Principle of Coordination," *Tinbergen Institute Discussion Papers* Nr. 00–017/1.

—— (2001a) "On the Principle of Coordination," *Economics and Philosophy*, 17: 221–34.

—— (2001b) "Rationalizing Focal Points," *Theory and Decision*, 50: 119–48.

Lewis, D.K. (1969) *Convention. A Philosophical Study*, Oxford: Blackwell.

Miller, S. (1991) "Coordination, Salience, and Rationality," *Southern Journal of Philosophy*, 29: 359–71.

Parsons, T. and Shils, E.A. (1951) "Categories of the Orientation and Organization of Action," in T. Parsons and E. Shields (eds.) *Toward a General Theory of Action*, Cambridge, MA: Harvard University Press, 53–109.

Pettit, P. (1996) *The Common Mind: An Essay on Psychology, Society, and Politics*, New York: Oxford University Press.

Provis, C. (1977) "Gauthier on Coordination," *Dialogue*, 16: 507–9.

Schelling, T.C. (1960) *The Strategy of Conflict*, Cambridge, MA: Harvard University Press.

Schmid, H.B. (2003a) "Rationality-in-Relations," *American Journal of Economics and Sociology*, 62: 67–101; reprinted in L.S. Moss and D. Koepsell (eds.) (2003) *John Searle's Ideas about Social Reality: Extensions, Criticisms, and Reconstructions*, Oxford: Basil Blackwell.

—— (2003b) "Can Brains in Vats Think as a Team?," *Philosophical Explorations*, 6: 201–18.

—— (2005a) "Beyond Self-Goal Choice: Amartya Sen's Analysis of the Structure of Commitment and the Role of Shared Desires," *Economics and Philosophy*, 21: 51–63.

—— (2005b) "Nostrism – Social Identities in Experimental Games," *Analyse & Kritik*, 27: 172–87.

Searle, J.R. (1990) "Collective Intentions and Actions," in P.R. Cohen, J. Morgan, and M.E. Pollack (eds.) *Intentions in Communication*, Cambridge, MA: MIT Press, 401–15.

—— (1995) *The Construction of Social Reality*, New York: Free Press.

—— (1998) "Social Ontology and the Philosophy of Society," *Analyse & Kritik*, 20: 143–58.

Sen, A.K. (2004) "Social Identity," *Revue de philosophie économique*, 7: 7–27.

Sugden, R. (1993) "Thinking as a Team: Towards an Explanation of Nonselfish Behavior," *Social Philosophy and Policy*, 10: 69–89.

—— (1995) "A Theory of Focal Points," *Economic Journal*, 105: 533–50.

—— (1996) "Rational Coordination," in F. Farina, F. Hahn, and S. Vanucci (eds.) *Ethics, Rationality and Economic Behavior*, Oxford: Clarendon Press, 244–62.

—— (2000) "Team Preferences," *Economics and Philosophy*, 16: 175–204.

—— (2003) "The Logic of Team Reasoning," *Philosophical Explorations*, 6: 165–81.

Thalos, M. (1999) "Degrees of Freedom: Towards a Systems Analysis of Decision," *Journal of Political Philosophy*, 7: 453–77.

Tuomela, R. (1995) *The Importance of Us: A Study of Basic Social Notions*, Stanford: Stanford University Press.

—— (2002) "Joint Intention and Commitment," in G. Meggle (ed.) *Social Facts and Collective Intentionality*, Frankfurt am Main: Hänsel-Hohenhausen, 385–418.

Tuomela, R. and Miller, K. (1988) "We-Intentions," *Philosophical Studies*, 53: 367–89.

11 Adding reasons up

William A. Edmundson[1]

1 Introduction

Economics is criticized from two directions. Moralists and moral philosophers scold it for its stunted conception of normativity. Psychologists and philosophers of mind and action chide it for its unrealistic models of practical rationality. The confluence of these two critiques lies within the domain of moral psychology, that part of the philosophy of mind that concerns itself with the question how norms (moral and otherwise) are realized in the psychology of those subject to them. In this chapter I want to explore these two lines of critique, with a view toward determining whether they are mutually reinforcing or dissonant. In particular, I will argue that the "maximizing conception" of rationality that economists are criticized for employing is one that moral philosophers cannot well do without. But the maximizing conception, though essential to identifying *what* reason requires that we choose, seems unsuited to the task of explaining *why* we choose what we do – even when we do choose as reason requires. In practice, the maximizing conception seems as unenlightening as an explanation of choice as it is hopeless as a decision strategy. I will conclude by suggesting that the two-system model of practical rationality that Kahneman and Tversky have pioneered (Tversky and Kahneman 1971) can be seen as a step toward reconciling the normative and positive aims of economics (compare Hausman and McPherson 1993 with Friedman 1953).

In the next section I will contrast two concepts essential to normativity: reasons and requirements. The two concepts are most naturally connected by the idea of maximization. Though qualifications and corrections are in order, the maximizing conception is uniquely suited to connecting what we have reason to do with what we are rationally required to do. But applying the maximizing conception needs still further qualification to avoid repugnant consequences: this is most evident in the case of moral reasons, but it is a general worry.

In the third section I focus on alternatives to the maximizing conception within the moral subdomain. I conclude that none of these alternatives –

sanction theory, voluntarism, and universalizability – can displace the maximizing conception, and that the subdomain of moral reasoning, which might have seemed especially uncongenial to maximization, cannot do without it.

In the fourth section I consider the recent critique of maximization advanced by John Broome (2003). Although much of Broome's critique can be deflected, it does suggest the point that it is not easy to see what the maximizing conception can lend to the empirical study of decision-making.

In the final section I explore some of the difficulties of transposing the reason/maximization/requirement framework from the realm of the normative to the realm of positive behavioral psychology. The basic problem is that the notion of a rational requirement does not share the ambidexterity of reasons, which familiarly play both justificatory and explanatory roles. I suggest that Kahneman and Tversky's distinction between intuitive and supervisory systems may create a niche for the idea of a "rational requirement" in explanations of behavior. Whether and to what extent the supervisory system realizes anything like a process of maximization is – as it should be – an empirical question and, as such, is not one that economics can be convicted of having begged.

2 Reasons and requirements

We and our actions are subject to reasons and to requirements. Reasons differ from requirements in that reasons are typically merely advisory while requirements are, as the term implies, mandatory (Grice 2001; Gardner and Macklem 2002). My focus is on reasons for action and requirements of actors in acting, rather than reasons for belief. Some of the reasons and requirements to which our actions are subject, though presumably not all, are moral reasons and moral requirements.[2]

We almost always have a wide range of options – possible actions – before us, and reasons to perform at least some among them. Rarely, if ever, is it the case that we have no reason to do anything. If there is any action, call it ϕing, such that we have reason to ϕ and no reason to do anything else (including no reason not to ϕ) then it would be irrational not to ϕ. Or, to put it differently, ϕing is rationally required in case there is reason to ϕ and no reason to do anything incompatible with ϕing.[3] But this too is a rare case; typically, within the range of possible actions available to us there are many that we have reason to perform and, again typically, it will not be possible for us to perform all of the actions we have reason to perform. The question arises: What does reason require in typical circumstances? The answer that springs naturally to mind is this: we are rationally required to do what we have most reason to do. This answer is the centerpiece of what we can call the "maximizing" conception of rationality. Every requirement has its reason, but not every reason is a requirement: some reasons to ϕ will be outweighed by others and so, though there is reason to ϕ, there is insufficient reason. What is required by reason is that we do what there is most reason to do.[4]

The maximizing conception of rationality may be too straightforward. Sometimes, it seems, reason requires a more indirect strategy. Sometimes direct pursuit of what we have most reason to do is counterproductive. As Joseph Raz (1990) has emphasized, our practical reasoning includes such things as rules of thumb, which operate as reasons not to act on the balance of all reasons, apparent or actual. If I am tired, for example, I might do better in attaining my financial goals by following a self-imposed rule against trading online after 6 p.m. Even if the balance of all reasons on a particular occasion would favor my making an after-hours trade to be executed on the Hong Kong exchange, my rule of thumb would exclude my so acting. Moreover, it might be rational for me to follow my rule rather than the balance of all reasons. Acknowledging the superiority of the indirect strategy is but a small departure from the maximizing conception, however, for the indirect strategy assumes the correctness of the basic account the maximizing conception offers of the relation between reasons and rational requirements. Reason requires that we do what we have most reason to do – but sometimes what we have most reason to do is to follow a rule of thumb that supersedes our more direct attempts to follow the balance of all reasons.[5] Collective action problems similarly illustrate the need for indirect strategies. Again, the maximizing conception isn't refuted by the need for refinements that take into account the fact that in many instances what we have most reason to do is best achieved by indirection.

Where do reasons come from? This is a matter of controversy. Desires, wants, values, interests, needs, pleasures, pains, aims, projects, commitments, intentions, ends, goals, beliefs, and facts – whether singly or in combination, shared or personal – have been said to furnish, or not to furnish, reasons for action. The focus here is not on the question "Where do reasons come from?" but on the distinct question "When do reasons ripen into requirements?" The intuitively irresistible answer to the latter question seems to be this: we are rationally required to do what we have most reason to do.

This answer has to face up to another complication. It asks us to suppose that reasons are capable of being assigned a weight, in some sense, and that such weights are capable of being added up and compared. In other words, the maximizing conception seems to assume that there is a certain kind of metric that reasons (in all their variety) are susceptible to, and which can at least in principle impose an order such that, for any given set of options available to an actor at a time, there is (absent a dead heat) a unique action such that that action is what the actor has most reason to do. This "metrical assumption" may seem fantastically implausible. A moment's reflection upon the vast range of options available to each of us at this very moment makes the metrical assumption look silly. Right now, for example, I am capable of doing (among many other things) any of the following: finishing this paragraph, going to the coffee urn, checking my e-mail, writing a check to CARE for famine relief, telephoning my sister, brushing my teeth, reading a manuscript, finishing a book review, unloading the dishwasher . . . etc., etc.

Two points should suffice here, I hope, to allay the worry that the maximizing conception has to be wrong because the metrical assumption is unbelievable. The first is that the metrical assumption is an abstract *post facto* reconstruction rather than a recipe for a decision procedure. It would indeed be hopeless to try to go about deciding what to do by enumerating all options, assigning a weight to all options, and then calculating which option scored the highest. But that is beside the point. The metrical assumption doesn't prescribe a decision procedure but, rather, an interpretive heuristic to be applied to reconstruct why someone may have done what she did or to predict what she will do – or as a critical heuristic to identify what she ought to have done or to do. Because, for example, I did finish the previous paragraph rather than check my e-mail, go to the coffee pot, or anything else that I might have done, it makes sense to say that I estimated that I had more reason to finish the paragraph than to do anything else, and that the reasons I had to finish the paragraph added up in a fashion that outweighed the weight I assigned to the reasons favoring each of the other options that came to my mind at the time.

The second point is that the maximizing conception needn't assert the metrical assumption; it will be enough to take it provisionally. In other words, the maximizing conception could be expressed this way: to the extent that it makes sense to make the metrical assumption, what reason requires is that we do what we have most reason to do. Does this make the maximizing conception a triviality? The case for thinking that some reasons are incommensurable or incomparable is far from conclusive (Chang 1997); and, even if that case were stronger, it would do only minor damage to the maximizing conception. Incomparability of reasons would only mean that sometimes – because there are reasons for different alternative actions and there is no fact of the matter as to which set of reasons is weightier – there won't be an alternative that has most reason going for it. But in such cases what results is an option, not a requirement that one do something other than what there is most reason to do (cf. Kagan 1994).[6] How often, in practice, incommensurabilities create rational options for us is a question we may put aside.

Now compare the maximizing conception of rationality to its more obviously non-trivial counterpart in the realm of moral reasons. Suppose we are morally required to do what we have most moral reason to do. What follows? Nothing drastic follows until we make some further observations about what moral reasons there are. Suppose there is a moral reason to help others, or at least to relieve extreme suffering. There is, as a matter of fact, quite a lot of extreme suffering in the world that we could do something about. Were the maximizing conception of rationality simply transposed to the moral realm, the moral reasons that are, as it were, thrust upon us by the suffering in the world might require us to take what steps we could to relieve as much of that suffering as we could. Morality might turn out to be, as the phrase has it, very strenuous and *demanding*; and if it were, we would be very remiss, for few of us are doing anything at all, at this moment, to relieve the suffering of others. The strenuousness problem, for some, is not a problem at all, but a valuable insight (for example Singer 1972). But many people think this conclusion can't be right, and the question becomes how to avoid it without retreating into a repulsively self-centered version of morality.[7]

The strenuousness problem (if it is a problem) isn't the fault of applying a maximizing conception of rationality to the moral realm, because the maximizing conception seems irresistibly true and to belong to an attractive unary account of rationality. Rather than customize our conception of how reasons are to be processed in the moral realm, a better treatment of the strenuousness problem might consist in keeping closer watch at the gate over what is to be admitted as a moral reason. One typical "gatekeeper" solution is to refuse to recognize certain types of consideration as moral reasons at all. For example, one might assert that moral reasons are one and all reasons against doing harm, and that there is no moral reason not to allow harm (although it might in some sense still be praiseworthy to prevent harm to others).

The strenuous problem is actually even more insidious than proponents of gatekeeper solutions have appreciated. There is a strenuousness problem that one has to confront even if one denies that there are moral reasons to help others, or admits that there are such reasons but denies that they are sufficiently weighty to overbalance moral reasons we have to concentrate on our own projects and pleasures. So long as one admits that there are any moral reasons at all, the maximizing conception will require the actor to perform that act which he has most reason, morally, to perform. If the only morally admissible reasons are reasons not to do harm, the maximizing conception will have the actor act so as to minimize harm – a strenuous undertaking in itself. If what one has most moral reason to do is to pursue one's own pleasure, then doing so is not morally optional but morally required (Kagan 1989).[8] The maximizing conception would put even the most insouciant hedonism to relentless work in morality's service. The point is not altered if we subtract the "moral" qualifier. If reason requires that I do what there is most reason for me to do, then it threatens to be constraining indeed.[9]

Rationality – moral or "prudential" – tends to become very demanding if the maximizing conception is applied to any set of reasons, unless the *de minimis* and the incommensurable are found (or, more likely, assumed) to be the normal case (cf. Raz 1999).[10] What I want to consider next are the possible alternative accounts of how moral reasons ripen into moral requirements. If the maximizing conception of rationality is set aside, how can one account for the logical passage from having a reason to φ to being required to φ, on pain of being convicted of a rational failing?

3 Alternatives to the maximizing conception in the moral realm

Sanction theories of duty

Sanction theories are probably the oldest theories of duty (I will use the terms "duty" and "moral requirement" interchangeably, and ignore any distinction between duty and obligation). In the stronger form, a sanction theory might purport to say both what makes a reason a moral reason and what makes a moral reason a moral requirement (viz., a duty, an obligation, something the non-doing of which is morally forbidden). In its strongest form, a sanction theory might hold that the sanction simply is *the* moral reason supporting moral requirements – that, in other words, moral reasons flow from moral requirements and not vice versa. In the weaker form of sanction theory, moral reasons have some independent source, but become moral requirements only when a sanction is added. For example, a divine command theory of morality might represent God as surveying the universe of moral reasons (which on the stronger view but not on the weaker, He will have created or simultaneously creates), and then choosing which of those moral reasons to make obligatory. He signifies this choice by coupling a sanction to the chosen reasons – "thou shalt . . . etc."

Sanction theories needn't be theistic. On some accounts, the sanction is a conventional, social one rather than a divine injunction. Nietzsche, for example, never denies that "herd" morality has something to be said in its favor. That is, he never denies that there may be some moral reason to do what will conform to ordinary morality. But Nietzsche did think that most people had failed to notice that, without God, the only sanction morality has is the sanction of social convention, which tends to make obligatory precisely those moral reasons that favor the weak and numerous at the expense of the stronger few. Nietzsche was no nihilist, but he was willing to doubt that the sanction of society was sufficient to elevate undoubted moral *reasons* to the status of universally binding moral *requirements*.

Sanction theories, divine or other, are hard now to take seriously (cf. Hacker 1973). The strongest form of sanction theory is the most repulsive: viz., the idea that the *only* reason that, for example, murder is wrong is that God or society has forbidden it. But even the weaker version seems muddled and incredible: wrongness is one thing; the sanctions that might be brought to bear upon wrongdoers is entirely another. True, the fact that a set of moral reasons has become a moral requirement may mean that a sanction of some sort for ignoring those reasons must at least be permissible to add. But the moral reasons drive the permissibility of the sanction, not vice versa.

Voluntarism

Voluntarism could be viewed as an extraction of "the truth in sanction theory," this truth being simply the fact that there is a gap between what there is moral reason to do and what one is morally required to do. The error of sanction theory, on the voluntarist view, is to look outside the actor (the duty bearer) for the extra element that closes the gap. To put the point differently, the "sanction" that converts a reason into a requirement is a sanction in the endorsement sense rather than in the threat sense, and is one that the *actor* freely adds to the reason. The paradigm of voluntaristic obligation is the promise. The reasons we have that favor our making a promise to ϕ do not normally obligate us to ϕ, but, having promised to ϕ, we become obligated (*prima facie*) to ϕ. Voluntarism hopes to generalize the paradigm case of promising to cover as many kinds of case as possible – if not all, then enough to displace the maximizing conception as the dominant picture of how moral reasons obligate.

The actor's endorsement is not to be construed as functioning simply to add yet another reason to the mix of reasons already applicable. In the paradigm case of promising, one's saying "I promise" is normally conclusive irrespective of the strength of whatever other reasons there are to do as one has promised to do. If promises obligated simply by adding a reason to do what was promised, voluntarism would become merely an (implausible) appendage to the maximizing conception, reiterating in effect that one is obligated to do what one has most reason to do, adding only that promising obligates by furnishing an additional reason for action that is of a strength that somehow happens to make performing what was promised into what one has most reason to do.

Voluntarism draws what plausibility it has from the fact that it uses as its paradigm a familiar phenomenon in which we can, as it were, experimentally observe obligations coming into being. Its plausibility suffers, though, as soon as we notice that, unless refined, it makes obligation both too easy and too hard. The first-person process of endorsement, whatever it might be, can't generally suffice to create obligations. Even promising seems to presuppose, if not a background of conventional practices, then at least the existence of a promisee who actually witnesses our intentional manifestation of our willingness to be bound (cf. Scanlon 1998). Something more is needed, obviously, which we might call reflective endorsement.[11] But it isn't easy to understand what reflection adds to endorsement. Reflection might prevent one from making hasty or ill-considered endorsements, but the work that needs doing is of a different nature. What we are looking for is an understanding of how moral reasons generate moral requirements. If reflection and endorsement have a distinctive contribution to make, it has to be something other than as a psychological process that helps or enables us to figure out what morally we have most reason to do. Otherwise, reflective endorsement would merely be an account of how we discover what we have most reason to do, rather than an independent account of what makes a set of moral reasons a moral requirement.

There is controversy over whether the individual actor's endorsement is or is not a necessary condition for a set of moral reasons to create a moral requirement of that actor. What seems to me to be the more plausible view, externalism, insists that moral requirements are not escapable by the easy-seeming technique of refusing to endorse them. The opposite view, internalism, is the view that for any person X, X's being obligated to φ presupposes that X is somehow motivated (or non-invasively motivatable) to φ.[12] Internalism perhaps ought to insist that what motivates has to amount to an endorsement, reflective or otherwise, of the reasons that ground the requirement. But internalism might not be so finicky: an internalist might be willing to say that those who are motivated to obey moral rules mindlessly are sufficiently motivated to be obligated. For the purposes of this chapter it isn't necessary to decide which is the better understanding of internalism; nor is it necessary to adjudicate the dispute between internalism and externalism. This is because internalists and externalists can agree that being motivated by moral reasons isn't itself sufficient to create a moral requirement (think of any case of supererogation – my sudden urge to spend the following weekend helping at the homeless shelter isn't in itself sufficient to require me morally to do so). More is needed; and that is what we are after here. Once that "more" is identified, the internalist will want to add that the "more" had better motivate; the externalist won't add that.

One of the attractions of a voluntarist or reflective endorsement account is that motivation would fall right out of the endorsement, thus finessing the internalist/externalist dispute. The problem at this juncture is that endorsement has so far presented at best a sketchy *epistemic* account of how actors get in touch with what they have most reason, morally, to do. That approach seems not to reach the main question: What makes a set of moral reasons into a moral requirement? In fact, this rendering of voluntarism seems tacitly to endorse the maximization conception, that we are morally required to do what we have most moral reason to do.

The spirit of voluntarism is not honored, however, by construing voluntarism purely epistemically. Voluntarism wants to depict the actor's role in becoming morally bound as a less passive one. It's not that the actor is simply exposed to moral reasons and she becomes subject to a moral requirement straightaway once she "gets it," or merely responds to those reasons in a certain (perhaps necessarily motivating) way. Somehow she must freely make a contribution of some sort – and what could that be? Her contribution can't be one of merely adding yet another reason, or can it? Two possible voluntaristic frameworks present themselves at this point: it will be handy to call the first the *evaluation model* and the second the *commitment model*. The evaluation model represents the actor as making a positive evaluation with regard to the action the reasons before her recommend. This evaluation itself constitutes a decisive reason, and (as noted earlier) does so in a way that should not be misunderstood as her merely adding another reason to the mix. The commitment model similarly represents the actor as endorsing what the reasons before her recommend, and doing so in a way that renders her subsequent actions subject to a moral requirement. But her endorsement is regarded as a commitment rather than as a judgment. Thus, the key difference between the two frameworks is that on the evaluation model the actor's endorsement supplies a decisive reason that (somehow, and non-additively) transforms what had been merely a set of moral reasons into a moral requirement, while still somehow reflecting those underlying reasons. On the commitment model, on the other hand, endorsement is a *commitment*, and that commitment does the job of moving *beyond* moral reasons to moral requirements. The underlying reasons are scaffolding, not part of the resulting obligation.

The evaluation model has the advantage that it allows for an explanation of how the actor might be mistaken about whether or not a certain set of moral reasons was "really" obliging. The evaluation model has the actor judge the weight of the competing moral reasons in the set relevant to her actions, and has the resulting judgment simultaneously displace those reasons and place the actor under a duty to act. The actor is not the mere agent of the underlying reasons, for she is not obligated in a direct way by them, but by her own judgment, which has now subordinated them. Her motive is her judgment, and the possibility of error exists in virtue of the fact that her judgment is fallible and (to some extent) revisable. To adapt a well-known example of Sartre's, if I judge that the reasons to take care of my ailing mother are weightier than the reasons to join the Resistance, two things happen. One, I am now morally required to care for my mother rather than join the Resistance (since we are assuming that I can't do both) and I am motivated to care for her not only by the pre-existing reasons I had, but now also by my judgment. Two, I could be wrong about the balance of reasons but (paradoxically, perhaps) I can't be wrong about what (having judged) is now my obligation.

The commitment model would render this version of Sartre's example differently. I am obligated and am motivated, and I can't be wrong about being obligated, just as on the evaluation model, but it is a false intellectualization to say that I have judged the balance of moral reasons to tip one way or another, or even to say that I judged them to be in equipoise, or incomparable. There is no judgment. The actor reflects and then commits. Saying, "Well, then you *must* have judged" is a mistake that inevitably tempts those who assume that the only proper outcome of a process of reasoning is something at least purporting to be cognitive (true or false). But the commitment model does not make this assumption. The commitment – and not any judgment – creates the obligation; therefore there is no possibility of being mistaken in that judgment, at least not in the sense made possible on the evaluation model.

The commitment model explains the durability of obligation by denying that the essential obligation-creating commitment involves any judgment that has to reflect (and thus be held hostage to) the underlying set of moral reasons. Endorsement is a new beginning, a sort of Kierkegaardian "leap." The evaluation model, in contrast, is more concerned with fidelity to the rational underpinning of obligation than with its durability. The independent life that obligation acquires is always somewhat backward looking, in the sense that the obligation-creating judgment is always capable of being called again to account by the underlying reasons. On the commitment model, there need be no looking back.

The commitment model has an additional attraction. If some moral reasons are incomparable or in equipoise, the evaluation model seems stuck with having to conclude that in such cases there is an option, and that after having chosen the actor must learn to live with the fact that moral reasons did not require her to do as she chose. In cases of equipoise or incommensurability, a stance like Luther's "Here I stand: I can do no other" is not honestly available. But on the commitment model it is. On the commitment model, the "no other" need not be supplied by reasons (although it may be). It is sometimes supplied by the actor himself. Robert Bolt might have had Thomas More justify himself to Norfolk in these terms: "It's not that I *can* do no other: it is that *I* can do no other."[13]

Because the commitment model represents endorsement as a process of, as it were, turning one's back to one's reasons, it is vulnerable, unsurprisingly, to the charge that it is unacceptably irrationalistic and subjectivistic. Voluntarism aspires to provide not merely an epistemic but a "metaphysical" account of moral requirements of action, but the trick is how to get the will in without seeming merely willful. The evaluation model does limit the will's discretion, and the question becomes whether, even on this construal of voluntarism, we have a plausible account of duty and its relation to reasons. The evaluation model creates room for the possibility of a reflective endorser not "really" being obligated, but that possibility teeters on the verge of paradox. What seems to be demanded is some further restriction upon the range of reasons that are admissible endorsement candidates or, instead, some restriction upon the process of endorsement even beyond the stipulation that it be "reflective." In this way two problems can simultaneously be treated: the first is the problem of the ornery or recalcitrant actor, who withholds his endorsement for no good reason; the second is the fallible endorser, who endorses what is at variance with what she has most moral reason to endorse. As the discussion in the following section shows, these further restrictions are typically characterized either as *formal* or as *procedural* ones.

Universalizability

A full exposition of the ideas at work here is not possible, but the basic idea is simple enough. Not every moral reason an actor (reflectively) endorses becomes a moral requirement; and moral requirements are binding even upon those who, for whatever cause (for example blindness, partiality, weakness, contrariness) do not in fact properly endorse the relevant moral reasons. The voluntarist account is unsatisfactory until and unless this pair of difficulties is addressed.

Formal conditions for proper endorsement: Some reasons, even admittedly moral ones, do not have the proper form to constitute moral requirements. They are not "universalizable," in the sense that their being acted upon by every actor would have logically paradoxical or otherwise chaotic or repugnant consequences. Only those moral reasons that are universalizable can constitute moral requirements, no matter whether the actor endorses them or not. There are two different ways to take the universalizability restriction. One way would be to treat it as a "gateway" restriction upon the range of reasons for action that can count as moral reasons. But this way of understanding universalizability is not favored. For one thing, it may be too restrictive, because a reason that may not be universalizable in a straightforward way may support a moral requirement in a less straightforward way (self-interested reasons, for example). For another, the gateway approach unhelpfully shortcuts the all-important process of reflective endorsement itself. Put differently, in the voluntarist spirit a universalizability test should be built into the process of reflecting upon moral reasons, rather than a gateway criterion testing whether they are worthy to be reflected upon at all.

The sufficiency of accessibility: Insisting upon universalizability may seem promising as way to address the problem of the fallible endorser. But what of the problem of the refusenik, the holdout, the non-endorser? What of the actor who fails to endorse a set of moral reasons that does pass the formal test of universalizability and would survive a reflective process applying this test? Is she or is she not morally bound? Internalists and externalists alike would like to be able to respond with a commonsensical "Yes, she is bound," but the only way to maintain this response is to relax the strict voluntaristic requirement of *actual* endorsement, at least insofar as that would be construed as waiting upon anything like an occurrent psychological event or mental act on the part of the actor. What seems to be an inviting and, hopefully, adequate substitute is the abstract accessibility of *the process itself*. Whether or not the actor has successfully gone through the process of reflectively applying the universalization test, if she did so she would endorse the relevant moral reasons in a way sufficient to put her under a moral requirement in acting. And this possibility is *itself* enough to obligate her.

This "procedural turn" is distinctive of the "ideal observer" theory of moral requirements, and it has affinities with "hypothetical consent" theories of political obligation (cf. Stark 2000). It also has a counterpart in the realm of non-moral rationality, and that counterpart appears to lend it support. In the realm of non-moral rationality it is a commonplace business to dictate what an actor is rationally required to do, based upon the outcome of a rational procedure operating upon the set of relevant reasons. Even with the assumption that the set of relevant reasons includes only those available to the actor, if she misprocesses them what she is rationally required to do tracks the *correct* process. Her error does not immunize her from criticism for acting (or tending to act) contrary to what reason requires and, by the same token, neither does her failure to endorse what proper processing yields. The process is objective. Turning back to universalization as an account of moral requirement, we see that proceduralizing similarly yields an objective (or an idealized subjective) account of the transformation of moral reasons into moral requirements. Voluntarism is honored in name only.

Universalization approaches may aspire to refine voluntarism, but their inevitable tendency seems to be to refine away the contribution of the will until nothing is left of it but, at most, an idealized ceremonial role. Furthermore, the work of transforming moral reasons into moral requirements, on a full account, seems hard to contrast to the work of transforming reasons generally into rational requirements of action. But this means that the maximizing conception has to be confronted again, and resisted, if resistance still seems worth mounting.

What would capitulation mean? To admit that the maximization conception is the right way to understand the relation between moral reasons and moral requirements isn't automatically to capitulate to consequentialism, for what we have moral reason to do needn't always be a matter of consequences. Capitulation to the maximizing conception does seem to mean, however, that the war against consequentialism has to be fought at the gates, that is, at the point at which reasons are certified as moral reasons or not. The consequences of action for welfare are seemingly irresistible candidates for certification as moral reasons. Whether the balance of such reasons alone is to determine what we are morally required to do will depend upon what other moral reasons there certifiably are, their weight, and (perhaps) their comparability. It will not depend upon the acceptance or rejection of the maximizing conception in the realm of moral reasons. That conception, I think we have seen, is really the only game in town.

4 Doubts about the maximizing conception

The maximizing conception of rationality flows easily from a general presumption I have made, following Joseph Raz, that the relationships between reasons and requirements are of central importance. But has the Razian "age of reasons" gone too far? That is, are there good grounds to resist the recent urge in analytical philosophy to reduce normativity generally to the study of reasons? John Broome (2003) believes so and, in particular, argues against the maximizing conception, in a discussion centered around several counterexamples.

Broome agrees that if X has most reason to ϕ, then X is required to ϕ. But is the reverse true, that is, is it the case that wherever X is required to ϕ, X has most reason to ϕ?[14] Broome points out that the phrase "most reason to φ" is ambiguous between two senses that are easily confused. In one sense, what he calls the "perfect reason" sense, to say that X has most reason to φ is merely to say that there is an explanation of the fact that X ought to φ. But it is not necessarily to say that that explanation is what he calls a "weighing explanation," that is, an explanation following the maximizing conception. To assert or assume that every explanation of a normative (practical or moral) requirement must be structured according to the maximizing conception is to commit the error that Broome calls *protantism*, a none-too-happy term fashioned upon the second sense of reason Broome identifies, which he calls "*pro tanto* reason." The defining characteristic of *pro tanto* reasons is their essential amenability to the metaphorical process of weighing, measuring, and aggregating that characterizes the maximizing conception. Protantism, or the maximizing conception, asserts that whenever X is required to φ that is because the balance of *pro tanto* reasons tips toward X's φing. And this is what Broome contests.

Here are Broome's counterexamples to the maximizing conception: one ought not, *ceteris paribus*, believe that it is now Wednesday and now Sunday; one ought not, in general, believe inconsistent propositions; one ought to will the means necessary to any end one wills (Kant's principle); a certain taxpayer X ought to pay £12,345 in taxes for a certain year; one ought in normal circumstances to do what the law requires; one ought not (for a Razian exclusionary reason rather than a weighing reason) to disobey the law merely to benefit oneself. Broome doesn't deny that for each of these putative requirements we can dream up extraordinary circumstances in which they do not hold. We might, for example, be rationally and morally required to believe a contradiction – or to disobey a law, or to will an end without its necessary means – if doing so is the only way to avoid catastrophe. But the fact that a principled constraint may be canceled in extreme circumstances shows at most that it is conditional in form; it does not show that it must be explained on the model of the maximizing conception. Moreover, even if protantism is correct, the *useful* explanation of a requirement needn't be one fashioned on the template of the maximizing conception. All sorts of other forms of explanation are possible and worth exploring, and, Broome concludes, "it would be a prejudice" (Broome 2003: 46) to insist that all of them be regimented according to the maximizing conception.

Broome's doubts call for a response. First of all, the "great variety" of other types of explanation of "ought facts" that Broome says we notice at work in his counterexample cases is not really that great. In fact, the variety boils down to three types. One type is conceptual, another is inherently anti-weighing, and another is an appeal to what could be called "constraintism." Finally (but not fourthly), there are instances that might just as well fit within one of these three types as within the typical maximizing mold. (I will discuss these three types in detail in a moment.) Broome is correct that the maximizing conception is not much in evidence in, say, the field of fluid mechanics; but he does not suggest that the variety of explanations of ought facts can include any that take the form of explanation typical of the physical sciences. So, at least in the normative dimension, the maximizing conception doesn't prevent hundreds of flowers from blooming, but at most only a few, which we should now look at more carefully.

Conceptual truths as requirements: It may be correct to say that conceptual truths, as rational requirements, do not comfortably fit within the maximizing conception. With a little shoehorning, such requirements as "never believe a contradiction" could be fitted into the maximizing conception as limiting cases, in which the reasons for the requirement are simply unopposed. Insofar as right reason is what the actor aims at, there is simply nothing to be said in favor of believing a contradiction, and quite a lot against. But this is a degenerate case of reasons ripening into a requirement, and no harm is done by classifying conceptual truths as sui generis.

When we turn to moral principles, however, there seems to be greater cause to resist the sui generis treatment that conceptual truths might merit. As Broome admits, it is harder to believe that the principle that the law is to be obeyed does not rest upon a "weighing explanation" in line with the maximizing conception. True, it is possible to insist that certain moral principles state requirements that are not to be understood as resting upon any operation upon underlying reasons. This is a view for which I've suggested the name constraintism.

Inherently anti-weighing requirements: Some requirements require that the actor not engage in weighing or not act upon the balance of reasons. Razian exclusionary reasons are of the latter type. As I suggested earlier, these do not really stand outside the maximizing conception because such anti-weighing requirements themselves rest upon an assessment of the balance of reasons, as Raz himself explains. Anti-weighing requirements are normally thought to be the best way of achieving the best outcome, practical or moral. To the extent that moral requirements such as the duty to obey the law and to keep promises forbid the actor to act upon the balance of reasons, they should be classified here rather than as sui generis moral truths – a more satisfactory treatment, I think many will agree, than constraintism.

Constraintism: This, as I have defined it, is the view that some moral requirements do not have what Broome calls a weighing explanation, and so are at a variance from the maximizing conception. They are more usefully understood as substantive or "synthetic" moral truths rather than merely definitional or analytic truths. Broome does not enumerate particular candidates for inclusion in this category, but does suggest that "even if protantism is true and every ought fact has a weighing explanation, the interesting explanation of an ought fact may include many facts that are not pro tanto reasons, and none that are pro tanto reasons" (Broome 2003: 46). The example of the tax liability of £12,345 is, he says, one in which

> we take it for granted that you ought to pay your taxes, and we are interested in why it is £12,345 that you ought to pay. This calls for an explanation consisting of complicated conditions and calculations . . . [but] this mass does not constitute a weighing explanation, and it includes nothing resembling a *pro tanto* reason for or against paying £12,345 in income tax.
>
> (Broome 2003: 46)

Is this an objection? This ought fact is easily understood as a derivative obligation (derived from the duty to obey the law plus a calculation of what the tax law requires of a particular taxpayer in a particular year), and so the interesting issue raised by constraintism is whether there are any non-derivative moral requirements that have or need no weighing explanation.

In the realm of the moral, is there a way of adjudicating between protantism and constraintism? Protantism, or the maximizing conception, seems more and more plausible the greater the degree to which we acknowledge that we exist amidst a multitude of plural and conflicting moral reasons. If a multitude of such reasons get past the gate (as value pluralism holds), then the maximizing conception alone seems able to give each its due. Constraintism picks favorites from the multitude, and has to say which ones and why, but without weighing and balancing. Constraintism would be more plausible if it could limit what is admissible as a moral reason right up front, which is why I suggested earlier that its battle has to be fought at the gates. Once the multitude of putative moral reasons is admitted, the maximizing conception begins to look irresistible.

Once the multitude is within, constraintism resorts to conditionalizing its putative constraints as its way of giving other moral reasons and their weight their due. But conditionalizing is hardly a faithful rendering of what goes on in cases of moral conflict. When, for example, Sartre's liberation fighter/ dutiful son contemplates the situation he finds himself in, it is artificial to portray him as trying to determine which of two apparent constraints upon his action is really of conditional form. Is he really best represented as asking which of the following is the operative pair of constraints: {"perform your filial duty" and "fight for your country's liberty, except where filial duties supervene"{or instead,} "fight for your country's liberty" and "perform your filial duty, except when you must fight for your country's liberty"}? If the actor's conflict gets resolved by determining which is the exceptionless principle and which the conditional one, there really never was a dilemma, only the appearance of one.

In cases of conflicting moral reasons, constraintism offers perhaps too much ease of conscience. The maximizing conception, in contrast, explains not only why the prevailing reason prevails, but also the tug the other, outweighed, reasons exert even after the balance has been taken. None of what I've said amounts to a decisive refutation of constraintism, but I think it suffices to put the question to it: if the maximizing conception does not govern the relation between moral reasons and moral requirements, what does?

Reasons are related to rational requirements, and moral reasons are related to moral requirements. It is appealing to think of moral reasoning as a specification of a more general reasoning process, and to think of the capacity to engage in moral reasoning as a specific aspect of a general capacity to reason. Therefore it may also be attractive to think of the relation between moral reasons and moral requirements as a straightforward modification of the more general relation between reasons and rational requirements.

One type of modification has already been suggested: moral reasoning takes as inputs a more restricted set of reasons than reasoning generally. Certain reasons that are admissible prudential reasons, for example, may be inadmissible in moral reasoning. What suits my convenience may be a perfectly good reason from a prudential perspective, but it may or may not be admissible for purposes of moral reasoning. Moral reasoning, in other words, may involve filters, which remove morally inadmissible reasons from the process.[15] What one is morally required to do is simply what one has most reason, morally, to do, which is simply what one has most reason to do, ignoring morally inadmissible reasons. John Rawls's (1971) celebrated "veil of ignorance" is a device of this type.

Another type of modification involves not filtration but supplementation. Moral reasoning, on this approach, operates upon a wider, rather than a narrower set of reasons than ordinary prudential reasoning. The set of reasons may be supplemented by considerations of the welfare of others, for example, which from a prudential perspective I may be free to ignore if they implicate no interest of mine or significant consequence for me. Or, as suggested by the universalization test associated with Kant, it may be that the set of reasons is supplemented by further reasons that reflect the logical or practical consequences of everyone's adopting a particular option of a type available to the reasoner. Moral reasoning, in other words, may involve *supplements*, which inject additional, morally relevant reasons into the process. What one is morally required to do is simply what one has most reason, morally, to do, which is simply what one has most reason to do, *noting* morally relevant though prudentially irrelevant reasons.

It may also be the case that both filters and supplements are distinctively involved in moral reasoning. At the extreme, moral reasoning may involve filters so strong that the only reasons that are inputs are supplements. The point is that both filters and supplements are perfectly compatible with the maximizing conception of rationality. What one is morally required to do is simply what one has most reason to do, after the relevant filtration and supplementation have been performed. Moral philosophy's gripe against economics can best be understood in these terms: economists are faulted for representing agents as failing to supplement their "agent-relative" reasons with the full range of relevant "agent-neutral" reasons (Parfit 1984: 27, 129;

Nagel 1986: 138–53). Economists lose touch with normativity, in other words, not by adopting a maximizing framework for reasons-processing, but by failing to police the gates to assure that all but only the proper inputs are admitted (cf. Broome 1995; White 2004). As I have argued, the maximizing framework is one that moral philosophy has to use as well. It is, as it were, a public right of way that all must share.

5 Do we maximize when we reason?

The "reason/maximization/requirement" framework I have been discussing is not easy to transpose from the realm of the normative to the realm of positive behavioral psychology. The basic problem is that the notion of a rational *requirement* does not share the ambidexterity possessed by the concept of a *reason*, which we are familiar with on both sides of the justificatory/explanatory divide. Perhaps merely coincidentally, *Homo economicus* also has a divided nature, according to the psychological model that has emerged from the pioneering work of Kahneman and Tversky (Kahneman and Frederick 2005). On their dual cognitive model, an agent's judgments are outputs of two systems: an intuitive one, and another, more deliberate, supervisory one. "Bounded" rationality, as revealed by empirical studies, can be understood in terms of the shortcomings of the intuitive system, which judges quickly, effortlessly, and usually correctly, but is prone to errors that the supervisory system cannot always catch in time. The dual model bears interesting resemblances to the distinction between internal and external reasons already noted, which has been prominent in recent disputes in moral psychology.

Some say that nothing is a reason for action for a given actor unless that reason is capable of motivating her. If a reason for action is understood in this way, it can do service both in explanations of her behavior and in criticisms of how well she performs according to canons of rationality (Williams 1981: 101–13). Call this view *reason internalism*. Those who deny reason internalism hold that one may have a reason for action whether or not one is motivated by it or is capable of being motivated by it by means short of conversion. Call this view *reason externalism*. Although reasons for action, understood this way, will not be as dependably usable in explanations of behavior, they will be more useful when what is at issue is not explanation but criticism (Scanlon 1998).

Reasons are ambidextrous as between explanatory and critical functions, in a way that requirements are not. That an actor had reasons for acting as she acted has explanatory power; that she was rationally required to act as she acted has (oddly) less – perhaps none – even after idealizing assumptions (such as closure under implication) are made about the actor's cognitive capacities.

To put the point differently, *requirement internalism*, the view that nothing is a requirement of action unless it is a motive, seems far less plausible than reason internalism. This could be because the vexed questions of freedom, responsibility, and the causal order incline us toward welcoming reasons as explanations of behavior, but at the same time make seem repellent and false any suggestion that an actor acted as she did because required to do so, whether by reasons or anything else. As a matter of critical and justificatory vocabulary, however, to say that an actor acted contrary to what reason required seems natural and unthreatening. *Requirement externalism*, which holds that what reason requires need not have a root in any given actor's motives, seems to that degree more plausible than reason externalism.[16]

Put yet another way, reason internalism is faithful to something like an intuitive system, which inclines us and typically explains what we do. The idea of an internal *requirement* seems alien, on two counts. For one, the actor is invested in her intuitive choices so deeply that their phenomenology seems immiscible with the coldly compelling notion of requirement. For another, "requirement" as a term of critical vocabulary, seems both futile and dictatorial, far more so than the term "reason" in its external guise.[17]

The reason externalist, on the other hand, is attuned to a supervisory system, which is relatively seldom cast in an explanatory role and is subject to norms that may lie at or beyond the limit of the actor's familiar cognitive repertoire. However ready an entry external reasons may have into that repertoire, becoming internalized, so to speak, external requirements remain just that: external. It may be that what is most troublesome about proposing that agents maximize something in their behavior is the idea that there is any sense to be made of the notion of an internal requirement.

It is thus appealing to combine reason internalism with requirement externalism in developing a general picture of rational and moral agency. But I will conclude by suggesting another possibility: that the concept of a supervisory system can make a home for the concept of an internal requirement. Whether such requirements are outputs of any identifiable process of maximization is an empirical question (Glimcher, Doris, and Bayer 2005). It may very well be that they are not. But behavioral economics hasn't begged this question; and given the inescapability of the reasons/maximization/requirements framework in normative theory, it is a natural hypothesis to put to the test.

Notes

1 I thank Matt Adler, Brian Bix, and Irit Samet-Porat for comments on an earlier draft of this chapter.
2 The commonsense thought that there is a special category of moral reasons has been called into question by contemporary philosophers of diverse persuasions (for example Gauthier 1986; Raz 1999). My discussion is not intended to prejudge this issue.
3 "Irrational" may be too strong. Raz (1999) suggests that "silly" will in trivial cases be the most serious charge that will stick. In any case, the agent who acts contrary to reason is subject to some form of criticism.

4 I ignore for now the complications that arise from the fact that the actor may be insensitive to certain reasons that apply to her.
5 If Raz's exclusionary reasons account is correct, then following the rule of thumb may be rationally required because it is the only reason left standing.
6 Michael Smith accepts a variant of the maximizing conception, which he traces to G.E. Moore (Smith 2003: 576-78). In Smith's formulation, what one is morally obligated to do is to perform that act which, of the available options, will bring about the most good and the least bad. This formulation can be criticized as (perhaps inadvertently) failing to guide the actor when no single action both maximizes good and minimizes bad.
7 See Kagan (1989) and Unger (1996).
8 Kagan (1989) sometimes denies that one is always morally required to do what one has most reason, morally, to do, but several of his arguments against moral options rely on the assumption that one is. As I have elsewhere suggested, if there is any room at all for moral options, it may have to be in the shelter of incomparabilities between reasons. Scanlon (1998) elaborates a contractualist account of morality according to which persons are assumed to seek agreement upon moral requirements that are binding unless reasonable to *reject*.
9 Weirich (2004) discusses and sets aside arguments against maximization that appeal to satisficing (Simon 1982) or to moderation (Slote 1989) which are distinct from the ones I discuss here.
10 Does an agent's utility function, reflecting her revealed preferences, map her reasons in a way that tends to wring out incommensurabilities? Raz (1999) and Scanlon (1998) deny that a desire or preference is *per se* a reason for action. Raz also denies that perfect rationality requires an agent to conform to all the reasons that apply to her: there are far too many. Moral reasons, however, must be conformed to whenever they apply.
11 Compare Korsgaard (1996).
12 The contrast is sometimes drawn in terms of "procedural" versus "substantive" practical rationality, rather than internalism versus externalism (Hooker and Streumer 2004; Parfit 1997).
13 "But what matters to me is not whether it's true or not but that I believe it to be true, or rather, not that I *believe* it, but that *I* believe it" (Bolt 1972: 52–3).
14 Raz (1999) and others doubt that reasons require anything unless they surpass a *de minimis* threshold. Nothing I say here is meant to prejudge this issue. If there is such a threshold then being what one has most reason, morally, to do will be sufficient to impose a moral requirement only if the threshold is cleared.
15 Unlike first-order reasons that happen to fall within the scope of a Razian exclusionary reason, reasons that are removed by filtration are not necessarily intended to be furthered, indirectly, by the process.
16 David McNaughton and Piers Rawling (2004) propose combining a reason externalism with a moderate requirement externalism. Rejecting Williams's arguments for reason internalism, they characterize requirements in terms of "what a reasonable person in [the] circumstances" would do or attempt (McNaughton and Rawling 2004: 126). They regard Williams's linking of the motivational and normative force of reason as a confusion (McNaughton and Rawling 2004: 122). My proposal is an attempt to preserve both the motivational and explanatory aspects of the notion of a reason, while acknowledging that the concept of a requirement (moral or rational) has little explanatory value, except perhaps in terms of a supervisory system operating in an individual's psychology.
17 Mark White (in correspondence) has suggested to me that Kantian perfect duties can be construed as internal requirements, insofar as they "take the form of the moral law as self-legislated will." Stark (2000) explores the tendency

of the "internal" to evaporate in the quest for the "perfect" or exceptionless requirement.

References

Bolt, R. (1972) *A Man for All Seasons: A Play in Two Acts,* New York: Vintage.
Broome, J. (2003) "Reasons," in P. Pettit, S. Scheffler, M. Smith, and R.J. Wallace (eds.) *Reason and Value: Essays on the Moral Philosophy of Joseph Raz*, Oxford: Oxford University Press, 28–55.
—— (1995) *Weighing Goods*, Oxford: Blackwell.
Chang, R. (1997) "Introduction," in R. Chang (ed.) *Incommensurability, Incomparability, and Practical Reason*, Cambridge, MA: Harvard University Press, 1–34.
Friedman, M. (1953) "The Methodology of Positive Economics," in *Essays in Positive Economics*, Chicago: University of Chicago Press, 3–43.
Gardner, J. and Macklem, T. (2002) "Reasons," in J. Coleman and S. Shapiro (eds.) *The Oxford Handbook of Jurisprudence and Philosophy of Law*, Oxford: Oxford University Press, 440–75.
Glimcher, P.W., Dorris, M.C., and Bayer, H.M. (2005) "Physiological Utility Theory and the Neuroeconomics of Choice," in *Games and Economic Behavior*, 52, 213–56.
Grice, P. (2001) *Aspects of Reason*, ed. R. Warner, Oxford: Clarendon Press.
Gauthier, D. (1986) *Morals by Agreement*, Oxford: Clarendon Press.
Hacker, P.M.S. (1973) "Sanction Theories of Duty," in A.W.B. Simpson (ed.) *Oxford Essays in Jurisprudence (Second Series)*, Oxford: Clarendon Press, 131–70.
Hausman, D.M. and McPherson, M.S. (1993) "Taking Ethics Seriously: Economics and Contemporary Moral Philosophy," *Journal of Economic Literature*, 31: 671–731.
Hooker, B., and Streumer, M. (2004) "Procedural and Substantive Practical Rationality," in A.R. Mele and P. Rawling (eds.) *The Oxford Handbook of Rationality*, Oxford: Oxford University Press, 57–74.
Kagan, S. (1989) *The Limits of Morality*, Oxford: Clarendon Press.
—— (1994) "Defending Options," *Ethics*, 104: 333–51.
Kahneman, D. and Frederick, S. (2005) "A Model of Heuristic Judgment," in K.J. Holyoak and R.G. Morrison (eds.) *The Cambridge Handbook of Thinking and Reasoning*, Cambridge: Cambridge University Press, 267–94.
Korsgaard, C. (1996) *The Sources of Normativity*, Cambridge: Cambridge University Press.
McNaughton, D. and Rawling, P. (2004) "Duty, Rationality and Practical Reasons," in A.R. Mele and P. Rawling (eds.) *The Oxford Handbook of Rationality*, Oxford: Oxford University Press, 110–31.
Nagel, T. (1986) *The View from Nowhere*, New York: Oxford University Press.
Parfit, D. (1984) *Reasons and Persons*, Oxford: Clarendon Press.
—— (1997) "Reasons and Motivation," *Proceedings of the Aristotelian Society* supplementary, 71: 99–130.
Rawls, J. (1971) *A Theory of Justice*, Cambridge, MA: The Belknap Press of Harvard University Press.
Raz, J. (1990) *Practical Reason and Norms*, 2nd edn., Princeton, NJ: Princeton University Press.
—— (1999) *Engaging Reason*, Oxford: Oxford University Press.
Scanlon, T.M. (1998) *What We Owe to Each Other*, Cambridge, MA: Harvard University Press.
Simon, H. (1982) *Models of Bounded Rationality, vol. 2: Behavioral Economics and Business Organization*, Cambridge, MA: MIT Press.
Singer, P. (1972) "Famine, Affluence, and Morality," *Philosophy and Public Affairs*, 1: 229–43.

Slote, M. (1989) *Beyond Optimizing*, Cambridge, MA: Harvard University Press.

Smith, M. (2003) "Neutral and Relative Value after Moore," *Ethics*, 113: 576–98.

Stark, C. (2000) "Hypothetical Consent and Justification," *Journal of Philosophy*, 97: 313–34.

Tversky, A. and Kahneman, D. (1971) "Belief in the Law of Small Numbers," *Psychological Bulletin*, 76: 105–10.

Unger, P. (1996) *Living High and Letting Die*, New York: Oxford University Press.

Weirich, P. (2004) "Economic Rationality," in A.R. Mele and P. Rawling (eds.) *The Oxford Handbook of Rationality*, Oxford: Oxford University Press, 380–98.

White, M.D. (2004) "Can *Homo Economicus* Follow Kant's Categorical Imperative?," *Journal of Socio-Economics*, 33: 89–106.

Williams, B. (1981) *Moral Luck*, Cambridge: Cambridge University Press.

12 Externalism, expensive tastes, and equality

Keith Dowding[1]

1 Introduction

In the "Equality of What?" literature the conception of and arguments proceeding from "expensive tastes" loom large. Expensive tastes are used by Dworkin and Sen against the idea that "welfare" or "utility" can be the currency or space in which to make judgments about equality.[2] They are used by Cohen and Sen against the idea that "resources" can stand as that currency – though they do not use them in the same way (see pp. 202–3). The arguments marshaled in this regard depend upon testing our (egalitarian) intuitions about the justness of distribution given the examples developed around the "expensive tastes" criterion and the logical and conceptual consequences drawn from those arguments. I put "egalitarian" in quotes since, whilst it is undoubtedly our intuitions in terms of equality that are being teased in these examples, it is not clear to me how far we can demarcate our intuitions about justness that are based on egalitarian instincts as opposed to other considerations.

My contention in this chapter is that all of the positive inferences drawn from our intuitions in these examples rely upon external or publicly perceptible factors of the cases discussed.[3] Those aspects which remain contentious – or plain silly – rely upon an assumption underlying all of that debate: that an internalist conception of the mind is the appropriate one. Internalism here is certainly the folk vision of our minds, and so we might say it is our intuition. But in no philosophy does intuition trump conceptual and logical argument; nor does it trump empirical evidence. And in this regard externalist accounts of our consciousness, experiences, and psyche are increasingly, I think, becoming dominant in the philosophy of mind. I am not explicitly going to defend externalism here but rather use it to try to convince readers that it is the publicly perceptible factors of what Dworkin calls "buzzes" (episodes of experiential enjoyment) and "ticks" (satisfactions of preference) that are relevant to any role such buzzes and ticks may play in our intuitions about the examples discussed. This means that any residual thoughts about those examples relying upon internalism can be safely discarded. I will also try to convince the reader that, so discarded, the at times somewhat esoteric debate engages much more directly with genuine policy issues. I do not comment on whether resources, welfare, capability, or any other concept is the best currency or space in which to measure equality.

My argument relies upon the impossibility of making global interpersonal comparisons of utility. However, I argue that to the extent that local comparisons between individuals and rough global comparisons between types of people can be made, these are made on the basis of demeanor and behavior. The expensive tastes argument relies upon the assumption that precise global comparisons between individuals are possible. Once discounted we can utilize the argument properly in terms of resource conversion to see how public policy can take into account rough global comparisons between types of people.

2 Expensive tastes and what they are not meant to show

Someone is said to have expensive tastes if it costs more to satisfy those tastes than it costs to satisfy the tastes of someone else. So Louis has expensive tastes if he gets the same amount of enjoyment from a glass of expensive wine that Louisa gets from a cheap one. He would gain less pleasure than Louisa from drinking a glass of the cheap wine that she enjoys drinking. Thus, if one thinks that enjoyment with regard to wine drinking should be equalized, then Louis is unjustly treated if he has only the same amount of money to spend on wine as Louisa. Dworkin and Sen think this is counterintuitive. Of course Louis's wine drinking should not be subsidized simply because he has fine tastes. Cohen responds that there is nothing "of course" about the matter. It is true that, on balance, we might not want Louis's wine drinking subsidized by the state. Nevertheless it is perfectly reasonable to be an egalitarian about enjoyment, and if Louis does have to suffer the cheap wine enjoyed by Louisa, then he has a legitimate complaint, even if it is not a complaint that we feel able to do anything about.

We must note here what, for Cohen, the expensive tastes argument is meant to demonstrate. The argument is not meant to show that the state should equalize over tastes. The expensive tastes example is only intended to show that welfare (which in this example I have termed enjoyment) is a legitimate concern over which we should recognize claims. In that sense he uses it against resources being the (only) currency of egalitarian justice. Cohen further wants to make much of this concern that the market does not recognize such claims and in that regard, at least, is inegalitarian and unjust. And this is so, even if there are other claims that might be made about the good(s) that markets provide. Equalizing initial resources and letting the market rip will not provide just outcomes, not simply because there will be unequal final resources, but because the expenditure of those initial equal resources will not provide initial equal enjoyment.

Sen also uses the expensive tastes argument against resources but in an entirely different way. Louisa is disabled, which affects her mobility. In order to get around she needs a wheelchair. She can only travel on kneeling buses which have large spaces for her wheelchair. She needs a specially equipped car and requires that buildings have ramps and large doors if she is to enter them. Special arrangements are also required for air or sea travel. If resources are not spent on providing those things her mobility is restricted. She has expensive tastes with regard to mobility. Sen appeals to our intuitions that equalizing resources between Louisa and able-bodied Louis is not egalitarian. We note here that welfare, enjoyment, or even satisfaction need have no part in our intuitions with regard to this example. As long as we recognize that mobility is a legitimate concern for justice, we can recognize the strength of the argument. Louisa's desire to travel is, almost, irrelevant.[4]

We should note here that the phrase "expensive tastes" is a misnomer in this second example. There is no natural reading of a person's mobility as being a "taste" of theirs. Indeed, insofar as the difficulty they have in getting around is an objective fact about their current abilities it has no reference to anything subjectively welfare-related. So the phrase "expensive tastes" in this example is at best a technical or quasi-technical term, and at worst seriously misleading. Indeed Sen usually sees this as a "conversion rates" problem: converting resources into some achievement, such as mobility. Part of my argument is that the conversion rates argument is sensible because it has no relevance to "tastes," though we might still see that utility functions are defined over achievements and not resources. To repeat, if we want to equalize (as far as possible) people's mobility there is no need to mention preferences at all.

3 Where expensive tastes come from

Luck egalitarians, such as Cohen, want to reduce inequalities dependent upon bad (brute) luck. That is, they see that there may be no unjust inequalities that are dependent upon agents' choices freely and responsibly made. Relevant to our intuitions over the expensive tastes examples is whether we want to consider inequalities amongst, say, enjoyment – dependent upon tastes freely and responsibly chosen – differently from those for which the person has had no choice. To the extent that we can, quasi-technically, describe Louisa's congenital disability as her taste, we can attach no responsibility to her for that expensive taste for mobility. In Louis's case, much ink has been spilled over whether we think he should be entitled to compensation for his love of fine wine if that taste were thrust upon him rather than carefully cultivated over the years. Originally Cohen and, for example, John Roemer argued that the precise responsibility for the origination of tastes for expensive wine should determine our attitudes here. Cohen (2004) has now refined his position (or perhaps made it clearer): he believes there is a legitimate claim for egalitarian compensation no matter how the tastes are generated. We will return to this issue. But let us first consider the clearer case of physical disability.

4 Physical disability

Do our intuitions tell us that we should treat identical disabilities differently depending upon their causes? Imagine five identical paraplegics: Louisa, paraplegic from birth due to "natural" genetic/environmental conditions; Lesley paraplegic from birth due to her mother taking a prescribed medicine whose potentially damaging side effects were hidden from public view by the pharmaceutical company which produced the drug; Lionel, injured whilst fighting for his country; Lina, who is paraplegic following an accident sustained during a dangerous sports activity; and Luigi, who inflicted his injuries on himself whilst in jail.[5]

We could have a long discussion of these cases. I will short-circuit that by suggesting the following. If we encountered each of these people in our everyday lives we would treat them identically. We would help if we saw them struggling to get through a door, or if they were neighbors we would support their application for a special disabled parking space outside their home; institutionally, however, we might not want to treat them equally.[6] Considering these cases in the context of a modern capitalist developed country such at the U.S. or U.K., we might think Louisa should receive some support to help her overcome her disabilities (how much depends on our politics); Lesley we might feel should get massive compensation from the pharmaceutical company; Lionel should be fully supported through a generous program run by a veterans' or similarly state-supported association. Lina's case is a little harder. Do we say it was her fault; she should have had private insurance and so deserves no support, or at least less state support than Louisa? Our answer might depend on how easy or obvious private insurance was for those indulging in dangerous sports. If she wantonly ignored the insurance available we might be harsh; if such insurance was not readily or obviously available we would be more generous. One answer is for the regular costs of participating to factor in the level of danger in order to pay for insurance. Luigi's case is likely to provoke the most disagreement. Some would suggest that he should receive full support just like Louisa; others would argue that as he brought his paraplegia on himself he should receive no (or only the most minimal) support. Within both groups of people some would probably want to know how it is possible for Luigi to damage himself in this manner in a jail and expect the authorities to try to stop such self-inflicted injuries.

My purpose in bringing up these five cases is not to argue that egalitarians should be committed to one course of action or the other, but rather that intuitions and arguments for how we should treat each case, if we do not think they should be treated equally, seem to rest on issues of responsibility. With no further information about the cause of the paraplegia we would treat each the same as the other. With information about how a person's disability may have been the result of their own actions we might wish them to bear certain costs. This intuition might result from one or both of two considerations. The first is scarcity. Everyone should be aware that whatever resources are devoted to one person means that equivalent resources cannot be devoted elsewhere. So fairness is not simply what a person deserves given their position, but what this entails for what someone else cannot have. And making people take responsibility for injuries that result from their reckless actions will allow greater resources to those whose disabilities are absolutely no fault of their own.[7] Second, it might result from a desire to change behavior: knowing that one will receive help in case of injury, whether health or social assistance, will change the nature of risk assessments and behavior.

After the event, we might soften our line. We might treat Louisa and Lina the same after the latter's accident; though beforehand we are likely to think Lina should bear the costs of the risks she is taking. Lionel is an interesting case. If someone is injured in the cause of their country, then we might wish more generosity, since the injury was incurred as a result of voluntary action but one of which we approve.[8] Luigi is the hardest case of all – at least in the sense that his case is likely to cause the greatest disagreement. Those who think he needs more help would probably argue that he is not responsible, in the sense that it takes a kind of insanity to inflict such disabilities on oneself (or he did not realize the true extent of the damage he was likely to cause); those who take a harder line towards compensation would expect him to bear full responsibility.[9] Extra generosity towards Lesley (often demonstrated in personal claims cases) is almost certainly due to the fact that someone else will be paying – the pharmaceutical company. We are usually happy to be generous with other people's money.

I have deliberately set the stories in a society recognizable to most readers. If I set the stories in a fully communist society, or a developing country, quite how we treat the cases might differ. But intuitions about justice do not hang in the air; rather, they are dependent upon the world in which we each live. And it is not my purpose to use these examples to analyze what the proper (all things considered) just society should do. Rather, it is to demonstrate that even in fairly clear-cut cases of physical disability where responsibility can be relatively easily assigned, our intuitions as a society are not complete and consistent (in other words, not everyone has the same intuitions). Furthermore, each of us may feel the pull of conflicting intuitions. Even in relatively clear-cut cases it is not obvious what (egalitarian) compensation is justified.[10]

5 Buzzes

Our intuitions about how to treat the paraplegics require no direct reference to their happiness or satisfaction. They do not require any reference to buzzes (episodes of experiential enjoyment). The Louis–Louisa wine-drinking example does. It is about whether or not Louis should receive higher income (or wine vouchers) because he gets less enjoyment from the cheap wine than does Louisa.[11] A short answer some give is that it is not the state's job to make people happy. But is the short answer correct even in terms of what the state should do? (Let alone against Cohen's argument which, remember, divorces egalitarian justice from what the state should do all things considered.) The state does subsidize enjoyment: in the form of culture, the arts, libraries, sports facilities, playgrounds for children, swimming pools. These subsidies are often justified in other terms. Playgrounds and sports facilities are justified because they help improve our health, culture for our spiritual health, and so on. Surely, however, parents who press for a playground in the park are thinking of the fun it will bring to their children, not how healthy it will make them.[12] Similarly, community centers in deprived areas exist for the enjoyment of their clientele, even though the public justification might be to reduce crime, create community spirit, and so on. Publicly justifying facilities on the grounds of the enjoyment they bring might seem too frivolous for most politicians, but I believe that the motivation for those who press the state to provide facilities is really the enjoyment they bring. Similarly, public provision of drugs for depression is related to experiential well-being, if not actual episodes of experiential enjoyment. All this is somewhat beside the point, however. The question is whether Louis has a legitimate claim of injustice because, let us say, he cannot afford to buy the wine he enjoys whereas Louisa can afford the wine she enjoys, even though both have the same amount of money for wine expenditure.[13]

If equalizing buzzes is an egalitarian aim, then there is nothing to debate. The correct distribution of buzzes is an equal one and that is the end of the matter. However, the logical question is not the issue and Cohen certainly does not argue that the egalitarian is concerned exclusively with buzzes. Rather, he argues for a pluralism of values for which, I take it, he thinks the correct currency is equal opportunity for advantage. His problem is that the latter is not a currency – it gives us no hint, for example, of how we might trade Louis's buzz for good wine with the irk Louisa feels struggling into a shop with wheelchair-unfriendly doors. And in fact this is the unexpressed assumption underlying the entire expensive tastes literature: that there is a currency – a way of judging Louis's and Louisa's respective buzzes – that is entirely separate from the measurement of the market value of what gives them those buzzes. Of course equality of opportunity for advantage is not such a currency, for there is no such currency. And if there were, it would be utility.

6 Comparing preference-satisfaction

The standard currency in economics for making cardinal comparisons is von Neumann–Morgenstern (VNM) utility. Required for the cardinality of their game theoretic formulations, VNM utility functions are generated, in theory, by individual choices over objectively measured sets of lotteries. The standard objection to making interpersonal comparisons using VNM utility functions is that different functions can represent the same behavior up to a positive affine transformation. This means that the same choice behavior can be represented by two utility functions u and v, where v can be calculated from u with multiplication with a positive constant k and adding another constant l. The idea is that the internal "happiness" of two people might be represented on an absolute scale underlying the two representative utility functions, so that v represents more happiness given the underlying l constant and each act a person takes represented by v, which gives greater increments of utility as given by the constant k. It follows that the external behavior cannot be guaranteed to represent the internal feelings and so we are not justified in making such interpersonal comparisons in VNM utility.

The question this objection begs is how we are to measure the internal or "experiential" utility if not through VNM utility.[14] If the answer is we cannot, then no comparisons can be made and there is no currency of egalitarian buzz justice. And that is the move many make: though it should be noted that the expensive tastes literature *requires us to make such comparisons* since we are told that Louis gets less pleasure from cheap wine than Louisa does. Taken at face value, the impossibility of interpersonal comparisons means we cannot make this claim and so we cannot be egalitarian with regard to experiential enjoyment. However, we *cannot* take this at face value, because we make judgments all the time based on what we take to be others' enjoyment. Think of Louis coming to dinner. You know he is fastidious about his wine, so you carefully choose some nice wine, spending more than you ordinarily would. When Louisa comes you know she enjoys any old plonk (though she is fussy about cheese) and buy accordingly. Thus you may well spend more on Louis than on Louisa, but that has little to do with how you feel about them generally and certainly nothing to do with how much you think they deserve overall. You make a judgment about what they enjoy and modify your behavior accordingly. How do you make that judgment? From what they say, how they react to different wines, what others have told you, and so on. Of course, there may be occasions when you realize that someone has hidden from you how appalling they find the wine you serve: what people really think can be carefully hidden. However, over repeated interaction people are actually very good at guessing others beliefs in such social situations even when those others try to hide them. Humans have had a long time to develop good signaling strategies, masking strategies, and antennae for picking up the signals.[15] But what is important in these interpersonal comparisons is that it is the behavior by which we make them, not any supposed buzzes that might come with them. We are, in a less rigorous manner, working out others' VNM utilities.

One way of trying to express this argument is the following. How could you judge *how much* you prefer one type of wine over another? It is not enough to say that, ordinally, I tend to prefer the Sauvignon grape to the Chardonnay. The question is *by how much* do you prefer it? I suggest the only way you could begin to quantify your preference is to note how often you choose one type of wine over the other, to note how much more you are prepared to pay for one type of grape over the other, and so on. There is no internal measure of preference – there is *only* the external one.[16]

Let us be clear what I am claiming here. We have experiences, and we may know that we find some activities more pleasurable than others. With regard to wine drinking we may know that we gain a better buzz, if you like, from some grape varieties than others. But that is not the question. The question is: How can we *measure* that difference? There is no internal yard-stick by which to take such measurements. If each of us wants a measure of *how much more* we prefer one grape variety over another, or how much more we enjoy some activities than others, the only measurements that it is possible to make are external ones. These involve seeing what choices we make, under different choice conditions, and the measurements will involve some yardstick in terms of relative quantity of choices, or some real (mone-tary) price. From these choices we can, in theory at least, develop a cardinal measurement of utility. That external cardinal measure is, in fact, the only measurement of utility for anyone. There is no alternative by which to compare it.

Now we cannot move from the fact that there is only the external measure of Louis's and Louisa's preferences to direct comparisons between their utility. Real Louis and Louisa have full and complex lives: they have different incomes, separate responsibilities, diverse lifestyles. Even if their income were the same and Louis spent much more on wine than Louisa, we could not, from that evidence alone, conclude that Louis achieved more enjoyment from wine than Louisa.[17] We could not conclude thus because Louis's wine buying is relative to the other products available to him (or that he has sampled), as is Louisa's consumption. She may simply have found other products she values more than wine (or have other needs). Maybe Louis would buy less wine if he discovered some of the cheeses Louisa spends her money on. But could we imagine a Louis and a Lewis where we might feel justified in comparing their utilities?[18]

Imagine the world of Louis and Lewis, whose behavior in all regards is absolutely identical. They do not inhabit the same spatio-temporal dimen-sion, of course, but their lifestyle in all regards is precisely the same. They live in identical houses, do identical things, buy identical products. What warrant would we have for suggesting their utility functions were not iden-tical?[19] It might be argued that they could still get different amounts of pleasure from their world even though they live externally identical lives. But what evidence could we bring for that inference? It is no good suggesting that Lewis might be depressed and Louis happy, since such claims are them-selves subject to inferences drawn from behavior. After all, Lewis and Louis could themselves only draw such relative inferences from their own and others' behavior. If it still seems intuitively wrong that we have no warrant for assuming the two individuals' utility functions are identical, then it might be that the example is too far removed from our experiences for us to have any intuitions about it. Perhaps we should look to animal behavior for the intuition. When we see a nest of worker ants busily running about – perhaps after we have poked the nest with a stick – do we infer that some worker ants have different utility functions from others? I would guess not. We would assume that each ant is interchangeable with each of the others. But I guess you do not feel any dog is interchangeable with another even if they are clones. Why? Because we base the judgment on their behavior. Ants simply don't behave differently enough from each other for us to make such inferences; mammals do. And that is why we cannot imagine two people having the same utility function.

My argument is simply that all inferences we make about differential buzzes, enjoyment, happiness, experiential utility, or whatever that people undergo are based upon their behavior. If this is correct, then it follows that we have no justification for assuming that two people have any measurable utility differentials if their behavior (truly) is identical. If we have no warrant for inferring any measurable utility differentials, what warrant have we for there being any differentials at all? Any residual feeling that there might still be some difference "inside" is left over from folk psychological thinking – unless, that is, someone can come up with a way of measuring such buzzes.

The problem of interpersonal comparisons of utility is simply that life (thank goodness) is too complex; people are too different; and the complexity of the interaction of these two factors means that we cannot have any confidence in the production of accurate comparisons of utility between people in terms of their overall utility at any given moment. This does not deny that there is an epistemological problem with interpersonal comparisons of utility. It simply claims there is no basis of sameness by which to make the comparison. However, we can have confidence in rough comparisons between people with regard to aspects of their lives, because there is rough sameness by which to make comparisons. And we can have such confidence because evolution has fitted us with the skills and abilities to do so in these limited contexts. So when they come to dinner we buy some nice wine for Louis and some special cheese for Louisa. In other words, we can and do make *local comparisons* all the time. We cannot be confident in making *global comparisons* between individuals. Local comparisons are all you need in ordinary social life. However, the state and the constitution of society require a more global comparison. We can only make such global comparisons across sets of people by making some assumptions that within each class there is an equal normal distribution of preferences for rival states of the world. We consider what this means for judgments of welfare in the final section.

7 Tastes and responsibility

I have argued that there is no difference between preference satisfaction and buzzes – at least not with regard to measurement. For Dworkin "ticks" are satisfactions of preferences and we can measure those in various ways through choice behavior. Dworkin discounts equalizing ticks, or satisfactions of preferences, as the correct currency of egalitarian justice. One reason is that he does not see ticks simply as expressions of VNM utility. Rather, he sees a "satisfaction of a preference" as a tick on a list of assignments. And there is no particular reason why we should want to equalize the ticks people give to their lifetime list of assignments. Some people may have extravagant or overly modest judgments about what a successful list of such lifetime achievements should be. In other words, when we carry out a survey of how satisfied people are with their lives and the opportunities they have, the answers we receive will be based upon their expectations. And those expectations will be determined by their personalities and the conditions under which they lead their lives. Those from wealthier or higher-status backgrounds will only be satisfied with better life-plans than those from poorer or lower-status backgrounds. Why should we reward those with an expensive or unrealistic list of ticks?[20]

We have not yet left Louis and his taste for expensive wine behind. One important aspect of Louis that has exercised egalitarians is the degree of responsibility we can assign to him for his tastes. Some believe that to the degree he is not responsible we should treat him much as we treat the paraplegic Louisa. Whilst I believe that circumstances do, of course, help determine our preferences, this aspect of the expensive tastes argument is the least satisfactory. Taste for wine cannot be considered on a par with physical disability unless we can globally judge satisfaction interpersonally as easily as we can globally compare interpersonal mobility. And we cannot. But that is not to say that we cannot make any global comparisons of satisfaction. I will briefly review some empirical evidence on such comparisons.

First, we can note that there is some evidence that reported happiness is correlated with genetic factors, much as other psychological features of humans are. We can also note that reported levels of happiness are correlated with family background: for example, people from single-parent families report lower levels of happiness on average throughout their life than people from stable nuclear families.

Survey evidence suggests that rich people report slightly higher levels of satisfaction than poor people. The poor (and especially the unemployed) report greater satisfaction with public services than do the middle or upper classes. This evidence suggests that levels of satisfaction (or happiness) are indeed based upon expectations, with the poor having lower expectations (both for the quality of public services and for their own life satisfaction). Relative levels of wealth are important. If your income rises relative to others, then so does your happiness, but if everyone's income rises your happiness rises only two-thirds as much. Furthermore, one's happiness depends upon one's income aspirations, which itself depend on what you think others in your community earn. This demonstrates that people do strive for status and self-respect; it does not show whether that striving would be lower or happiness higher in egalitarian societies – though there is some independent evidence that happiness overall is higher the more egalitarian the society.

More pertinent to the expensive tastes debate, however, is that whilst the rich are happier than the poor, they are only slightly so. Similarly, paraplegics and those with life-long disabilities report lower levels of happiness – but only slightly so. If someone gains a windfall, their reported happiness shoots up for a while but then returns to around what it was prior to the windfall. And those who suffer financial disaster – or serious long-term disability – self-report much lower happiness immediately after the disaster but then return to much the same level (though slightly lower) than before. In other words, reported happiness is relevant to one's circumstances, but we do adapt to those circumstances.[21] The evidence seems to support Dworkin's claim that our plans are created relative to our expectations, but also that there are advantages to being rich and fully able bodied in happiness as well as in more obvious terms.

What we should learn from this evidence is that there are structural factors affecting the self-reported general happiness or satisfaction of people measurable across social classes. It goes without saying that these reports concern generally expressed feelings of well-being and not buzzes. But are we justified in making global comparisons between classes of people? We are justified in thinking that the rich, on the whole, are marginally happier than the poor; the fully able-bodied marginally happier than the disabled; that community spirit increases happiness; that spiritual well-being increases happiness; and we are justified in thinking that a more democratic society increases our feelings of well-being. What does this tell us about the wine-drinking habits of Louis and Louisa?

It tells us that, no matter how Louis gained his taste for fine wine, if he has more money than Louisa, then on average he is likely to report greater satisfaction with life. Of course, if his income falls dramatically – meaning his wine consumption (among other things) suffers – then he may well report much lower satisfaction with life. Our intuition that Louis should not receive a subsidy for his wine consumption derives from two aspects. First, as we are never justified in thinking that Louis and Louisa have identical satisfaction from life beyond their wine drinking we cannot use any local comparison over wine drinking to satisfy the claim that Louis overall is unjustly treated.[22] Of course Louis might have a legitimate complaint against a friend who serves the best wine to Louisa, who cannot appreciate it, whilst giving Louis the plonk. But, due to his taste for fine wine alone, Louis has no complaint if he cannot afford the wine he enjoys even when Louisa can afford the wine she likes. This is so no matter what the provenance of Louis's love of wine.

Second, we suspect that the rich gain (on average) greater satisfaction from life than poorer people, and even if they do not, we see other aspects of lives of equal or greater importance than propping up the self-esteem of the rich. However, we may feel that the Louis's of the world require support when they fall on hard times and we can see that the higher you are the greater the fall. That is what self-reported satisfaction shows – though these effects are not long term. Our level of satisfaction with life is partly based upon our expectations, and it is the unfulfilled expectations of Louis that we feel might require support – at least in the short term. States do recognize these hardships when, for example, (short-term) housing support takes into account the level of mortgage repayment, which generally means those with larger mortgages (gained through higher income) get greater support. It is not unusual, in the U.K. at least, for bankrupts' housing, private education, and regular monthly bills to be taken into account when giving orders about repayment to debtors. This means that the rich are treated more generously than the poor. Whether these practices are egalitarian (based on experienced privation) or conservative (Burkean) "based on expectations" is open to debate.

We may wish to take responsibility into account when compensating for privation, but Louis and his penchant for expensive wine do not tell much us about such responsibilities. His past life may have led him to have expectations about his future life that we may want to take into account when he suffers a loss. However, suffering a loss should alter his expectations about his future life from the point in time of the loss. Helping people through difficult times is for the short term only.

We cannot generalize from local judgments about interpersonal comparisons – what wine we serve for Louis and Louisa – to global comparisons about their overall utility. Global comparisons across classes of people are possible, using objective characteristics, including behavior and stated satisfaction through survey evidence. These do require making assumptions – which may not always be justified – about the normal distribution of preferences for ways of life across classes of people. So we provide facilities for the disabled to enable mobility, ignoring any logical possibility that some might not desire greater mobility. Only when we face the most obvious responsibilities for a disability, such as the case of Luigi, might we reconsider special arrangements. We may wish the Linas of the world to face the true costs of their activities, but the idea of not supporting those injured through dangerous sports is only really an issue when scarcity of resources bites hard.

The expensive tastes argument around the Louis wine-drinking example can only be taken seriously if measurement of internal utility is taken seriously. I have argued that it cannot. We have no warrant for such an assumption since one can only measure one's own cardinal utility through examining one's own behavior. Local interpersonal comparisons are relatively easy, which allows us to take account of others' tastes in our everyday lives. For overall egalitarian calculations, however, a currency is required, and we do not have one. Rough global comparisons can be made, but only across classes of people, and exceptions made only where the preference assumptions are obviously biased (as in the case of Luigi) or where humans' notoriously bad judgment for low-level risk with a high price for failure kicks in. Let us leave the bad arguments concerning "expensive tastes" behind us to think more about real policy concerns.

Notes

1 Earlier versions of this chapter were given at the International Network for Economic Method session on "Economics and Philosophy of Mind II: Choice, Utility and Agency" at the Allied Social Science Associations conference, Philadelphia, January 8, 2005; to the Choice Group, London School of Economics, October 12, 2005; and to the Nuffield College Political Theory Workshop, November 7, 2005. I would like to thank participants, particularly Richard Bradley and Christian List, for their comments.

2 Whether "space" or "currency" is the correct way of conveying the difficult-to-phrase question about what it is egalitarians should want to equalize depends upon one's hopes for a comprehensive such measure. Sen prefers "space," believing that only partial orderings are possible; Cohen – despite his avowed pluralism – prefers the term "currency." And it is not unimportant for the critique that he needs some concept (the most obvious being "utility") by which to measure all the elements he claims are important in an account of justice (see Dworkin 2004: 342). I will use the term "currency" here for ease of phrasing, though I mean to imply no commitment to the idea that a complete measure of equality in some item of "stuff" is possible.

3 It is difficult to make claims based on "our" intuitions, since yours might be very different from mine. But I do not want to claim that my argument is simply based upon my own intuitions. I do want to claim general (though not universal) acceptance. How far readers find my argument persuasive will be one measure of how justified such a general claim might be. In this regard my appeal to intuitions is no greater than those I discuss, and I can see little way out of utilizing "intuitions" in moral arguments of this kind. See Dowding and van Hees (2005: sect. 2) for a short consideration of the use of intuitions in political philosophy.

4 I say "almost" irrelevant, since if, say, such disabilities were always accompanied by a psychological predisposition not to want to travel anywhere (and, say, that this predisposition exists even after resources are devoted that enable mobility for the disabled), then Sen's example would almost certainly fail to generate the relevant intuition. In Sen's terms, Louisa would lack the capability for mobility no matter what her desires are. If those desires could never be present (say) in such disabled people, then the lack of capability might not be thought to be morally important. So there is a sense in which welfare (in the guise of desire or motivation) is indirectly important in Sen's example too.

5 The final example was suggested to me by Brand-Ballard (2005) and is based on a real case.

6 I've specified five identical cases, but intuitions get in the way. Would we treat mad-eyed tattooed ex-con Luigi the same way as gentle Louisa as he struggled through a doorway? Almost certainly not; and if Luigi was a bad (or maybe just a slightly frightening) neighbor, that might affect our attitude to the parking space too. Replying, "Those intuitions are not egalitarian ones" invites the response "But they are not equal cases: look at Luigi's demeanor."

7 The scarcity of resources underlies many of the arguments in the U.K. for denying National Health Service resources for heavy smokers.

8 How much of that intuition is derived from wanting to give soldiers the right incentives?

9 Also note that differential treatment in private lives as suggested in note 6 is likely to derive from differences in the demeanor and behavior of the five paraplegics

and so differential treatment there is likely to derive – at least indirectly – from ascriptions of responsibility.

10 Let's be clear what is being argued here. If you want to equalize mobility, then there is no room for discussion. All get treated equally. That is a matter of logic, not intuition. The question is whether or not our (egalitarian) intuitions lead us to want to equalize mobility or something else.

11 Why give money to Louis? Why not subsidize the expensive wine, allowing Louisa and Louis to buy it as they wish? Well, if the wine is expensive because it is rare, then the distribution based on monetary expense will be replaced by one based on time expense. Who gets the best wine will depend on how long they are prepared to queue, and Louis might get more pain from queuing than Louisa. And Louisa might end up drinking the fine wine and not being able to tell it is any different from the cheap stuff.

12 The silliest argument of all is the provision of swimming pools in order to save lives. In the U.K. (and especially in Australia when I last visited) there are campaigns to teach children to swim on the grounds it will save them from drowning. Nonsense. Most people who drown can swim. Non-swimmers do not go swimming, and are much more careful around water. Swimming is good because it is fun. But teaching your children to swim increases, not decreases, the risk they will drown over the course of their lives.

13 I prefer to put it this way since it should not matter to Cohen's position even if Louis could afford to buy his preferred wine but chooses to spend too much on other things. Louis and Louisa do not have to have the same income. Louis might be vastly more wealthy than Louisa, but as long as they are equally happy minus wine drinking, how much they spend to get that happy is irrelevant to the question of Louis's claim about their relative buzz vis-à-vis wine drinking.

14 Roemer (1996: 16) simply assumes this calculation can be made in his account of the failure of interpersonal comparisons of VNM utility.

15 And it is hardest to pick up when those signals proceed from self-deception. But who is most likely to spot self-deception – the person him- or herself or others?

16 That is not to say that there cannot be an objective measure of "buzzes." Brain scans pick out different brain activity when people are shown happy or sad pictures. And self-reported degree of pain on receiving a hot pad applied to the leg correlates with different levels of activity in the appropriate part of the cortex. But these are correlations of neuronal activity with external factors – photographs and reported speech acts – not measures of something otherwise "internal."

17 That is the most natural reading of what an "expensive taste" implies: how much someone is prepared to spend on a product relative to their other expenditure.

18 I turn Louisa into the male Lewis for the example, because it requires us to imagine identical behavior. I simply cannot imagine this for a male and female. They require different personal hygiene products, for example.

19 And we might add that I mean such behavior no matter what test we subject them to.

20 We should note here that those who argue that VNM utility is the correct object of equality are not straightforwardly subject to Dworkin's criticism. Harsanyi, for example, uses a contractual device of choosing a distributive mechanism behind the veil of ignorance for maximizing expected utility specifically designed to avoid such a critique; or, again, uses the notion of empathy (with some preference laundering).

21 This is by no means a comprehensive review. See Van Praag and Ferrer-i-Carbonell (2004) or Layard (2005) for evidence.

22 If Louis is depressed, then buying him some wine might cheer him up. If he is suffering clinical depression, then he needs help, but such a global comparison

does not justify subsidizing his wine consumption. Indeed it might justify the opposite.

References

Brand-Ballard, J. (2005) "Sen's Capabilities Approach Is Unfair, Additive, and Elitist . . . Looks Good to Me!," paper presented at the American Political Science Association annual meeting, September.

Cohen, G.A. (2004) "Expensive Tastes Rides Again," in J. Burley (ed.) *Dworkin and his Critics*, Oxford: Blackwell, 3–29.

Dowding, K. and van Hees, M. (2005) "Counterfactual Success and Negative Freedom," unpublished manuscript (http://personal.lse.ac.uk/DOWDING/Papers. htm).

Dworkin, R. (2004) "Ronald Dworkin Replies," in J. Burley (ed.) *Dworkin and His Critics*, Oxford: Blackwell, 339–95.

Layard, R. (2005) *Happiness: Lessons from a New Science*, London: Allen Lane.

Roemer, J. (1996) *Theories of Distributive Justice*, Cambridge, MA: Harvard University Press.

Van Praag, B. and Ferrer-i-Carbonell, A. (2004) *Happiness Quantified: A Satisfaction Calculus Approach*, Oxford: Oxford University Press.

Index

abstinence 33, 34
ACT *see* Adaptive Control of Thought model
action theory 1–2, 6, 144–47
actions 1, 77, 146, 149, 152, 181–82
active externalism 89, 92, 93 *see also* vehicle externalism
Adams, F. 106, 109
Adaptive Control of Thought (ACT) model 64, 65
adaptive preferences 140
addiction 18, 33, 38, 52, 53, 153
aesthetic value 22
Ainslie, G.: bundling and resolute choice (downside of personal rules 37–39; multiple selves and bargaining 31–33; overview 2, 4, 29, 30, 31; predicting 36–37; strategic interaction and prediction 33–34; what kind of model 34–36); emotion 11–26 (bounded willpower 12–18; overview 3, 11–12, 25–26; sub-personal interaction 4, 41, 45, 50; will 6, 145, 147, 149, 152–53, 155
Aizawa, K. 106, 109
akrasia *see* weakness of will
Allais, M. 59
altruism 18–19, 23
Alzheimer's disease 93, 94, 95, 106, 108
amygdala 15
Anderson, E. 177
Andreou, C. 5, 115–24
anger 26

animals 131, 132, 208, 209
anti-weighing requirements 192, 193
ape rationality 145, 146
appetite 23, 24
architecturalism *see* vehicle externalism
Arrow, Kenneth 5, 45; *see also* Impossibility Theorem
art 22
artifacts 95
assignment of function 77, 78, 81, 82, 83, 84
audience game (Ainslie) 34, 35
Austrian school of economics 2, 83, 87
autobiographical memory 63, 64, 66, 68
automation 25
autonomy 50, 173
axiomatic decision theory 1–2

Bacharach, M. 168, 170, 171
"Background" (Searle) 5, 78, 83, 86
bargaining: Ainslie's bundling 31–33, 35, 37; emotion 18, 19; Nash model 35, 39; will 147
barter 80, 91, 100–104, 110
Bayesian theory 151, 168
Bechara, A. 15
Becker, G. 153
Beecher. H. 19
behavioral economics 58–71; cognitive psychology, identity and memory 62–65; neuroeconomics and identity 67–70; overview 4, 58–59; personal

identity 65–67; preferences 59–62; social interactionism 70–71
behavioral psychology 7, 181, 196
Berns, G. 45
Berridge, K. C. 14, 18
Binmore, K. 51
Black–Scholes model 45
Boettke, P. 2, 87
Bolt, R. 189
bounded rationality 2, 12, 144, 196
bounded self-interest 18–25; altruism and vicarious pleasure 18–19; emotion as reward dependent 20–21; overview 12, 26; role of facts 21–22; vicarious reward 22–23
bounded willpower 12–18, 26
brain: behavioral economics, neuroeconomics, and identity 59, 66–71; buzzes 214; emotion 14–15, 20, 22–23; language and monetary exchange 79; sub-personal interaction 42–46, 48, 49, 52, 53; vehicle externalism 104
brain imaging 14–15, 42, 44, 66, 67, 214
Bratman, Michael: collective rationality 2, 6, 159–60, 168–69, 174; will 6, 152, 155
breakdowns of will 37, 38, 39
Breiter, H. 45
Brennan, T. 146
"bright lines" 32, 33, 35
Broome, J. 7, 125, 144, 181, 191–94
bundling choices: Ainslie 29, 31–35, 37; emotion 13, 17; freedom from choice 128, 130
buzzes 201, 205–9, 211, 214

capabilities approach (Sen) 6, 127, 128, 139
Chalmers, D. : economic examples 97–100, 103–5; extending mind into economic activity 96; integration principle 105, 108; vehicle externalism definition 93–96; vehicle externalism overview 5, 89–92, 109, 110

character 143, 148, 150–53, 155
cheater-defector module 66, 67
Chisholm, R. 154
choice: Ainslie's bundling 4, 29–34, 36, 38; behavioral economics 60, 61; collective rationality 169; economics 1; emotion 3, 11–17, 25; freedom from choice 5–6, 127–29, 134–37, 140; preferences 5, 60–61, 119–25; vehicle externalism 96; will 6, 143–49, 153–55
chosen preferences 119–25
Churchland, Patricia 68
Clark, A.: economic examples 97–101, 103–5; extending mind into economic activity 96; integration principle 105, 108; vehicle externalism definition 93–96; vehicle externalism overview 5, 89–92, 109, 110
cognitive architecture 93
cognitive biases 144
cognitive bloat 89–90, 92, 95, 99–100, 105–9
cognitive enhancement 90–91, 94–95, 97–98, 103, 108–9
cognitive integration 89, 92, 105–8, 109
cognitive psychology 2–3, 58–59, 62–68, 70–71, 147
Cohen, G. A. 201–3, 206, 213, 214
"cold shower paradigm" 152
Coleman, J. L. 1
collective intentionality: collective rationality 6, 159–60, 168–69, 172–77; language and monetary exchange 76–80, 81–84, 86
collective preferences 119–20, 122–24
collective rationality 159–76; coordination 162–65; group mind 172–75; irrationalist position 165–67; overview 159–60; team thinking 167–72; trouble with deconditionalization 160–62
collective subject (group mind) 173, 174
commitment model 187, 188, 189
commodity money 102

compensation 203, 204, 205
compromise 32, 33, 35
conceptual truths 193
Condorcet's paradox 115–16, 122, 123, 124
conflict: freedom from choice 130–32, 134; language and monetary exchange 76, 77; reasons 194; will 153
connectionism 53, 67
conscious mind 94
consequentialism 191
consilience 43
constitutive rules 77–79, 82–85
constraintism 192, 193, 194
consumer choice 144
consumptionism 139
content dependence 135, 136
content externalism 92
content independence 127, 128, 129, 134, 135
context dependence 135, 136
context independence 127, 128, 129, 134, 135
conventions 159, 161, 162, 166, 185
cooperation: Ainslie's bundling 35, 36, 37, 38, 39; collective rationality 159; language and monetary exchange 76, 77; sub-personal interaction 45
coordination: collective rationality (deconditionalization 161; definition 162–65; irrationalist position 165, 166, 167; overview 6, 159, 175, 177; team thinking 168–72); sub-personal interaction 43, 47
Cooter, R. 147
coupled systems 93, 97–99, 100, 104, 108, 109–10
coupling-constitution fallacy 106
cowardice aversion 125
Cubitt, R. 125
culture 46, 48, 50–52, 55, 78

databases 50
Davidson, D. 125, 144, 147
Davis, J. B. 2, 4, 58–71, 176

decision theory 1–2, 29, 30, 144
declarative knowledge 63, 64
deconditionalization problem 161–65, 169, 177
democratic collectives 122, 123, 124
Dennett, D. 3, 4, 41, 46, 49, 54
depression 206, 214
Descartes, R. 89, 94, 147, 175
descendent selves 69, 70
desire/belief model 144, 146
determinism 145, 147, 149, 154
dictatorial collectives 123, 124
disability 202, 203, 204–5, 211, 212, 213
discounting *see* exponential discounting; hyperbolic discounting
discovered preference hypothesis 61
division of labor 5, 96, 97, 98
dorsal striatum 45
Dowding, K. 7, 201–13
drugs 18, 19
dualism 48, 147
duty 185, 189
Dworkin, R. 201, 202, 209, 210, 211, 214

ecological scale 52
economic-institutional reality 82
economic transactions 96–100, 107, 108
Edmundson, W. A. 6–7, 180–97
egalitarianism 201–7, 210–12
eliminative materialism (eliminativism) 68
Elster, J. 140, 150, 152, 153
emotion 11–26; bounded self-interest 18–25 (addition to orthodox economies 23–25; altruism and vicarious pleasure 18–19; reward dependence 20–21; role of facts 21–22; vicarious reward 22–23); bounded willpower 12–18; overview 3, 11–12, 25–26
emotional reward 20–24, 26
empathy 22
endorsement 186, 187, 188, 189, 190
enforcement 38
enjoyment 201, 202, 205–6, 207, 208, 209

entrepreneurs 84, 86
environmentalism 89, 92 *see also* vehicle externalism
episodic memory 63, 64, 66
equality: buzzes 205–6; expensive tastes 202–3; overview 7, 201–2; physical disability 204–5; preference satisfaction 206–9; tastes and responsibility 209–13
equilibrium behavior 45, 48
ethics 144, 148
ethology 49
evaluation model 187, 188, 189
evolution 13
evolutionary game theory 43
evolutionary psychology 54, 66
exchange goods 102, 103
exchange rates 91–92, 100–101, 103–4, 110
exclusionary reasons 192, 193, 198
executive power 33–34
expectations: Ainslie's bundling 36; collective rationality 161, 162, 169; emotion 14; expensive tastes and equality 210–12; sub-personal interaction 42, 43, 45, 47
expected utility theory 59, 60, 61
expensive tastes 7, 201–3, 205–7, 209–14
experienced preferences 130–33, 136, 139–41
exponential discounting 11, 12, 13, 18, 19
extended mind hypothesis 91–93, 95–96, 100, 104–6, 108–9
externalism: expensive tastes and equality 7, 201–2, 208; reasons and requirements 187, 196–98; vehicle externalism 89, 92, 105; *see also* vehicle externalism

facts 21–24, 76–77, 79, 81–82
fasting 128, 136, 137
Ferejohn, J. 96
fictions 20, 21, 23
first-order scarcity 41
fission cases 69, 72

Fitzpatrick, D. 5, 89–109
fMRI *see* functional magnetic resonance imaging
food 19, 20
formal conditions for endorsement 189, 190
formal individualism 174, 175
Frank, R. 21, 51
Frankfurt, H. 6, 131–35, 139, 147
freedom from choice 127–39; content- and context-independent preferences 128–29; content dependence and free will 134–36; Gandhi and freedom 136–38; overview 5–6, 127–28, 138–39; reasoned scrutiny and metapreferences 130–34
free riders 38, 65
free will: bounded willpower 14; freedom from choice 128, 131–34, 139; will of Homo economicus 6, 146, 149, 153–55
Freud, S. 41
Friedman, M. 51
functional magnetic resonance imaging (fMRI) 2, 44, 55
functional parity 91, 94, 97–99, 104
functionings (Sen) 128, 139
fusion cases 69, 72

gambling 21–22, 23, 24, 53
game theory 29, 43, 52, 155
Gandhi, M. 128, 136, 137, 138
Gasper, D. 139
Gauthier, D. 162, 163, 164, 176
Gazzaniga, M. 66
George, D. 5–6, 127–39
Gilbert, M. 2, 6, 159, 168, 169, 173
given preferences 119–22, 123–26
Glimcher, P. 45, 53, 54
global comparisons 209, 212
God 185
group mind 6, 160, 170, 172, 176

happiness 7, 205–11
Harsanyi, J. 168, 214

Hayek, F. A. von: economics and philosophy of mind 2, 3; language and monetary exchange 5, 75, 79–85; subpersonal interaction 51

"herd" morality 185

Hicks, J. R. 42

higher-order preferences 130, 147

Hobbes, T. 154

Holton, R. 148, 151

Horwitz, S. 2, 5, 75–87

Houthakker's axiom 43

Hume, D. 1, 41, 154

hungers 20, 23, 24

Hurley, S. 177

hybrid mind thesis 106

hydraulic conception 145

hyperbolic discounting: Ainslie's bundling 4, 29, 30, 34, 39; economics and philosophy of mind 2, 3; emotion 12–13, 16–17, 19–20, 23, 25–26; neuroeconomics and identity 68; will 147, 150

hypothetical consent theory 190

ideal observer theory 190

identity: behavioral economics and neuroeconomics 4, 58–59, 62, 65–71; collective rationality 176; economics and philosophy of mind 2; subpersonal interaction 47

imagination 165, 166

Impossibility Theorem (Arrow) 5, 116, 122, 124

impulsiveness 12, 13, 18, 37

incentive salience 14

income 144, 210, 211

independence, and identity 69, 70

independence axiom 30, 59, 60

individual: behavioral economics, neuroeconomics, and identity 4, 58, 61–62, 65, 67–71; collective rationality 6, 168, 170, 172; economics and philosophy of mind 2; preferences 123, 124; vehicle externalism 104

individual expected utility maximization 161, 162, 168

individual intentionality 168, 169, 173, 174, 175

individualism 44, 172, 174, 175

individuation 70, 71

information technology 50

institutional facts 77, 79, 81

institutional reality: history and unintended consequences 79–82; monetary calculation and order of market 82–87; Searle on mind, language, and society 77–79

institutional scale 52, 53

institutions: behavioral economics 65, 66; bounded self-interest 25; language and monetary exchange 76, 79–82, 85, 87; vehicle externalism 96, 98, 104

instrumental facts 21

integration principle 5, 89, 92, 105–8, 109

intentionality: collective rationality 159, 168, 169, 173, 174, 175; language and monetary exchange 76–77, 78–81, 83

interaction 4, 33–39, 53, 66, 71

internal conflict 130, 131, 132, 134, 153

internalism: expensive tastes and equality 7, 201; reasons and requirements 187, 196, 197, 198; vehicle externalism 89, 93, 105, 106

interpersonal bargaining 18, 37

intertemporal bargaining 16, 18, 19, 35, 37, 147

intuitions 201, 203–5, 208–9, 213

intuitive cognitive systems 7, 181, 196, 197

irrationality: Ainslie 24, 29; collective rationality 160, 161, 165–67, 169, 172; preferences 117–18, 121, 124, 125; reasons and requirements 181, 189, 197; sub-personal interaction 45; will 145

Janssen, M. C. W. 165, 170–71

Jevons, W. S. 110

Jolls, C. 12

justice 205, 206, 207, 210

Kagan, S. 198
Kahneman, D.: behavioral economics 2,
    60; emotion 3, 12; preferences 126;
    reasons and requirements 7, 180, 181,
    196
Kant, I. 6, 153, 154, 192, 195, 198
Kavka, G. 15
Kavka's problem 15, 16
Keynes, J. M. 42
Kihlstrom, J. 66
kin dynamics 55
Kirsh, D. 93
Klein, S. 66
knowledge 63–64, 66, 83–85, 87
Kuran, T. 140

labor 5, 96, 97, 98
Laibson, D. 139
Lamarck, J. B. 49
Lange, O. 85
language 75–87; history and institutional
    reality 79–82; monetary calculation
    and order of market 83–87; overview
    5, 75; Searle on mind, language, and
    society 75–79
larger, later (LL) goods 11, 12–18, 20
Lavoie, D. 84
law 71, 139, 150, 192–94
Lewis, D. 161
LL goods *see* larger, later (LL) goods
local comparisons 209, 211, 212
Locke, J. 4, 58, 59, 62, 63, 72
Loomes, G. 125
loss 12, 24, 35–36, 60, 68, 212
lotteries 24, 206
luck egalitarians 203
Luther, M. 189
Lutz, M. 145, 154
Lux, K. 154

macroreduction 49–54
Maglio, P. 93
manipulation thesis 106

markets: emotion 11, 12; expensive
    tastes 202, 206; language and mone-
    tary exchange 5, 75, 82–87; vehicle
    externalism 105; will 144
Marx, K. 51
maximization 6–7, 180, 181, 196, 197
maximizing conception of rationality
    180–84, 186, 187, 191–96, 198
McCain, R. 155
McClennan, E. F. 2, 4, 29–39, 125
McNaughton, D. 198
meaning-based self-concepts 62, 63
memory: behavioral economics and
    neuroeconomics 4, 58–59, 62–65, 66–
    69, 71, 72; bounded willpower 16;
    vehicle externalism 94, 95, 101, 106
Menary, R. 105, 106, 109
Menger, C. 5, 80, 91, 100–103
menu dependence 125, 140
metafreedom 128, 138
meta-knowledge 64, 66
metapreferences 5–6, 127, 130–34, 136,
    138–40, 148
metrical assumption 182, 183
Mill, J. S. 148
Miller, K. 168
mirror neurons 22
Mises, L. 5, 75, 83, 87
modules 46–49, 52, 53, 66
monetary exchange 75, 79, 82–87
money: bounded self-interest 21–22;
    language and monetary exchange 5,
    76, 77, 80–82, 84–87; vehicle exter-
    nalism 91, 100–104, 107, 109–10
money pumps 11–12, 51, 116–21, 125
money sieves 116
Montague, P. R. 45
Montero, B. 1–7
Moore, G. E. 198
moral philosophy 180, 195, 196
moral reasons: doubts about maximizing
    conception 194, 195; overview 181,
    183, 184; sanction theories 185;
    universalizability 189, 190, 191;
    voluntarism 185–89

moral requirements: doubts about maximizing conception 193, 194, 195; overview 181, 184, 198; sanction theories 185; universalizability 189, 190, 191; voluntarism 185–89
More, T. 189
Morgenstern, O. 30, 39
motivation 12–13, 15, 20, 187–88, 196
multiple utilities 148, 155
Murphy, K. 153

narratives 47, 50
Nash, J. 35
Nash model of bargaining 35, 39, 45, 53, 155
natural language 86, 87
natural selection 48, 49, 51
negative emotions 22, 26
negative empathy 22
neoclassical economic theory 47, 51, 58, 61, 62
neuroeconomics: behavioral economics and identity 58, 59, 67–70, 71; bounded self-interest 20; economics and philosophy of mind 2; sub-personal interaction 4, 42, 44–46, 48–49, 52–54
neurons 22, 45, 46, 48, 53, 54
neuroscience 2, 14–15, 66–67, 69–70
Newcomb's paradox 152
Nietzsche, F. 185
normativity 180, 191, 195
Nozick, R. 6, 152, 155
nucleus accumbens 15, 53
Nussbaum, M. 129

obligation 185, 186, 188, 189, 190, 194
observer-relative phenomena 76, 77
ought facts 192, 193, 194

pain: buzzes 214; emotion 18, 19, 25; freedom from choice 137, 138; neuroeconomics and identity 68; preferences 117, 125; reasons and requirements 182

Pareto optimality 35, 37, 164, 165
Parfit, D. 4, 59, 69, 70, 71
parity principle: economic examples 97–100, 101, 104; integration principle 105–8; vehicle externalism definition 93, 94, 95; vehicle externalism overview 89–92, 108, 109
passions 1, 21, 154
payoff dominance 164, 168
perception-based self-images 62, 63, 66
perfect reason 191
personal identity: behavioral economics and neuroeconomics 4, 58–59, 62, 65–71; collective rationality 176; economics and philosophy of mind 2; sub-personal interaction 47
personal rules: Ainslie's bundling 29, 31, 32, 34, 37–39; emotion 14, 18–20, 22; sub-personal interaction 50
personal scale 52
PET *see* positron emission tomography
Pettit, P. 128, 129
physical determinism 149, 154
physical disability *see* disability
physical sciences 48, 192–93
Piaget, J. 17
picoeconomics: economics and philosophy of mind 2; emotion 12, 18; sub-personal interaction 4, 41–43, 45–46, 48–49, 52–54; will 147
planning 30, 31, 32, 83, 85, 152
Plato 41
pleasure 18, 20, 184
pledges 15, 16
Plott, C. 61
plural agency 2, 6
plural subject 173
positive behavioral psychology 7, 181, 196
positron emission tomography (PET) 44
precedents 29, 32, 34, 152
precommitment strategy 33, 34, 38
prediction 34, 36–37
preference rankings 130, 131, 136, 138, 148
preference reversals 30, 31, 41, 44, 45, 59

preference satisfaction 143, 144, 206–9, 210
preferences 115–24; Ainslie's bundling 30, 31, 37; behavioral economics 4, 58, 59–62; collective rationality 169, 170; definition 119–22; expensive tastes and equality 206–10, 212; freedom from choice (content- and context-independent preferences 128–29; content dependence and free will 134, 135; Gandhi and freedom 136, 137; overview 5–6, 127–28, 138–40; reasoned scrutiny and metapreferences 130–34); given and chosen preferences, and Condorcet's paradox 122–24; money pumps, self-torturer puzzle, and preferred-option claim 116–19; overview 5, 115–16, 124; sub-personal interaction 41, 44, 45; transitive-preferences claim and money-pumps 116; will 13, 143, 144, 147, 148
preferred-option claim 5, 115, 117–19, 121–22, 124
prices 83–87, 91, 102, 104, 144
primary induction 15
priming effects 64, 65
principle of coordination 164, 168
prisoner's dilemma: Ainslie's bundling 31, 35; collective rationality 159; emotion 14, 26; freedom from choice 131, 132
probability distributions 147, 149, 150, 151, 152, 153
proceduralizing 189, 190, 191, 198
procedural knowledge 63, 64, 66
profit and loss 86
promises 186, 193
property rights 50, 83, 86, 88, 100, 140
propositional knowledge 63, 64, 66
prospect theory 45, 60
protantism (pro tanto reason) 192, 193, 194
Provis, C. 176
psychic trauma 47
psychological determinism 145, 149, 154

psychology *see* behavioral psychology; cognitive psychology; social psychology
public goods 65

quantum theory 48, 149, 155
quasi-memory (q-memory) 63, 67
Quinn, W. 117, 118, 119, 120, 125

Rachlin, H. 53
rational agency 147, 148
rational choice theory (RCT): economics 2; emotion 11, 14, 25, 26; preferences 115, 116, 122, 125; vehicle externalism 96; will 144
rational expectations theory 42, 43
rational fools 6, 47, 51, 54, 172
rationality: collective rationality (coordination 162–65; group mind 172–75; irrationalist position 165–67; overview 159–60, 175–76, 177; team thinking 167–72; trouble with deconditionalization 160–62); economics and philosophy of mind 3; emotion 12; preferences 5, 119–21, 123, 124; reasoned scrutiny 132; reasons and requirements 180–84, 190; will 6, 143–46, 153
Rawling, P. 198
Rawls, J. 195
Raz, J. 182, 191, 197, 198
RCT *see* rational choice theory
reasoned scrutiny 132, 133, 134
reason externalism 196, 197, 198
reason internalism 196, 198
reasons 180–97; alternatives to maximizing conception 185–91; doubts about maximizing conception 191–96; overview 180–81, 196–98; reasons and requirements 181–84; sanction theories 185; universalizability 189–91; voluntarism 185–89
reciprocity 65, 66, 67
reductionism 42–44, 46, 48–49, 51, 54, 68–69

reflective endorsement 186, 187, 189, 190
regret aversion 125
Reid, T. 153, 154
remembering 64, 106, 107, 108
repeated prisoner's dilemma 14, 26
requirement externalism 197, 198
requirement internalism 196
requirements 180–84, 186–87, 191–93, 195–98
resolute choice 30, 34, 38, 39
resources 201–3, 205, 212, 213
responsibility 204, 205, 210, 212, 214
rewards: Ainslie's bundling 37; bounded self-interest 20–24; bounded willpower 13–18; emotional reward 20–24, 26; sub-personal interaction 45, 53
risks: Ainslie's bundling 30; behavioral economics 60, 61; collective rationality 168; emotion 24, 26; equality 205, 212; vehicle externalism 110
Rizzello, S. 1, 3
Roemer, J. 203, 214
Ross, D. 2–4, 41–54, 147
r-rationality 177
rules: Ainslie's bundling 29, 31–34, 36–39; behavioral economics 60; emotion 14, 18–20, 22; language and monetary exchange 77, 84, 85, 87; reasons and requirements 182, 198; sub-personal interaction 50
Rupert, R. 106
Ryle, G. 147

saleableness 102, 103
salience 162, 163, 164, 165, 166
Samuelson, P. A. 11
Samuelsonian theory 44, 45, 46
sanction theory 7, 50, 180, 185, 186
Sartre, J. P. 188, 194
satisfaction: collective rationality 176, 177; emotion 24; expensive tastes and equality 201, 203, 205–9, 210–12; will 143, 144
satisficing 12, 198

Satz, D. 96
scaffolding 101, 109
Scanlon, T. M. 198
scarcity 41, 204, 212
Schelling, T. 41, 45, 161, 165
Schmid, H. B. 2, 6, 159–76
science fiction 118
Searle, J.: collective rationality 6, 159, 160, 168–69, 173–74; economics and philosophy of mind 2, 3; language and monetary exchange 5, 75–79, 80–83, 84–87; will 6, 143, 145, 146, 149, 153–55
second-order preferences 127, 130, 132, 133, 140
second-order scarcity 41
self-as-memory 59, 63, 64, 67, 70
self-concepts 63
self-control 13, 15, 33–35, 147, 152, 155
self-images 63, 66
self-interest 12, 18–25, 65, 67, 148
self-prediction 34
self-reference effects 64
self-torturer puzzle 117–18, 120–22, 124, 125
Selten, R. 168
selves: Ainslie's bundling 31–33, 34–36, 38, 39; behavioral economics and identity 62, 63, 64, 66, 67; sub-personal interaction 47, 50, 52, 55
semantic memory 63, 64, 67, 72
Sen, A.: collective rationality 176; expensive tastes and equality 201, 202, 213; freedom from choice 127–39 (content- and context-independent preferences 128, 129; content dependence and free will 134, 135; Gandhi and freedom 136, 138; overview 5–6, 127, 139, 140; reasoned scrutiny and metapreferences 131, 132, 133, 134); sub-personal interaction 47, 51; will 155
separability principle 30
Shackle, G. L. S. 145

Shaftsbury, A. 1
shared intentionality 160, 168, 169, 170, 174
Shoemaker, S. 72
Simon, H. 2, 3
single preference function 61, 62
Skog, O. -J. 153, 155
smaller, sooner (SS) goods 11, 12–16, 18, 20
Smith, A. 1
Smith, M. 198
Smith, V. 59, 65, 66, 72
smoking: Ainslie's bundling 33, 34; emotion 14, 15; freedom from choice 129, 139; sub-personal interaction 52; tastes and responsibility 213; will 150, 155
social facts 76, 77, 82
social identity 176
socialism 83, 85
socially extended cognition 95, 96, 108
social memory 67, 68
social psychology 59, 70–71
social reality 3, 75–76, 78–79, 87
social scale 52, 53
sophisticated choice 33, 35, 38, 39, 125
split-brain transplants 69
spontaneous order theory (Hayek) 5, 81
SS goods *see* smaller, sooner (SS) goods
Stark, C. 198
Starmer, Chris 59, 60, 61
status functions 79, 81, 82, 85, 87
Stich, S. 68
stigmergic algorithms 101
strategic prediction 33–34, 35, 36
strength of will 143, 148–50, 151–52, 153
strenuousness problem 184
striatum 14, 45
Strotz, R. H. 39
subjective individualism 174, 175
subjectivity 70, 71, 174, 175
sub-personal interaction 41–54; macroreduction 49–54; modules, rational fools, and people 46–49;

neuroeconomics, picoeconomics, and reduction 44–46; overview 4, 41–44
Subrick, R. 2
suffering 183, 184
Sugden, R. 2, 6, 125, 159, 168, 170–72, 177
supererogation 187
supervisory cognitive systems 7, 181, 196, 197
supplements to moral reasoning 195
symbolic utility 152
symbolization role of language 75, 76, 79, 81–82, 85–87

tastes *see* expensive tastes
taxes: maximizing conception 192, 193, 194; vehicle externalism 5, 98–100, 107, 108
team reasoning 170, 171
team thinking 2, 6, 159, 167–72, 174
teletransporter cases 69, 72
temptation: Ainslie's bundling 30, 33, 35; emotion 14, 15, 18, 22; preferences 121; sub-personal interaction 52; will 143, 149–52
tertiary circular reactions 17–18
texts 20, 21, 22, 23
texture 24, 25
ticks 201, 209, 210
transcranial magnetic stimulation (TMS) 44
transformation thesis 106
transitive-preferences claim 5, 115–19, 121–24
transplants 69, 72
trembles 155
trust game 65, 66
Tuomela, R. 2, 6, 159, 161, 168–69, 173, 177
Tversky, Amos: behavioral economics 60; economics and philosophy of mind 2; emotion 3, 12; preferences 60, 126; reasons and requirements 7, 180, 181, 196

ultimatum game 65, 66

universalizability 7, 180, 189–91
universalization test (Kant) 195
utility: Ainslie's bundling 30; behavioral
    economics 59–62; collective ratio-
    nality 161; expensive tastes and
    equality 7, 201–2, 206–10, 212, 214;
    sub-personal interaction 45, 47, 48;
    will 143–45, 148–49, 152–53

value 11, 20, 21, 23, 26
value pluralism 194
vehicle externalism 89–109; definition
    92–96; economic examples 96–100,
    100–105; extending mind into
    economic activity 96; integration
    principle 105–8; overview 5, 89–92,
    108–9
veil of ignorance 195, 214
Velleman, J. D. 145–46
ventral striatum 14
vicarious reward 19, 22–23, 26
"virtual" entities 48, 49
VNM *see* von Neumann–Morgenstern
    utility
volitionist conception of rational agency
    147, 153
voluntarism 7, 180, 185–89, 190, 191
Von Neumann, J. 30, 39

von Neumann–Morgenstern (VNM)
    utility 206–7, 210, 214

Wallace, R. J. 6, 143, 145, 147–48, 152–
    53
weakness of will 145, 151, 153, 154
wealth 210, 211
Weber, M. 170
Weber–Fechner law 13
weighing explanations 192, 193, 194
Weirich, P. 198
welfare 201, 202, 203
welfare economics 25
White, M. D. 1–7, 143–53, 198
will 143–53; agency and choice 143–46;
    Ainslie's bundling 34, 37, 38, 39;
    emotion 14, 26; freedom from choice
    131, 134, 135; introducing the will
    146–48; model of choice 148–50;
    modeling character change 150–53;
    overview 6, 143, 153–55; reasons and
    requirements 189, 191; *see also*
    willpower
Williams, B. 198
willpower: Ainslie's bundling 33, 38, 39;
    bounded willpower 12–18, 26;
    modeling character change 151; *see
    also* will

For Product Safety Concerns and Information please contact our EU
representative GPSR@taylorandfrancis.com
Taylor & Francis Verlag GmbH, Kaufingerstraße 24, 80331 München, Germany